BUSINESS VALUATION FOR BUSINESS OWNERS

Master a Valuation Report, Find the Perfect Business Appraiser and Save Your Company from the Looming Disasters That You Don't Yet Know About

Zachary M. Sharkey, CFA, CPA/ABV

BUSINESS VALUATION FOR BUSINESS OWNERS

Master a Valuation Report, Find the Perfect Business Appraiser and Save Your Company from the Looming Disasters That You Don't Yet Know About

Copyright © 2016 Zachary M. Sharkey

All rights reserved. No part of this publication may be reproduced, distributed, or transmitted in any form or by any means, including photocopying, recording, or other electronic or mechanical methods, without the prior written permission of the publisher, except in the case of brief quotations embodied in reviews and certain other noncommercial uses permitted by copyright law.

This publication is designed to provide accurate and authoritative information regarding the subject matter covered. It is sold with the understanding that neither the author nor the publisher is engaged in rendering legal, accounting, or other professional service. If legal advice or other expert assistance is required, the services of a competent professional person should be sought.

The scanning, uploading, and distribution of this book via the Internet or via any other means without the permission of the author or publisher is illegal and punishable by law. Please purchase only authorized electronic editions and do not participate in or encourage electronic piracy of copyrightable materials. Your support of the author's rights is appreciated.

Book cover design by Ida Fia Sveningsson
Editing Manager: Stefanie Williams

ISBN-10: 153296384X
ISBN-13: 9781532963841

Dedicated to the many business owners, attorneys, accountants, financial advisers, valuation practitioners and clients who asked for a better way.

TABLE OF CONTENTS

Acknowledgments	1
Introduction	2
SECTION ONE: WHO, WHY AND HOW	**4**
Chapter 1: The History of Business Valuation	6
Chapter 2: Reasons for a Valuation	10
Chapter 3: Credentials and Professional Valuation Organizations	18
SECTION TWO: LAYING THE FOUNDATION	**26**
Chapter 4: Getting Started	28
Chapter 5: Standards of Value	37
Chapter 6: Levels of Value	45
Chapter 7: Premises of Value	50
SECTION THREE: VALUATION APPROACHES AND METHODS	**55**
Chapter 8: The Income Approach	57
Chapter 9: The Market Approach	78
Chapter 10: The Asset Approach	99
Chapter 11: The Excess Earnings Method	113

SECTION FOUR: THE APPRAISER'S TOOLKIT — 122

Chapter 12: Cost of Capital 124

Chapter 13: Valuation Discounts and Control Premiums 150

Chapter 14: Navigating through a
Business Valuation Report 171

SECTION FIVE: THE LANDMINES YOU DON'T SEE — 181

Chapter 15: Why Your Company Is in Danger 183

Chapter 16: The Business Owner's Solution 201

Chapter 17: Eliminating the Level of Value
Quandary in Your Buy-Sell Agreement 226

Chapter 18: EBITDA: The Anti-Valuation Multiple 236

Chapter 19: Choosing an Appraiser (and Getting
the Most Bang for Your Buck) 242

About the Author — 253

Acknowledgments

Many people helped support the composition of this book. Even more helped push me in life to reach this point.

First, I need to thank my parents who were always supportive of my decisions, whether or not they initially agreed with them. Mom, thank you for always being the perfect mother a son could have. You taught me how to treat all people with the utmost dignity and respect. My empathy and passion to pleasing others for the greater good is a gift you taught me, and I thank you. To my Dad, you taught me what truly measures a person's worth – integrity. Without you, I wouldn't be the stubborn achiever that I am today.

My wife Pam, this wouldn't be remotely possible without you. I don't know of a single person who would go through what you've been through with me. Graduate school, CFA®, CPA, ABV, RPLU, additional graduate school, this book, articles, work – none of my achievements would have been possible without your help. You're a wonderful mother to our children and the best teammate in life.

To my three children, Matthew, Natalie and Mary Anne; you are my life. Thank you for understanding the sacrifices I had to make by being away from home several nights for many months. Always remember to do your best, no matter how others perceive your success.

I also need to thank my father and mother-in-law for believing in me when few others did. Guy and Lynn, you have always supported me, despite knowing how hard my absence was on your daughter. Your collective resilience never fails to amaze me. Thank you for raising such an amazing individual.

I want to thank my Grandparents – both Sharkey and Lashbrook. Each day I leverage the tools and life lessons you instilled in me. I'm fortunate to have been blessed with such wonderful role models, confidants, and teachers in my life.

Finally, to my editor and friend Stefanie – thank you for everything. Your help in areas beyond editing has improved this book exponentially.

Introduction

In today's fast-paced world, knowing the right steps to take in managing and planning your business for the long-term is more confusing than ever. When was the last time you read about business valuation on the Internet, discussed it in conversations with friends, or heard about it from advisers and ended up more confused than when you started? How do you know where to begin? Who should you choose to value your business? How much does a valuation cost? What kind of appraisal do you need? So many questions!

Now there is a book that answers your critical business valuation issues in an easy to read format. *Business Valuation for Business Owners* has been designed to address your questions and concerns in a concise and easy to understand manner. This book is for people who want to protect their company, drastically improve its value, find the best business appraiser for the lowest possible price, and uncover the landmines that every company has (but doesn't know).

As a professional business appraiser of both operating businesses and investment partnerships, I've read hundreds of the best books and articles on the subject of business valuation. After years of answering questions from my business valuation clients, I've mastered the art of explaining these complex issues in an easy to understand manner, breaking down the pertinent and valuable information you need.

Years of experience working in the trenches and witnessing the pitfalls that strike closely-held businesses has provided me the tools to guide you away from disaster before it occurs. Adding to the experience, I'm also one of the few (of only a select number in the country) licensed CPAs to hold the CFA® charter and Accredited in Business Valuation (ABV) designations. Having both the experience you need and in-depth education you require, this book gives you the answers to avoid unnecessary catastrophe. The Business Owner's Solution (Chapter 16) has never been available to the public – until now. The Business Owner's Solution is a tested and proven system that will help save your company from avoidable disaster, all while growing your firm's value and lowering its total risk.

Seasoned business owners, entrepreneurs and many others who struggle with "what's my business worth?", "how do I know I'm getting a good appraiser?" or "what does this valuation report even mean?" have already experienced great success by implementing the tips and tricks found in this helpful how-to book you're about to read.

I promise that if you follow the book chapter by chapter (no skipping), you will not only understand business valuation better than most advisers (and many appraisers), but you will save money and get the most bang for your buck. Even better, by following this book's pointers, I promise that you'll reduce the omnipresent anxiety in the back of you and your fellow business owners' minds.

Don't be the person who misses out on opportunities in life because you take too long (or wait until it's too late) to prevent avoidable disaster. Be the kind of person other people admire. Be the kind of person other business owners see and think "I don't know how they do it." Be the kind of person who takes action and does so immediately.

The valuation tips and tricks you're about to read have been proven to create positive results and increase firm value. All you have to do to make sure you heed the right path is to keep reading. Each chapter will give you new insight as you gain a practical understanding of how business appraisers determine your company's value. You'll have the information you need to improve your business's value, reduce costs, avoid heartache and discover the looming disasters just waiting to happen (and they're there – I see them all the time).

Take control of your company's future right now, make it productive and enjoy the new business (and life) you'll be creating in no time. All you have to do is turn the page.

SECTION ONE
WHO, WHY AND HOW

The first part of this book examines the industry of closely-held business valuation. Knowing the history of how the industry began and the direction the industry is heading provides color about who you should and shouldn't engage for your business valuation. Finance professionals and business owners often wonder (I field these questions frequently) why accounting professionals dominate the industry in the sheer number of practitioners, yet the scope of the work – "valuation" – requires knowledge and experience in finance and economics. You'll learn the answer to that, along with how the industry is changing and moving forward.

My specialty as a business appraiser is in estate and gift tax valuations, which is a natural fit in closely-held business succession planning. Despite my experience in this industry, I remain in awe of the number of reasons why valuations are needed. Not just closely-held business valuations, but other types of appraisals that require a business appraiser. Increased regulatory scrutiny and enforcement have led to a boom in the valuation of financial instruments and intangible assets. In this section, you will learn about the reasons why valuations are needed.

To end Section One, we assess the various participants who appraise businesses. Also discussed are the professional business valuation organizations and the different credentials they offer. You will learn how easy it is to earn some of these designations due to reciprocity agreements between the organizations. Many practitioners like to accumulate designations after their name in the hope of gaining perceived credibility. The hope – which is often true – is that closely-held business owners will know none the better between designations and that by playing "alphabet soup" they are perceived as thought leaders. Nothing could be further from the truth.

• • •

This book was designed for you, the business owner. It would be brazen of me to claim full credit for its contents because this book was written to answer the questions most often asked to me by my clients. Instead of my clients heading into a business appraisal blind, I want them to know what I'm doing and why I'm doing it – and I want the same for you.

The valuation industry is broad and reaches into many areas inapplicable to most closely-held business owners. As a result, I decided to capture the core of business valuation and speak to it in general terms, not the technical jargon of a specialized field. In this book, you'll learn how to find and choose a business appraiser that is qualified to meet your needs, and understand how the appraiser will do his job and what he'll need to do it.

Finally, I wanted to add some of my experience in this book by helping you avoid the most problematic areas I see on a regular basis. Business valuation is a passion of mine. Meeting business owners and learning their stories is incessantly fascinating. I believe you will find the key business valuation information you are looking for while reading this book, and, if I've done my job right, you will also discover a few areas where your company can improve.

Thank you for taking the initiative to learn more about the field I am so passionate about, and I can't wait for you to learn about The Business Owner's Solution that will help protect and grow your firm's value. Let's begin this section with the history of closely-held business valuation.

Chapter One

The History of Business Valuation

Introduction

Business Valuation for Business Owners is for closely-held business owners of small to medium-sized entities to understand the nuances of business appraisals. To fully grasp a business valuation, it is important first to know how the industry came to be. Before discussing the history, however, we need to clarify some terminology: Business Valuation and Equity Research. In this book, business valuation refers to the appraisal of private, closely-held companies. The terms business valuation and valuation will be used interchangeably throughout this book. Equity research applies to the valuation of publicly traded companies. Equity research applies to hedge funds, mutual fund companies and other entities in pursuit of building portfolios, managing investment strategies, or writing newsletters on publicly traded companies. A publicly traded company is one traded on the New York Stock Exchange, NASDAQ or other exchange that has an active market (significant shares traded daily). In this book, we're not talking about those. Our focus is on estimating the value of a closely-held company or investment partnership (companies) that isn't exchange traded. Investment companies may be new to you, but don't worry. We'll cover them later when we discuss Family Limited Partnerships (FLPs) in Chapter 10. Finally, you will also see the terms business appraisal, business valuation, valuation and appraisal mixed throughout this book. In nearly all instances the terms are used interchangeably.

History

You can thank the IRS for spurring the need for valuation of closely-held companies in the United States. In 1920, the IRS published the Appeals and Revenue Memorandum 34 (ARM 34) in response to Congress amending the Constitution by enacting Prohibition. Yes, alcohol helped fuel the engine for the closely-held business appraisal industry by providing a valuation formula for companies in the alcohol industry to "get out" after the passage of the 18th Amendment. Known as the Excess Earnings Method, or the Formula Method, it lives on today and is one of the most inappropriately applied methods in the valuation world. Many of these companies had little value regarding tangible assets (assets that can be touched) after the government banned their use in the alcohol trade. These companies, however, were otherwise very profitable. Consequently, the government was faced with a valuation impasse. The excess earnings method became the solution to provide a formulaic way to measure the Intangible Value (a value that's there, but can't be touched). Owners of companies no longer permitted to participate in the alcohol industry were able to receive an equitable price based on their business's tangible and (higher) intangible values.

Twenty-nine years later the IRS was at it again, publishing Revenue Ruling 59-60 (RR 59-60). Written to guide tax courts and appraisers with estate and gift tax valuations, RR 59-60 has become instrumental in guiding appraisers in many other areas of valuation. As you'll learn in this book, the ruling's reach has extended far beyond estate and gift tax valuations. Moreover, the decision laid the groundwork for the three major approaches used in valuation today: the (1) Income, (2) Market and (3) Asset approaches. Don't worry if these terms don't sound familiar. We'll discuss them later.

Successive rulings have also impacted the valuation community since RR 59-60, but their effects are not as widespread as those mentioned above. My guess is that you prefer to stay awake instead of reading about more IRS rulings, so we'll keep this high-level to what primarily matters.

If you're like me, the three letters "IRS" make you a bit uneasy. If taxes come to mind, your brain links the term to accountants. After all, taxes are what accountants do, right? And the license required to be a professional accountant is a CPA. So why were so many CPAs doing valuation (finance) work instead of finance professionals (CFA® charterholders and finance Ph.D.'s)? You may have guessed one reason, but let's discuss a couple.

The acronyms "IRS" and "CPA" are a natural fit. Think long ago (or not so long for us dinosaurs) before TurboTax and other Internet software made online tax filing a cinch. Back then your CPA was the go-to guy for accounting, and ultimately some finance work. If you needed a valuation, there was a small sect of CPAs who learned a thing or two about finance and were able to perform the work. Being the trusted accounting adviser to your business, your CPA was it. Few, if any, alternative options were available. People tend to conduct business with individuals they trust, and most small businesses lever their CPA as their makeshift CFO. Consequently, CPAs ruled the valuation world for years.

And then the Internet happened. Software developers brought us tax filing programs. Not only could we file our personal taxes with ease, but we could do them from the comfort of our home, at any time, and at a much lower price. Goodbye to $500 CPA fees and hello to $50 do-it-yourself software. Accounting firms that failed to adapt died. Smaller firms and solo practitioners either retired or escaped into the corporate world. Some, however, looked for alternative methods of income to save their practices. Business valuation services was a solution. Not only did it add additional revenue to the firm, but the cyclicality of the traditional tax accountant's practice was balanced. Think about it: similar to today, the income tax season's busiest period began in January and ended on April 15th each year. CPA firms rejoiced on April 16th to celebrate the end of 80-hour workweeks, and many took comfort in two-week vacations to restore sanity lost from sleep deprivation. When the relaxation and holidays were over, the chirping of crickets awaited their return. Providing business valuation services was a way to kick the crickets out, maintain a steady flow of income during the non-tax season and decrease the firm's reliance on fading tax revenue that software was pilfering. As CPAs furthered their reach into the valuation industry, a quagmire became noticeable to outside finance professionals. Why were CPAs doing finance work? The answer: because nobody else was doing it. That was about to change.

A man named Dr. Shannon Pratt helped pioneer the valuation world to new levels. A CFA® charterholder with a doctorate in business (finance emphasis), he wrote "Valuing a Business," which non-finance appraisers used to help fill the finance gap. Today the field has evolved remarkably. More CFA® charterholders are entering the practice of closely-held business valuation, bringing new theories and concepts to a previous afterthought of finance. Business valuation organizations have emerged to help practitioners hone their craft and educate the masses on the art and science of business valuation, and have given credibility to this niche area of finance. While not yet common (but much more-so than a decade ago), today you'll find licensed CPAs who are also CFA® charterholders and accredited in one of the major business valuation organizations (we'll discuss them later). CPAs now have the tools to learn the most critical parts of business valuation – finance and economics.

Valuation software has yet to take off as a viable, competent solution in the business valuation arena. On the other hand, real estate and other fields of valuation, notably divorce appraisals where equitable distribution of assets reigns king, have benefited from software applications. Divorce valuations, however, are governed by legal precedence at the state level, with no two states alike. Consequently, the results are (as you guessed it), state by state. Business valuation software's strengths lie in its ability to provide less-educated finance professionals a tool to perform valuation work. Its weaknesses are rooted in the fact that no two businesses are the same. Applying identical costs of capital, valuation discounts, growth forecasts, etc., to two companies that may look similar on paper but have fundamental differences behind the scenes (management, growth projections, succession planning – the list is endless) provides incorrect estimates of value based on the specificities of the company. As you'll read throughout this book, valuation is both an art and a science. Today's software can wrestle a portion of the science but very little of the art.

Conclusion

The closely-held business valuation field has come a long way since it gained steam in the early 1900s. An industry once dominated by public accountants has been shaken up and improved by finance professionals. While public accountants retain a strong presence in the industry, individuals with finance backgrounds – as opposed to accounting – are joining the industry and improving product quality. Valuation software to help practitioners perform appraisals has emerged. As of this writing, however, the software lacks the rigor needed to handle specialized and complex projects.

Chapter Two

Reasons for a Valuation

Introduction

This book examines closely-held business valuation. More specifically, the valuation of non-healthcare-related entities. Nonetheless, appraisals are needed for numerous purposes that extend far beyond the scope of this book. Also, the purpose of a valuation can change the scope of the project. Assume, for example, that your company needs an appraisal for tax-related purposes. The appraiser's required skill-set to perform this type of work would differ from an appraiser valuing your business for merger and acquisition purposes. In addition to business valuation, appraisals are needed for company assets, and services performed by professionals. Intangible asset valuations and goodwill valuations are some of these common purposes.

You will see that valuations are needed for countless reasons. Consequently, I narrowed the field down to reasons I believe would be most applicable to you – the business owner. The reasons discussed were selected from my experience, combined with feedback from other practitioners and professionals who work with small to medium-sized closely-held business owners. You may require an appraisal for reasons outside those discussed or listed in this chapter. The field continues to grow with increased regulation and advances in financial engineering. That very reason is why you should always select a specialist to perform your business valuation – a theme that will be mentioned repeatedly throughout this book.

Reasons for a Business Valuation

Business valuations (appraisal and valuation will be used interchangeably throughout this book) and the reasons for having one performed are both numerous and confusing. I'm often asked "do I need a valuation?" or "why do I need a valuation?"

My usual answer to the first question is "it depends." A word of caution: be careful who you ask the "do I need a valuation" question. Asking an appraiser whose livelihood depends on appraisal fees is akin to asking a barber if you need a haircut. If in doubt, seek legal counsel or a trusted adviser before approaching an appraiser.

Answering the second question, the most common reasons necessitating closely-held business owners to procure a business valuation are discussed below, with other less common reasons listed after that.

Estate Tax

If you're invested in a family limited partnership (FLP), own closely-held business interests, or hold other non-publicly traded investments (i.e. not traded on a stock exchange), your estate will need to provide a price to the IRS upon your death. Partnerships that hold publicly traded stocks are permitted valuation discounts (we'll get to that later) which lower the value of the Partnerships, and thus, the amount of tax paid to the government. Even if your estate isn't taxable, a valuation establishes a cost basis for the successor of your investments.

Gifting

Gifting strategies can be quite complex, so let's hit the major points. During your life, you can gift shares/units/partnership interests without tax as long as those shares fall under the annual gifting exclusion. The exclusion (adjusted annually for inflation) was $14,000 in value per recipient for 2015 and remained at $14,000 for 2016. Two important caveats to the exclusion are significant. First, the exclusion applies on a per-recipient basis. In 2016, an individual could make tax-free gifts of $14,000 per person to as many people as desired. Therefore, a husband and wife could make the maximum tax-free gift to each of their five children, passing along $140,000 tax-free annually. Second, the amount is in "value," meaning assets other than cash apply. A strategically written closely-held business succession plan often includes annual gifting of company stock to descendants over an extended period. With thoughtful planning and keen foresight, families can transition value to their offspring with minimal taxes paid.

Several business owners I have worked with have divided company stock into voting and non-voting shares. Following the split, owners make annual gifts of the non-voting shares to family members. Doing so: (1) decreases the taxable estate upon death, resulting in significant tax savings, (2) keeps the business within the family or whomever the owner desires, (3) allows the owner to maintain control of the company by retaining the voting shares, and (4) allows for successful succession planning of the business and estate's value.

Buy-Sell Agreements

Buy-sell agreements are instrumental to any private, closely-held company. The owners dictate terms and pricing in case a triggering event occurs. Should a triggering event occur, the buy-sell agreement states who has the first right to purchase the shares, the transaction's terms, the price paid, etc. Buy-sell agreements often apply in divorce proceedings, the death of a shareholder, disability of a shareholder, disputes of shareholders, succession planning – just about any reason a transaction would need to take place in either a predictable or unpredictable fashion.

Marital Dissolution

A word of caution: valuations for divorce purposes are quite different than those for estate tax and gifting purposes. Divorce courts are courts of equity. The game is different, and so are the rules. If you or your spouse own non-publicly traded interests in a closely-held company or investment partnership, a business valuation will be necessary for the court to opine on equitable distribution between the parties. Because each state has its respective rules, you should consult with your attorney if an appraisal for divorce purposes is needed.

Mergers & Acquisitions (M&A)

Since M&A valuation purposes are nearly endless, let's focus on a common reason. Suppose Company A is interested in purchasing Company B, and both agree in principle on the terms but haven't agreed to a price. Company A wishes to pay the least amount of money to acquire Company B while Company B wants to maximize its value in the sale to Company A.

Company A will consider (in its valuation) the synergies (cost savings) realized after acquiring Company B and the appraiser will incorporate those synergies and increased revenue to determine a fair value for Company A. Company A will know its maximum price point to acquire Company B to have the acquisition "make sense."

Company B's appraiser will value Company B given the foreseen circumstances (excluding a merger), and likely incorporate a premium into its price knowing that Company A will realize synergies (but not knowing what they are).

Accordingly, each appraiser will arrive at different value estimates. Let the negotiations begin!

Collateralized Stock Loans

Closely-held companies are increasingly allowing their employee-owners to hypothecate employee-held closely-held stock as collateral for bank loans. This incentive has grown as closely-held companies compete for talent with their publicly traded counterparts (industries fight for specialized talent — notably the software development, engineering, science and healthcare fields have been quick to adopt these programs because of talent shortages). Because this could help you (as a business owner) acquire an otherwise unattainable employee (or retain an employee offered a competing incentive that you can't match), let me provide additional color on how these are structured. I have been at the forefront of this area for years now and believe the structure will increase because it provides a win-win-win scenario.

Banks, as an industry, thrive on borrowing money at a low rate and lending at a higher rate (loans), earning a net interest margin. Increased regulation coupled with sound management practices has grown loan portfolio diversification. A loan portfolio consisting of a concentrated asset class (for example, residential/home mortgages) proved disastrous in the housing collapse of the late 2000s and took down many banks — hence the need for increased diversification and lower risk. Collateralized stock loans help provide banks these diversification benefits.

To illustrate, assume your company has a banking relationship with Capital Bank (fictitious name for example purposes only). You have a line of credit with Capital that you draw on from time to time. Like most closely-held companies, you have a few key employees that, if gone, would cause your business to incur hardship. These key employees are critical to achieving a healthy bottom line. Also assume these key employees are minority owners of your company (they collectively own 20 percent, for example).

When minority shareholders are key employees and non-family members, many closely-held companies tie bonuses and options to business value. Determining the closely-held company's annual value requires a business valuation. Here's where you can use that valuation for additional purposes, earning a greater return on your business valuation investment. (A note of caution before proceeding: make sure you inform the business appraiser of all intended purposes of the business valuation so that it is incorporated in the engagement letter, otherwise the bank may require an additional appraisal performed solely for this purpose. If you plan on using the valuation for both compensation and collateralized stock loan purposes, inform the appraiser of all intended uses.) The key employees, by your governing documents, are severely restricted from liquidating their ownership interests in your company. Perhaps they receive distributions or dividends on their ownership in the business, in addition to the annual bonuses tied to its value, but they are otherwise unable to tap into the interest's value. Unlike a publicly traded company's stock where pressing "sell" can provide a tidy sum of cash three days later, these employees lack such enjoyment. Collateralized stock loans provide an additional benefit to critical employee owners, and are commonly structured as follows.

Capital Bank and your company agree to a collateralized stock lending program. Under the program, the key employee-owners can borrow money from the bank at lower interest rates, using the employee-owned interest as collateral. Capital Bank agrees to lend 70 percent of the appraisal value, providing a safety net to the bank in case of default on the loan by the key employee. Your company agrees to the program with Capital. Because liquidity is of the essence to your business, should the 20 percent interest be fully indebted as collateral (which would be 14 percent of the total appraised value, 70 percent of the 20 percent), you set a maximum dollar threshold with the bank that meets your comfort level. Limits (i.e. thresholds) are typically adjusted periodically, and I recommend including an "as-needed" clause in times of economic hardship. People tend to need money when the economy is sour – the very time companies need it most. An as-needed threshold adjustment protects your business from a negative liquidity event.

Collateralized stock loans become a win-win-win scenario because:

1) **Shareholders** can access funds otherwise unattainable. Because the loan is collateralized, the interest rate is lower than the market rate, allowing the key employee to borrow at a below-market rate. Liquidity of otherwise non-liquid stock is gained, in addition to lower borrowing costs for the employee.

2) **Banks** further diversify their loan portfolio, reducing risk exposure. The independent appraisal provides a value which is further comforted with the loan-to-value limit (70 percent in this example). Also, because the bank's underwriting process and standards apply to the individual's credit worthiness, the bank is receiving a market rate on the individual's credit grade. The rate is reduced only by the safety net of your company's stock (the collateral). Two layers of collateral support the bank's loan — the borrower's personal assets followed by the insurance (collateral) of the company stock.

3) **Your company** can attract and retain key employees. Providing this option becomes an important sales component to your executive employee-owner benefit plan. The company's cost is minimal, especially if an annual independent business valuation is performed for your firm already.

Family Limited Partnerships (FLPs)

FLPs function as non-operating holding companies consisting of assets (real estate, publicly traded stocks, etc.) and are used for estate planning. While structured as a limited partnership, the general idea of an FLP can take many forms (e.g. LLCs and other pass-through entities). Accordingly, they are also referred to as Investment Partnerships.

FLPs provide an efficient manner to transition wealth from one generation to the next with the aid of valuation discounts. Valuation discounts are available as a result of the size of the interest transferred (if minority) and the Limited Partnership's restrictions. The size of the valuation discounts depends on the extent of the interest and the Partnership Agreement's restrictions (Chapter 13 examines valuation discounts). If it seems like FLPs are a smart idea — it's because they usually are. As with any great idea that mitigates taxes, however, the IRS has been hammering down on FLP valuation discounts. In 2015, the IRS threatened to change the laws applicable to FLP discounts but later rescinded. As of this book's writing, the tax code has not been amended to disallow or otherwise impact FLP valuation discounts.

Other

Other popular reasons to procure a business valuation include:
- Economic damages
- Intangible instruments
- Goodwill (an economic residual often lumped as an intangible, but different for financial reporting and allocation)
- Preferred stock
- Private debt, convertible debt, employee options, derivatives and other financial instruments
- Litigation (owner disputes)
- Employee Stock Ownership Plans (ESOPs)
- Life insurance
- Oppressed and dissenting shareholder purposes
- Fair value/financial reporting (for accounting statements)
- Private practice buy-ins and sales (popular with professional service firms)
- Executive compensation (e.g. executive bonuses and options tied to the company's performance, often measured by the increase in stock price. Without a public market, the business appraiser fills the void of the market and estimates the closely-held company's value.)
- Purchase price allocation
- Recapitalization (converting from a C-corporation to an S-corporation would be an example)
- Internal business planning purposes
- Succession planning
- Bankruptcies
- Income tax and ad valorem tax purposes
- Professional services
- Fair value of compensation
- Healthcare (a myriad of reasons exist in healthcare and continue to grow as technology expands and regulatory scrutiny increases)
- Other as needed or unique circumstances

Conclusion

Business valuations are performed for many reasons. Closely-held business owners of small to medium-sized companies often engage appraisers to perform valuations for transactions, planning, and tax-related purposes. Divorce valuation rules are dictated primarily by legal precedence that varies from state to state. Enterprises that change legal structures require an appraisal for allocation purposes. Mergers and acquisitions often necessitate valuations for purchase price allocation. Depending on your business's industry and size, intangible asset or goodwill impairment testing appraisals may be required for financial reporting purposes. Companies with employee stock ownership plans (ESOPs) must have appraisals performed in adherence to the U.S. Department of Labor's guidelines.

Collateralized stock loans are a growing field of business valuation. These loans allow a closely-held company to compete better for talent with publicly traded companies. The risk in providing this guarantee is small to the enterprise and can be hedged effectively with minimal effort. Providing employee-owners the option of hypothecating stock to achieve lower than market interest rates is a win for the employee, the bank or lender, and the closely-held company to attract and retain talent.

Valuing a company takes many forms and depends on the size, purpose and scope. An appraisal for tax-related purposes will differ discernibly from an appraisal needed for marital dissolution reasons. Because the differences are vast, and most engagements require significant expertise, a closely-held business owner would be wise to seek a specialist when an appraisal is needed.

Chapter Three

Credentials and Professional Valuation Organizations

Introduction

Business valuation of closely-held companies is both an art and a science. The goal, however, is to reduce the art component as much as possible because of its inherent subjectivity. Business valuation's science component lies in the quantitative or measurable elements that are customarily more easily supported if correctly quantified. Because business valuation includes the word "valuation," you should be wary of the many practitioners claiming to be experts in the business appraisal field. Accounting is not finance. To fully understand the core of valuation, one must be well educated in finance and economics. Security analysis is another core skill for the practitioner to have. Cost of capital is extracted from publicly traded companies, a skill taught in security analysis. Creating and understanding complex cash flow models – and then selecting the most appropriate model to use – are also ingrained in security analysis.

In this chapter, you will learn about the different credentials conferred by the four professional valuation organizations. An introduction to each organization is provided, along with the requirements needed to obtain the respective organization's credentials. You will also learn that many of these organizations have reciprocity agreements, allowing appraisers who have one credential to easily add on others. Finally, we will observe the difference between quality and quantity of credentials, why quantity is prevalent with many practitioners, and why you should always select quality over quantity.

Credentials and Professional Valuation Organizations

In the late 1980s, a non-profit organization named The Appraisal Foundation adopted the Uniform Standards of Professional Appraisal Practices, often referred to by its acronym USPAP. The Appraisal Standards Board of The Appraisal Foundation was the first major organization to promulgate business valuation standards, creating uniformity and quality control by providing guidelines for business appraisers to follow. Other professional valuation organizations would later emerge.

The four professional business valuation organizations that confer designations and enforce valuation guidelines are:
1) The American Society of Appraisers (ASA)
2) The American Institute of Certified Public Accountants (AICPA)
3) The Institute of Business Appraisers (IBA)
4) The National Association of Certified Valuation Analysts (NACVA)

(1) The American Society of Appraisers

Credentials: Accredited Senior Appraiser (ASA), Accredited Member (AM)

Sponsored by The Appraisal Foundation, this organization's foothold reigns in real estate, with branches including personal property and business valuation. To become a credentialed member, one must have a four-year college degree (or its equivalent) and meet the education and experience requirements.

Education

After passing the ASA Ethics and USPAP exams, the credential seeking candidate must complete one of the following to fulfill the education requirements:
1. Pass the ASA sponsored exams,
2. Pass the 8-hour Challenge Exam, or
3. Pass an equivalency exam administered by other appraisal organizations (ABV, CBA, MCBA).

Experience

The candidate must have five years of valuation experience to earn the ASA (Accredited Senior Appraiser) designation. Members who have two years of experience but fewer than five years can receive the AM (Accredited Member) designation. A comprehensive appraisal report completed within the past two years must also be submitted for peer review and approved by the review board. The experience requirement can be partially waived by holding select professional credentials.

(2) The American Institute of Certified Public Accountants (AICPA)

Credential: Accredited in Business Valuation (ABV)

Sponsored by The American Institute of Certified Public Accountants, to receive the ABV designation the candidate must be a Certified Public Accountant (CPA), meet experience requirements and pass two examinations.

Education

1. Hold a valid and unrevoked CPA certificate or license **and**
2. Pass 2 computer-based examinations within 12 months to receive credit for passing the ABV Exam, or
3. Hold the ASA or AM credential.

Experience

ABV candidates must have completed a minimum of either:
1. 6 business valuation engagements, or
2. Obtained 150 hours of BV experience within the 5-year period preceding the date of the credential application.

(3) The Institute of Business Appraisers (IBA)

Credentials: Certified Business Appraiser (CBA), Master Certified Business Appraiser (MCBA)

Founded by valuation pioneer Ray Miles, the IBA promulgates credentials for valuation and ancillary services. Business valuation credentials include the Certified Business Appraiser (CBA) and Master Certified Business Appraiser (MCBA) designations. Furthermore, the IBA sponsors the Business Valuator Accredited for Litigation designation (BVAL) which is relevant to appraisers who focus their practice in expert testimony and litigation.

Education
To complete the education portion, the candidate must:
1. Complete the Business Valuation and Certification Training Center (BVTC) program *and*
2. Complete and pass the 5-hour CBA written exam *and*
3. Complete the Comprehensive Certified Business Appraiser Workshop (CCBAW).

The CBA offers an accelerated process for candidates holding the following designations: ABV, ASA, CBV, CFA®, CFE, CVA, and MAFF. These individuals are "fast-tracked" through the steps above but must meet the review and experience requirements.

Experience
CBA: The candidate must submit professional references and two reports for a juried peer review with a detailed critique. Recertification is required every three years, consisting of 36 hours of additional education.

MCBA: Candidates must hold the CBA for no less than ten years and have a minimum of 15 years of full-time experience as a business appraiser. Additional requirements are also required to receive this designation.

(4) The National Association of Certified Valuation Analysts (NACVA)

Credentials: Certified Valuation Analyst (CVA)
NACVA confers three types of credentials, with the CVA (Certified Valuation Analyst) credential focusing solely on valuation. Originally targeting CPAs, NACVA has since expanded the CVA to include non-CPAs. Non-CPAs must have a bachelor's degree and an MBA (master of business administration) or higher business degree, or have a bachelor's degree and meet NACVA's definition of having "substantial experience." Non-CPAs must demonstrate having substantial experience in business valuation, whereas CPAs are not required to do so. Government employees are subject to a slightly different credentialing process.

Education
The education requirements apply to CPAs and Non-CPAs alike:
1. Pass a 5-hour multiple-choice exam.

Experience
The candidate must meet NACVA's "Experience Threshold" by completing a case study or by submitting a valuation report performed within the previous year for peer review. The standard of value must be fair market value (FMV).

NACVA also sponsors the Accredited in Business Appraisal Review (ABAR) and Master Analyst in Financial Forensics (MAFF) designations.

• • •

I cannot over-emphasize the importance of this enough: when choosing an appraiser, ensure that the individual holds (at minimum) a credential from one of the four professional valuation organizations. For many valuation purposes (SBA loans, ESOPs, etc.), holding a designation from one of the four professional appraisal organizations is required. The term "qualified appraiser" usually means the appraiser holds a designation from one of these bodies. If you're not sure, make sure. Your hard-earned money will thank you later.

The CFA Institute
Another organization that you should know about is the CFA Institute. The CFA Institute confers the global CFA® (Chartered Financial Analyst) designation. CFA® charterholders have entered the business valuation field in greater numbers in recent years. The valuation community has benefited profoundly from their contributions as thought leaders, pushing modern valuation theory forward in what was previously an accounting-centric field. The CFA® designation is a global credential and considered by many as the "gold standard" in finance. To sit for the CFA® examinations, the candidate must have a college degree.

Education and experience requirements needed to earn the CFA® charter include:

Education
Pass 3 levels of the CFA exam in succession (pass level I to take level II, pass level II to take level III).

Experience
Acquire 48 months of "acceptable professional work experience."

The process is grueling, and statistics of completing and earning the CFA® charter are grim with pass rates declining over time. From 2003-2012 the weighted average completion rate (those earning the CFA® charter) for candidates who sat for the Level I exam was 14%.[1] Otherwise stated, 86% of candidates who attempted the CFA® charter failed to complete the program.

The exam is given annually across the globe in early June. Level I is proctored twice per year, with the additional exam given in December. Candidates must pass each level before progressing to the next.

Bringing It All Together

The four professional business valuation organizations provide direction and structure to their members, bringing credibility and quality control to professional closely-held business valuation that was once non-existent. The ASA, ABV, and CBA offer education reciprocity. Therefore, after earning one credential, the candidate can "fast track" to another. Many practitioners believe having multiple designations provides added credibility. However, the barriers to obtaining additional credentials amount to the administrative burden of completing paperwork. Having "alphabet soup" after one's name does not necessarily infer quality.

The ASA is often considered the most stringent of the four because of the experience requirement. The experience requirement, however, does not necessarily promote it to the top as it reciprocates education requirements with the ABV, CBA, and MCBA. The ASA and AICPA have harmonized many of their standards, requiring credentialed members to follow similar

---

[1] "1963 - 2012A CANDIDATE EXAMINATION RESULTS" (PDF). cfainstitute.org. Archived from the original (PDF) on 2012-08-20.

guidelines. The bottom line is that choosing an appraiser based solely on the professional business valuation credential would be a poor decision.

Because valuation is rooted in finance and economics, ignoring the appraiser's understanding of finance and economic theory would be ill-advised. CFA® charterholders, despite their limited numbers across the globe due to the program's abhorrently low pass rates, have entered the business valuation field in greater numbers in recent years. As sell-side research has dwindled, more CFA® charterholders have found homes in the business valuation profession. The ASA designation is a natural fit for CFA® charterholders (the ASA is well respected and doesn't require a CPA license) and is one that many pursue as their business valuation credential. Others push to master both finance and accounting, earning the CPA in addition to the CFA® charter, while also obtaining a business valuation credential(s) (usually the ABV or ASA – or both). These highly educated individuals are out there, albeit in limited quantities, but their numbers are slowly increasing.

My biased independence (an oxymoron – I know) recommends that you find a business appraiser holding both the CFA® charter and a business valuation credential. Doing so helps ensure your appraiser has a fundamental understanding of the service (valuation) you are seeking, yet is also familiar with the nuances of closely-held business valuation (and is held to professional standards). To secure a top notch appraiser you should find, if possible, an appraiser with the CFA® charter or Ph.D., CPA license and a valuation credential. Senior designations or degrees in finance (CFA® or Ph.D.), accounting (CPA) and closely-held business valuation helps provide peace of mind that your appraiser understands the subject matter and can fulfill your needs while adhering to professional guidelines.

I should note that there are excellent valuation professionals who do not have two or more of the designations/degrees mentioned (e.g. CFA®/Ph.D.). Many CPAs who find a passion for finance and valuation (and I can't blame them, I love it!) obtain a valuation credential and work extremely hard to fill the knowledge gap. Designations alone do not make a sound appraiser – but they sure help qualify one.

Conclusion

When choosing an appraiser, you are well advised to conduct thorough due diligence. I've provided you the tools to understand the alphabet soup after business appraiser names. You now know that quantity doesn't always correlate to quality. Don't give a free pass to referrals from trusted advisers. While your trusted advisers are likely to steer you in the right direction, you don't know the relationship between the two. Moreover, the adviser may not know the ability and skill-set of the appraiser, but has used the appraiser because "that's who we've always used." Aim for the quality and experience that you deserve.

SECTION TWO
LAYING THE FOUNDATION

In the first section, you learned about the fundamental differences between business appraisers. If you were surprised to see the reasons why valuations are needed, you aren't alone! Demand for highly educated finance professionals continues to grow as demand for specialized valuation needs increases. You also learned that anybody can provide a business valuation, but many government organizations require a qualified appraiser. One thing you will hear throughout this book is that cheap usually costs more. I'm not plugging my business valuation services or those who have certain credentials or backgrounds. By action of purchasing this book, you asked for quality advice. The advice I give predicates from years of witnessing unnecessary headaches and weak jobs that ended up costing clients unexpected financial expenses and stress.

Sometimes cheap gets the job done, especially when business owners have no choice but to go cheap due to budgeting. For such predicaments I refer business owners to outside appraisers who I know will perform the minimum requirements needed, but only if cheap will work for the given circumstance. For most projects, however, you're better off paying a small premium up front instead of paying an unforeseen sum later.

Moving on to Section Two, we'll examine the "next steps" of engaging a business appraiser. Even with an appraiser selected, many owners remain uncertain about what exactly it is they need the appraiser to value. Business valuation has many technicalities, and this section delivers the guidance necessary to communicate the particulars which you will likely encounter. Section Two also surveys the types of reports issued and which report type you should choose for a particular project.

The engagement letter is an important piece of any business valuation engagement. I'll give you the tools needed to avoid the troubles many business owners encounter. Don't be a statistic here – especially when the problems are avoidable. This section alone could save you a princely sum of time and money.

Going beyond the engagement letter, Section Two introduces the fundamentals of business valuation. Knowing the correct standard, premise and level of value are critical. Both you and the appraiser must be on the same page when defining these, so pay close attention to the differences.

Chapter Four

Getting Started

Introduction

Chapter 19 of this book, "Choosing an Appraiser," is positioned at the end of this book to give you the tools needed to make an informed decision and get the most of your valuation dollar. Even if you're tempted to skip ahead – don't do so. The book's contents are organized to educate you about business valuation and give you the edge needed when selecting an appraiser and understanding the business valuation process.

In Chapters 2 and 3, you learned why appraisals were necessary and the differing valuation credentials. Despite these variances, a similar process is followed for most business valuations. The depth and variation of steps taken during your business valuation will depend on your particular engagement. Control interest appraisals of operating entities mandate significant attention and research by the valuation analyst whereas a minority interest appraisal of an FLP will be on the lighter side (in most instances). If you haven't noticed by now, many questions in the valuation community are answered with "it depends." Each appraisal is unique. Fortunately, there are some commonalities among a good number of business valuation engagements.

What Type of Appraisal Do You Need?

The four professional valuation organizations offer differing levels and types of valuation reports that its members can provide. When referring to levels, I'm talking about how in-depth the appraiser needs to dig into your company, industry, etc. A full appraisal report will be comprehensive whereas lighter reports (which have different names depending on the professional valuation organization) may only consist of a few pages and involve agreed-upon calculations. Oral reports are also allowed under many of the professional organizations.

The type of report required will depend on your particular need. Perhaps you'd like to know the value of your company for internal planning purposes. One of the "light" reports may be your best bet. On the other hand, if somebody passes away and the estate is taxable, nothing less than a full appraisal report should be ordered.

Prices for lighter reports are lower because of the reduced time commitment and resources required to complete the report. A lighter product will be significantly less thorough than a full report, which, from a price perspective, works to your advantage if you don't need the rigor of a full report. On the flipside, I've seen the lighter Calculation Engagements performed for decedents with taxable estates – all for the sake of saving money (something I strongly advise against).

So which one do you choose? Again, leveraging the most repeated phrase in the valuation community, the answer is "it depends."

Scenarios are virtually unlimited, so let me offer this as a high-level guiding light.

If the stakes are high – go with the full report.

If the report is internal and the consequences of the value being "off" are minimal – a lighter report will usually do the trick.

Law mandates full narrative appraisal reports in certain circumstances (ESOPs) whereas a lighter report can suffice for internal planning purposes (notably smaller firms). If you're still unsure, contact a legal or tax professional for help.

The Appraiser

Once you complete this book (including Chapter 19 – but don't skip to it now!) you will ultimately select an appraiser. Because each valuation is unique, the appraiser will request that you provide a variety of information. Be ready to send the appraiser any governing documents (e.g. partnership agreements, operating agreements, etc.), financial statements and tax returns. Many small businesses don't have formally prepared financial statements performed on a regular basis. If you find yourself without formal financial statements, it isn't usually a problem, although the appraiser may charge more for the appraisal because of the additional work needed to convert the tax-return numbers into working financial statements. Most appraisers will ask for a minimum of three years of historical financial (or tax) statements.

You might find yourself uncomfortable providing private financial information to a stranger (the appraiser). Many closely-held business owners enjoy the privacy and freedom of being a privately-held company. If that's the case, have the appraiser complete a Non-Disclosure Agreement (NDA). I complete many of my valuation engagements through an attorney (I perform a large number of estate and gift tax valuations for high-net-worth business owners). The attorney serves as the manager of the engagement representing the client. Because my practice is niche, most of my clients operate in the same manner and the customer's attorney usually drafts the Non-Disclosure Agreement on behalf of the customer. However, not having an attorney does not preclude you from having an NDA executed. Even if you are comfortable providing your financial information to the appraiser, I still recommend having the appraiser sign an NDA. To help facilitate the process, I've included a sample NDA on the website **www.valuationforowners.com**. Feel free to use this as a template and augment the language to fit your needs. Remember, however, that I'm not an attorney, I do not practice law, and I am not providing legal advice. An attorney is your best means of securing a bullet proof NDA.

If the appraiser hesitates at your request of executing an NDA, find a different appraiser. Not only am I comfortable signing NDAs – I expect to sign them. As a licensed CPA and holding the CFA® Charter, I'm bound to client confidentiality regardless of the situation. Discussing private matters in a public setting or with non-related parties is unethical, license or not. To ensure privacy, get an NDA signed.

The Price

Once the appraiser reviews your information, a price will be quoted as either a fixed price or as a price range. Many CPA firms cannot escape the billable hour. When providing price quotes for valuation engagements, they estimate the hours they believe will be needed to complete the engagement. Multiplying projected time (hours) to perform the project by the practitioner's hourly rate, the appraiser will quote an estimated fee. In addition to the estimated fee, there will be a clause stating that the price could differ depending on the final amount of time spent on the project. An hourly rate (or rates) will also be provided for any excess time dedicated to the project.

I quote fixed rates, and I recommend you request a flat rate as well. When you purchase a car, do you care how many man-hours were spent designing and building it? Of course you don't. Likewise, should you be penalized by an archaic practice (the billable hour) that costs you more money if the appraiser takes longer to complete the valuation? You care about the product – not how long it took to complete it. Time is the appraiser's problem. A fair practice is to request a fixed price so you know upfront what the cost will be. If an appraisal takes longer than budgeted for, it's the appraiser's fault, and you shouldn't have to pay for the appraiser's mistake. Don't fall victim to the billable hour.

If the scope of the original agreement changes during the appraisal process, however, a Change Order may be requested. Change Orders are separate contracts that amend the original contract. Because a shift in scope occurred, the appraiser is now required to use additional time and resources on a separate item not included in the original agreement. Change Orders should also have a fixed price and a detailed scope.

Finally, avoid going with cheap business appraisers. Instead of focusing on the cost, think of the value received by choosing a quality appraiser. This book discusses the pitfalls of cheap appraisers. I rarely have to re-do appraisals completed by quality business appraisers. When I'm asked to review IRS deficiency valuations because the IRS rejected the initial valuation, I can usually predict with pretty good accuracy which firm performed the appraisal. Most quality business appraisers have completed graduate school and received professional designations that required years of additional training. My wife jokes that I should have become a medical doctor because I was either in school or working towards an advanced designation longer than my doctor friends. All joking aside, when it comes to price think of the value received and potential consequences of going the cheap route. In Chapter 19 I provide a real example that illustrates how cheap is usually (much) more expensive.

The Engagement Letter

You and the appraiser have reached a consensus about the standard, level and premise of value (you will learn more about these in Chapters 5 through 7). You have also agreed upon the effective date, price, expected completion date; information needed (financial statements, compensation of directors – the list can be long) and any project-specific items. At this point, the appraiser will send you an Engagement Letter. An engagement letter is a legal contract that specifies the details above. It binds the appraiser to complete the assignment as defined in the engagement letter and holds you accountable to pay for the product/service.

Most engagement letters include contingent and limiting conditions that both the appraisal and appraiser are mandated to follow. The conditions outline what the appraiser relied on, what the appraiser is not responsible for, what the engagement can and can't be used for, etc. Review these contingent and limiting conditions. Do not merely gloss over them and provide your signature! The engagement letter is a legal document that can (and will) be enforced if needed. Many business owners have felt the scorn of blindly signing what they believed was an agreement in principle.

For example, disclaiming responsibility for real estate values in the limiting conditions – without verbally telling the client about the disclaimer – is a prominent maneuver frequently exercised by low-quality business appraisers. In other words, the business appraiser is saying they take no responsibility for the value of any real estate held by the company (or FLP, which can be disastrous as FLPs often own property). Real estate, however, is an asset that will most likely be in your appraisal, and at a minimum, considered when estimating your company's value. To save time and money, the business appraiser will use either the book value of real estate from the balance sheet provided by you or the assessed value of a county assessor's website. Because the business valuation is valid as of a particular date, however, either of the values will be incorrect. The assessor's value will probably be more accurate than the book value since real estate assessments are periodically updated. If using the balance sheet's carrying amount, and the company has owned the property for a length of time, the disparity can be monumental due to the accounting treatment of real estate. Unlike depreciable assets (e.g. buildings, machines, etc.), real estate is a non-depreciable asset and is not updated on the accounting balance sheet to reflect its current value. Real estate purchased for $50,000 thirty years ago could be worth twenty times that amount now. The difference between a $1 million and $50,000 value assigned to the same asset is unquestionably material. If the appraisal is for tax purposes, the estate tax differential between the two values is likely several hundred thousands of dollars (depending on the circumstance and client tax bracket) – further exemplifying how cheap becomes expensive.

In this example, a quality appraiser would request that real estate appraisals be performed as of the effective date so that the business valuation date and real estate appraisal dates align. Because the appraiser is not making a valuation judgment about the property values, and instead leaving it to real estate valuation professionals, the language in the limiting conditions will mention that disclaimer. At this stage, the property appraisals are unlikely to have been ordered yet. The engagement letter's limiting conditions will say that the business appraiser acknowledges the company owns real estate, that real estate appraisals will be ordered and incorporated into the valuation, and that the business appraiser disclaims any opinion of the value of the real estate. IRS engineers are trained to review the contingent and limiting conditions as part of their initial examination. Language absolving the appraiser of non-business valuation estimates (e.g. real estate) with no direction as to how these values were determined is an easy way to become an audit candidate. This example was a tax-related item for comprehension purposes, but the scenario could be for any purpose. If you don't feel comfortable reading the limiting terms and conditions, hire an attorney to do it. No matter the course you choose, make sure that you read, understand, and agree to the limiting terms and conditions before signing the engagement letter.

After reading and agreeing to the engagement letter's constitution, you will be asked to sign the letter and return it with a retainer fee. Most appraisal firms request half of the total fee upfront as a retainer, with the remaining balance due upon completion of the valuation. This practice can vary and usually depends on the purpose of the valuation. Litigation retainers are similar to attorney practices. What may become the entire fee could be requested upfront because the practitioner is unsure of the work and time that will be required to complete the project. Litigation pricing is different than most closely-held business valuation project purposes, and the fee practices are different. You probably won't find a fixed-fee practitioner in a litigation project.

If the appraiser requests the engagement letter be signed and delivered, make a copy for your records. You don't want to fall victim to inaction or misinterpretation that would invalidate the agreement.

Information Requests

The appraiser will ask for an abundance of information. The list may be arduous and can include: governing documents, by-laws, financial statements, tax information, lease agreements, prior appraisals, ownership percentages, executive management profiles and executive compensation. If the information request list looks ridiculous, call the appraiser and ask why the list contains perceived non-essential items. Going back to the "quality vs. quantity" assertion, cheap appraisers usually send a boilerplate information request list asking for non-applicable items. Don't put yourself through the stress and hassle of retrieving useless documents if you don't believe them to be pertinent. Call the appraiser first and make sure it's needed. Quality business appraisers take the time to ensure you aren't left wasting yours, and that includes the information request list. Note that if the appraiser works for a large firm, the appraiser (quality or not) may be instructed to send a boilerplate request list. Some liability insurance carriers require practitioners to issue particular forms for all valuation engagements. Again, if you find yourself in this situation call the appraiser and ask what is needed.

If possible, procure and deliver the information requested electronically. Password-protect all documents. One way to secure documents is to save each form as a pdf, assign passwords and change the security settings. Doing so helps protect changes from being made to the document. Another way to secure documents from manipulation is to scan the forms and then convert the scanned file into pdf instead of converting the documents straight to pdf files (i.e. Word to pdf conversion). Scanning the paper creates a picture of the file and removes text manipulation features found in many pdf software packages. Once scanned, convert the file into a pdf and add the security measures previously mentioned. Flash drives work well for delivery for two reasons. Flash drives are inexpensive, will hold the files needed and can be easily delivered. Second, you can (and should) assign a password to the flash drive to further protect your data. The recipient of the flash drive will need two passwords to access your data: the flash drive password and the file(s) password(s). Online portals are also growing in popularity as a means to securely transfer files.

Site Visits

Your appraiser may or may not ask to perform a site visit. Whether or not the appraiser conducts a site visit rests on the ever-popular valuation answer of "it depends." Most controlling interest valuations of closely-held operating companies will mandate a site visit. Minority interest valuations may or may not, with the decision based on the nature of the company's business and the valuation engagement. Valuations of FLPs, control or non-control, are void of the possibility of a site visit in most circumstances since the FLP's assets are liquid securities and real estate. On the other hand, if the FLP holds positions in closely-held companies, a site visit of these enterprises may be required, depending on the scope, size and nature of the valuation. Do you see why the most common answer to many valuation questions is "it depends?" The scenarios are infinite.

The extent of a site visit will depend on the size and complexity of the valuation and your company. Valuing a single entity with no subsidiaries will usually require half a day up to a day. If your company or the project is complex and extensive, appraisers often spend several days. A single day is typical for most companies.

Your goal is to minimize time spent with the appraiser while also answering all relevant questions. To expedite the process, request from the appraiser a list of questions the appraiser plans to ask during the visit. Quality business appraisers will send these questions to you beforehand. Like the information request list, the question list may also be boilerplate (and overwhelming). If that's the case, ask the appraiser which questions are relevant and require attention. Before the visit, ask what the appraiser what he would like to learn from his time spent at your company's premises. Because the appraiser will want to speak with executives and key employees, find a time that works best for your staff and schedule meetings to minimize time spent with the appraiser, yet enough to adequately answer all questions asked. Minutes dedicated to planning will save hours of you and your employees' time.

The appraiser will review your company's premises, looking for outdated assets, excess inventory and anything that stands out as abnormal. More importantly, the appraiser is there to gain a better understanding of how your company works. You know your business better than anybody. The appraiser is there to learn. Personally speaking, site visits are my favorite part of a valuation engagement. Business owners make business valuation fun (well, most of them). Listening to the passion of a founder or subsequent generation family business owner tell his story about how the company came to be, the struggles, achievements, how the company is better than its competitors, what makes them unique – it's all exciting and educational. Don't expect an audit. That's not why the appraiser is there. Let the experience be enjoyable. Share your story. The appraiser wants, and needs, to know it.

Conclusion

The type of report required will depend on your particular need, and the answer will be "it depends" until the purpose is explicitly defined. Before handing out your financial information, always have a Non-Disclosure Agreement (NDA) signed by the practitioner. Pricing will depend on your particular need, but request a fixed price if possible. Accounting firms remain entrenched with the archaic practice of billing by the hour, something you should try to avoid. The engagement letter should be read and scrutinized for clauses that could lead to negative consequences for you and your firm. Question any confusion or concerns, and the appraiser must provide a sufficient answer. Once both parties sign the engagement letter, deliver the requested information as timely as possible but use the security precautions mentioned to protect the data's integrity. Finally, the appraiser may perform a site visit to gain a better understanding of your company. Sharing your business's story and educating the appraiser about your firm will best serve all parties in procuring a reliable valuation estimate.

Chapter Five

Standards of Value

Introduction
Before an appraiser can begin the appraisal process, the appraisal's Standard of Value must be known. Defining the standard of value is fundamental to any valuation engagement. Consequently, it is mission-critical that you clearly communicate the intent and purpose of the valuation to the business appraiser. If unsure, seek counsel from an attorney or trusted adviser. Differing standards of value exist, each telling the business appraiser to proceed in a distinctly different way. One way to think of the standard of value is that of a direction. If the appraiser is told to go north but you meant south, the appraisal will be incorrectly performed.

Standards of Value
Appraisers use four common standards of value in closely-held business valuation engagements. Some standards of value apply more than others, and the standard of value chosen depends on the purpose of the appraisal. You will also see that there are subcategories of the primary standards of value, notably fair value. This chapter delivers the needed information from a business owner's perspective to comprehend the various standards of value.

(1) Fair Market Value

Perhaps the most well-known of all, fair market value is the requisite standard of value for nearly all tax-related valuations. The United States Treasury has defined it as:

> "The fair market value is the price at which the property would change hands between a willing buyer and a willing seller, neither being under any compulsion to buy or to sell and both having reasonable knowledge of relevant facts."[2]

The International Glossary of Business Valuation Terms defines Fair Market Value as:

> "The price, expressed in terms of cash equivalents, at which property would change hands between a hypothetical willing and able buyer and a hypothetical willing and able seller, acting at arm's length in an open and unrestricted market, when neither is under compulsion to buy or sell and when both have reasonable knowledge of the relevant facts."[3] *The definition varies slightly in Canada. Instead of the term "price" in this definition, Canada uses the terminology "highest price."*

The appraiser will ask you to define the "effective date" or "as-of date" before starting the valuation (the date will also be in the engagement letter). The fair market value standard implies the transaction takes place on a specific date (e.g. "effective date" or "as-of" date). For simplicity, let's refer to it as the effective date going forward. Just be aware when speaking to a business appraiser that he may use either of the terms and that they mean the same thing.

An interesting quagmire, however, is now presented. Unlike publicly traded companies, closely-held companies cannot be valued in real time. You can't log into your online brokerage account and view the current price of a closely-held private company's stock. Therefore, the effective date will be in the past. How far in the past depends on each circumstance, and can vary from days to years.

From the appraiser's perspective, only information known or knowable as of the effective date can be used. The appraiser must hypothetically travel

---

[2] Treasury Regulation 20.2031-1.
[3] http://bvfls.aicpa.org/Resources/Business+Valuation/Tools+and+Aids/Definitions+and+Terms/International+Glossary+of+Business+Valuation+Terms.htm.

back in time and consider only information known or knowable on the effective date. Simple on paper, this concept is often perplexing in practice. Assume, for example, that a business owner holding 20% of a closely-held company's stock passes away in June of 2010. The owner's estate was taxable, requiring a full narrative valuation. After careful consideration, the attorney presiding over the estate chooses a business appraiser, and the appraiser then begins working on the appraisal. Two days before the appraiser issues the final appraisal report – and one week before the estate tax return is due – the closely-held entity sells itself to another firm. The business appraiser's price estimate is 15% higher than the subsequent, more recent sale price. Which value is most appropriate for the estate's tax return?

The 20% interest was a minority position in a pass-through entity and the governing document required a three-quarters vote to sell the company. At the time of death, management had no anticipation of selling the company. Eight months later a feud broke out between management and owners of the enterprise while a key employee-owner was going through a divorce. None of these events were occurring at the time of death or six months following the decedent's passing (i.e. the "Alternative Valuation Date"). Since the information was not known or knowable at the time of death (the effective date), the appraiser's value is the correct value to use.

(2) Fair Value

Fair value has two variations: one for financial reporting and another for legal purposes.

(2.a) Fair Value for Financial Reporting is determined by accounting bodies. The Financial Accounting Standards Board (FASB) defines Fair Value for Financial Reporting Purposes as:

> "The price that would be received to sell an asset or paid to transfer a liability in an orderly transaction between market participants at the measurement date."[4]

Because this book has been written specifically for closely-held business owners, note that the financial reporting definition of the fair value standard is less applicable than other standards of value for most closely-held companies. Closely-held businesses with significant intangible assets, however, are probably familiar with this standard of value variant. Firms that have converted legal structures (C-corporation to an S-corporation)

---

[4] Statement of Financial Accounting Standards No. 157: Fair Value Measurements, p. 2.

or that have been part of an acquisition or merger are also familiar with this definition of fair value.

Rules governing the application of the fair value standard for financial reporting purposes differ under the accounting code and are beyond the scope of this book. One distinction to fair value for financial reporting is that it represents an exit value. An exit value is a price "received to sell an asset" or "paid to transfer a liability" and differs from fair market value which assumes hypothetical parties transact at arm's length (an entry value). Fair value for financial reporting purposes is the value received for selling (exiting) an asset or paying to absolve a liability (exiting a debt obligation). The nuances may appear subtle, but the rules governing each definition are involved. Fair market value defines the transacting parties as "hypothetical," "willing and able," "acting at arm's length" in an "open and unrestricted market," and neither party is "under compulsion to buy or sell" and "both have reasonable knowledge of the relevant facts." Fair value for financial reporting purposes, on the other hand, is less open and descriptive. Accounting governance has established rules to follow for each of the terms within the fair value definition, from "price" to "measurement date" – the methods and tests required under the fair value standard for financial reporting purposes differs from fair market value.

(2.b) Fair Value for Legal Purposes differs from state to state, and its definition is based primarily upon legal precedence. When the term "legal" enters the valuation conversation, you are wise to think "equal." Courts predominate as domiciles of equitable resolution. The fair value for legal purpose standard is customary in marital dissolution appraisals, stockholder oppression cases, and shareholder disputes. Because the purposes above are contentious, and courts seek equitable resolution, fair value for legal purposes is the common standard of value in such matters.

Some states have adopted the Revised Model Business Corporation Act (RMBCA) and follow its definition of fair value for legal purposes. Some states follow the RMBCA's definition with modifications. Other states follow their respective state-defined interpretation. To provide some clarity of Fair Value for Legal Purposes, the RMBCA's definition reads as follows:

> "Fair value means the value of the corporation's shares determined: (i) immediately before the effectuation of the corporate action to which the shareholder objects; (ii) using customary and current valuation concepts and techniques

> generally employed for similar businesses in the context of the transaction requiring appraisal; and (iii) without discounting for lack of marketability or minority status except, if appropriate, for amendments to the articles pursuant to section 13.02(a)(5)."[5]

As you can see, significant leeway and ambiguity exist in the RMBCA's definition of fair value. Consult with an attorney if fair value for legal purposes is your standard of value.

(3) Investment Value

The International Glossary of Business Valuation Terms defines Investment Value as:

> "Investment Value is the value to a particular investor based on individual investment requirements and expectations."[6] *The definition varies slightly in Canada. Instead of the term "value," in Canada, the correct terminology is "value to the owner."*

Not much of a definition, is it? The easiest way I explain investment value to my clients is that investment value is "the value that you believe the investment is worth." The words "you believe" are critical to the spirit of the definition. In my experience, using an example to help define investment value works well.

Pretend you own a company that creates and manufactures cooking oil sprays. You create the sprays' chemicals, which are in liquid form. You contract the process of completing the conversion of liquid to oil spray, packaging, etc. to another company. The company that finishes your product is the only company within ten states that has the capability and capacity to perform these vital functions. At lunch one day, you learn that the owner of the "finishing company" is looking to sell the business. Because investment value is the value "based on individual investment requirements and expectations," we need to examine the "individual" perspectives.

From your vantage point the company is treasured. It's the only company around that can do what you need to be done to survive as a business. Not only is the company vital to your firm's success, but, after performing some rough calculations, you determine that acquiring the company would make your business exponentially more valuable. Owning the

---

[5] Model Business Corporation Act § 13.01(4)(ABA 1999).
[6] http://bvfls.aicpa.org/Resources/Business+Valuation/Tools+and+Aids/Definitions+and+Terms/International+Glossary+of+Business+Valuation+Terms.htm.

company would reduce your business's overall risk. Instead of relying on a separate entity to complete an integral process, you would have control. Reduced compensation and other expenses would lead to greater cost efficiencies. Instead of two owner salaries, acquiring the finishing company would eliminate the target company's owner's compensation expense. Your business already performs the accounting, finance, and information technology services in-house, and can handily add on the added load of work received post-acquisition. Therefore, an added layer of expenses is eliminated by purchasing the company. Greater economies of scale, scope, and increased market power are additional benefits possible from this transaction, known as vertical integration.

What kind of value do you think the owner of an excavation company would assign to the same company? The answer is quite evident.

As you can see from this example, investment value considers the value based on particular circumstances. Parties to the acquisition are not hypothetical, and expectations (benefits) to be enjoyed are included as part of investment value. Thus, investment value is inherently different from fair market value and fair value. Acquiring the firm would be a no-brainer to you whereas the excavation company owner would likely want nothing to do with it. The value of the finishing company is much greater to you than to the excavation company owner.

The key takeaway is that the investment value standard states that value is unique to the parties at hand and considers investor attributes and expectations.

(4) Intrinsic Value

The International Glossary of Business Valuation Terms defines Intrinsic Value as:

> "Intrinsic Value is the value that an investor considers, on the basis of an evaluation or available facts, to be the "true" or "real" value that will become the market value when other investors reach the same conclusion. When the term applies to options, it is the difference between the exercise price and strike price of an option and the market value of the underlying security."[7]

---

[7] http://bvfls.aicpa.org/Resources/Business+Valuation/Tools+and+Aids/Definitions+and+Terms/International+Glossary+of+Business+Valuation+Terms.htm.

Intrinsic value is a foreign term if I'm wearing my CPA hat. As a CFA® charterholder, however, intrinsic value is burned in my brain. Interpreting the differing standards of value definitions requires wearing different hats.

You've likely heard the name Warren Buffett. If not, he's one of the wealthiest individuals on the planet and one of the greatest investors in modern times. He earned his wealth through a series of acquisitions, investments, and other investing strategies. Decades ago, Mr. Buffett was the apprentice of a valuation pioneer named Benjamin Graham. Often referred to as the "father of value investing," Benjamin Graham first published his formula for intrinsic value in the book *The Intelligent Investor*. Years later he changed the intrinsic value formula, but the conceptual definition remained the same. The simplest way to define intrinsic value is that it is the value a stock *should be* priced at based on a company's fundamentals after performing fundamental analysis. Fundamental analysis is deeply embedded in finance and economic theory, but is non-existent in accounting coursework – further exemplifying the importance that the business valuation analyst you choose must be well versed in finance and economics. (This importance becomes apparent in Chapter 16, when you will learn how to incorporate an appraiser's finance knowledge in growing your firm's value.) Value investors (like Warren Buffett) seek to purchase companies priced significantly below what they believe they should be priced at (below the company's intrinsic value). Determining what they "should be priced at" requires fundamental analysis of the enterprise. Investors should purchase companies priced below their intrinsic values and sell companies whose prices exceed their intrinsic values.

Conclusion

Business owners of small to medium-sized closely-held companies tend to encounter the fair market value standard more than the other standards of value. Succession planning, mitigating taxes through gifting strategies and accumulation of wealth from running successful enterprises lead them down this path. These purposes are ancillary to taxes in one fashion or another, where the fair market value standard applies. Business appraisers who specialize in marital dissolution engagements, fair value valuation for financial reporting or shareholder oppression appraisals would, of course, disagree with that sentiment. Small to medium-sized closely-held companies, however, are only occasionally subject to those instances.

Fair value for financial reporting is less used for smaller closely-held companies unless they hold significant intangible assets or have changed the legal structure of the enterprise. Fair value for legal purposes is hopefully seldom introduced since it usually accompanies a dispute requiring judicial resolution.

Investment value and intrinsic value are probably familiar to most business owners, especially those who make, or have considered making acquisitions. The former is based on the value of an investment unique to a specific individual while the latter is rooted in fundamental analysis and finance/economic theory of what a company's price "should" be. Both standards of value help the company make M&A and investment decisions.

Chapter Six

Levels of Value

Introduction

The standard of value tells the appraiser which direction to follow. Now the appraiser needs to know how deep to dig or how high to jump. The Level of Value answers this dilemma. In this chapter, we examine the levels of value commonly used today. You should note, however, that additional levels of value have been uncovered over recent years as more advanced finance and valuation professionals have entered the closely-held business valuation field. Correctly defining the level of value is important because the differing levels of value can result in significantly different value estimates.

Levels of Value

Expanding levels of value have emerged as more sophisticated individuals with backgrounds in finance and economics have entered the business valuation field. Various schools of thought exist regarding the levels of value, and more are likely to emerge. As a practical matter, let's discuss the four current mainstream levels of value. Extensions of the four general levels of value are outside the scope of this book.

The following picture illustrates the four levels of value. As you can see, investment value is the highest level of value whereas nonmarketable minority value is the lowest.

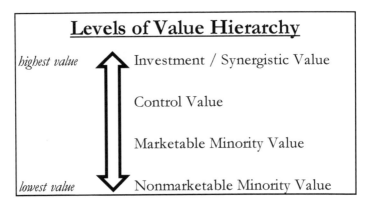

(1) Investment Value

Investment value is similar to Synergistic Value because the value includes synergies. The "level" is higher because the value is considered to be a controlling level of value with synergistic benefits included. In most cases, the term synergy implies cost savings. Investment value and synergistic value are occasionally disunited as separate levels, with the synergistic level seen as a slightly higher level than investment value. Other practitioners consider the two to be similar. I believe the two to be slightly different. The business valuation community, however, typically uses the two interchangeably. Accordingly, I have included what you are most likely to encounter.

(2) Control Value

Control value usually means greater than fifty percent ownership. This level of control, however, can represent different forms depending on the applicable standard of value used. For example, some states require a simple majority vote (greater than fifty percent) to execute corporate actions, whereas other states mandate a two-thirds or greater vote, usually called a "supermajority" vote. Control has many shades of gray. Furthermore, some appraisers and states argue whether control is marketable or nonmarketable. Marketable implies the interest enjoys marketability similar to publicly traded stocks. Nonmarketable means the interest is worth less because of the lack of marketability, or liquidity. Language determining the degree of control (or lack thereof) is in the company's operating/partnership agreement or other governing document (collectively referred to in this chapter as "Agreement" or "Agreements").

Control powers are valuable. Having control, defined as owning greater than fifty percent, allows the interest owner to make day-to-day decisions of the business entity. Under most Agreements, control owners can make distributions, enter into contracts on behalf of the company and hire/fire company employees. Major events, however, such as recapitalizations and liquidations, almost always require the approval of three-quarters of the voting shareholders.

Implied within control is the benefit of marketability. Marketability is similar to liquidity. At this level of value, the assumption is that shares can be liquidated quickly with minimal transaction costs. Nearly all private closely-held companies have limited marketability. Unlike companies traded on an active stock exchange, a shareholder owning an interest in a closely-held company is not able to sell the shares and receive cash three days later.

Marketability is similar, but not entirely congruent to liquidity. Because transaction costs of selling interests in closely-held companies are greater than those of publicly traded companies, an illiquidity discount to compensate for transaction costs is often applied. Note, however, that the discount reflects transaction costs of gaining liquidity and not marketability because control typically affords the ability to sell the shares, but at a greater cost compared to publicly traded companies.

(3) Marketable Minority Value

Marketable minority value implies that the owner does not have control powers of the entity, but the shares are marketable. Control, as previously defined, enables the shareholder to make and enforce entity-level decisions. Minority shareholders, acting alone, lack such power. Minority shareholders may gain control by combining votes with other minority shareholders, together summing up to a greater than fifty percent voting interest. Alone, however, the shareholder is not able to unilaterally enforce change. Less power, or none, equates to a lower value.

The same traits of marketability apply at this level as they do at the control level. As the interest assumes marketability similar to a publicly traded equivalent, no marketability discounts have been implemented. At this level, there is an implied discount for lack of control (DLOC). The primary difference that separates the higher level of value (control) from the marketable minority level of value is the ability to control operations of the company. Minority owners expect a discount from the control level of value to compensate for this lack of control. In Chapter 13 we examine DLOCs.

Marketable minority value is analogous to owning 100 shares of Apple stock on the NASDAQ stock exchange. Holding 100 shares of the 5.5 billion-plus shares outstanding does not give you the power to impact (control) the company's decisions. With 100 shares you aren't able to declare dividends and fire employees. Minority shareholders of publicly traded companies hold these shares with the intent of receiving capital gains (appreciation of the stock), dividends, or both.

(4) Nonmarketable Minority Value

Nonmarketable minority value assumes ownership at a minority level, as opposed to control, and that the shares are not marketable. Investors require two levels of discounts to induce investment at this level. Similar to marketable minority interests, the ownership interest lacks voting control. The nonmarketable minority level takes another valuation discount – a discount for lack of marketability (DLOM) – to compensate for the few, if any, options for selling the interest. At this level, the interest is assumed to be nonmarketable. Valuation discounts for marketability can be significant and depend largely on the restrictions in the company's Agreement. In Chapter 13 we discuss DLOMs.

Most gift strategies are performed at this level because of the significant valuation discounts afforded, which in turn lowers the value of the interest gifted. The lower value estimate reduces the taxable amount, and concurrently the tax liability. Further discounts, although minimal, are sometimes given to interests without voting power.

Accurately defining the levels of value in Agreements governing a company, in addition to clauses within these Agreements, is critical to deflect future infighting and misconceived value pricing. Defining the levels of value is one of the most neglected items in Agreements. Chapter 16 provides you the tools needed to "insure" you, your company, your family and fellow shareholders against these landmines that currently exist in your Agreement. Chapter 17 illustrates how neglecting level of value specificity can lead to alternative value estimates. The chapter also provides you (or your attorney) with remedies that solve this problem.

Conclusion

The level of value is of particular importance when calculating valuation discounts. Using the Levels of Value Hierarchy, the appraiser applies discounts or premiums to reach the desired level of value. Investment value is the highest level of value and is assigned the highest price estimate (although many practitioners view synergistic value as a greater level of value). A control level of value also has significant worth and is priced marginally below investment value. The difference between the two depends on the particular facts and circumstances of the subject interest.

Nevertheless, both investment and control levels of value assume control of the entity. The marketable minority level of value is similar to the level of publicly traded stocks on an active stock exchange. The term "marketable" implies that the shares can be freely transferred with minimal restrictions and costs. Minority specifies that the interest, or shares, lack control of the enterprise. A nonmarketable minority level of value has one important distinction from a marketable minority level of value in that there is no active market for a nonmarketable interest. Owners of nonmarketable minority level of value interests lack control of the enterprise and are not able to easily transfer their interests with minimal transaction costs or price concessions. Because they lack control and marketability, this level of value receives the lowest price estimate.

Chapter Seven

Premises of Value

Introduction

In addition to the standard and level of value, the appraiser must also know the Premise of Value when appraising an entity. Business valuation prescribes two general premises of value. These two general premises of value, however, have discernible subcategories. Application of these subcategories is a function of the standard of value. In other words, the particular premise of value used will depend on the purpose of the appraisal. You should also be aware that other valuation areas – notably real estate – have additional premises of value. Matching the premises of value is important when incorporating real estate into a business valuation.

Premise of Value

The International Glossary of Business Valuation Terms defines Premise of Value as:

> "Premise of Value is an assumption regarding the most likely set of transactional circumstances that may be applicable to the subject valuation."[8]

In this chapter we'll discuss the two premises of value used in business valuation: Going Concern Value and Liquidation Value (as well as those employed in other valuation fields). The latter part of this chapter dives

---

[8] http://bvfls.aicpa.org/Resources/Business+Valuation/Tools+and+Aids/Definitions+and+Terms/International+Glossary+of+Business+Valuation+Terms.htm.

deeper into the premises of value used in business valuation as they relate to the standard of value. All of the material (while dry and admittedly dull – I'm not going to sugarcoat it) is relevant and important to know.

(1) Going Concern Value

Defined by The International Glossary of Business Valuation Terms as:

> "Going Concern Value is the value of a business enterprise that is expected to continue to operate into the future. The intangible elements of Going Concern Value result from factors such as having a trained workforce, an operational plant, and the necessary licenses, systems, and procedures in place."[9]

Going concern value for a business entity means the company plans to continue operations without foreseen plans of liquidation, and the appraiser should value it as such. The company plans to continue to operate as a "going concern," hence the name. This premise of value reigns king for most closely-held company valuations.

The latter portion of the definition from the International Glossary of Business Valuation Terms discusses the intangible elements of a going concern enterprise. Intangible elements take many forms and a thorough discussion about intangible factors is beyond the scope of this book. When asked about intangible elements, the answer that seems to resonate with my clients is that intangible items are those that cannot be seen or touched, but are real. Unlike a truck, which is a tangible asset and can be seen and felt, an intangible element has real value but is not in physical form. An example of an intangible asset is a license to practice law. An attorney is legally entitled to practice law because of the license promulgating the attorney to do so. Without it, practicing law and holding oneself as being in the business of practicing law is illegal. The license has incredible value to the attorney. Software companies and web-based applications credit nearly all of their value to intangible elements. As of year-end 2014, Facebook's collective intangible assets and goodwill comprised almost 55 percent of the company's total assets, whereas tangible assets represented less than 10 percent of Facebook's total assets. For this example, both common-size ratios exclude current assets. Facebook's current assets consist primarily of cash and investments since Facebook is a service company and has no physical inventory to sell (as of early 2016).

---

[9] Ibid.

Goodwill is an intangible asset "arising as a result of a name, reputation, customer loyalty, location, products and similar factors not separately identified."[10] Some intangible assets are identifiable. Goodwill represents an intangible value that is not identifiable but is known to exist. Companies that purchase other firms will customarily acquire goodwill as it represents the value that doesn't "fit" with any other assets. Unlike intangible assets, goodwill is a residual value. It's what's left over after accounting for all other values. Goodwill is "tested" for impairment. If impairment exists, the impaired amount is expensed in the income statement. The impairment value is also removed from the goodwill balance on the balance sheet. United States GAAP and the IFRS used in Europe and other countries differ in their treatment of goodwill.

(2) Liquidation Value

Liquidation Value is defined by The International Glossary of Business Valuation Terms as:

> "Liquidation Value is the net amount that would be realized if the business is terminated and the assets are sold piecemeal. Liquidation can be either orderly or forced."[11]

An Orderly Liquidation Value is "the liquidation value at which the asset or assets are sold over a reasonable period of time to maximize proceeds received."[12] A Forced Liquidation Value is "the liquidation value, at which the asset or assets are sold as quickly as possible, such as at an auction."[13]

Important distinctions between the two include time and price.

Time

An orderly liquidation value provides a reasonable amount of time to locate a buyer. A forced liquidation value prizes immediacy of execution over reasonableness of price. Real estate serves as an example of the difference between the two premises. Most home sellers (in general) wish to maximize the price received to sell their home and expect to wait for a customary amount of time for an optimal buyer to purchase the home at its highest price. An estate sale, on the other hand, requires certainty of execution. Accordingly, most estate sales are conducted as auctions.

---

[10] Ibid.
[11] Ibid.
[12] Ibid.
[13] Ibid.

Price
An orderly liquidation value almost always exceeds a forced liquidation value. Having reasonable time to market and sell the asset increases the probability of receiving a higher price. On the other hand, a forced liquidation value requires execution certainty and usually results in a lower price.

If appraising your business using either of the two liquidation premises of value, the appraiser will deduct from the value administrative expenses to obtain the final estimate. Taxes, legal, accounting and other fees related to disposing of the asset are also netted from the price.

Which Premise of Value Should the Appraiser Use?
Under the highest and best use principle, in most circumstances the appraiser will value the interest at its highest and best use. Most operating entities are appraised on a going concern premise because their calculated values exceed their liquidation value estimates. Companies in liquidation or under a plan of liquidation will use liquidation value as the premise of value. An operating company with no plan of liquidation, however, could be valued on a liquidation premise of value. If the appraised interest meets the highest and best use test (worth more in liquidation than as a going concern) and the interest has the right to liquidate the entity, a liquidation premise could (and arguably, should) be used.

Premise of Value as It Relates to the Standard of Value
As discussed in Chapter 5, each standard of value defines the parties of a transaction differently. Fair market value defines the parties as "a hypothetical willing and able buyer and a hypothetical willing and able seller," whereas the fair value for financial reporting purposes defines the parties simply as "market participants." Because of the differing standards of value, the appraiser must establish who value is attributed to. Two premises used in the valuation of closely-held companies answer this question.

The *Value in Exchange* premise assumes that the interest will be changing hands via a transaction of some sort. The fair market value standard applies the value in exchange premise with the assumption of a hypothetical willing buyer and seller. This premise assumes the payment of cash proceeds, and that valuation discounts are allowed.

The *Value to the Holder* premise is frequently pertinent when the standard of value is investment value. As the name implies, this premise represents the value in its current form considering the owner's (holder's) vantage point. It does not assume a transaction. Value to the holder is the value as it currently is in form and ownership.

The fair value standard uses both of the premises above. The particular premise chosen depends on the scope of the appraisal. Most fair value appraisals will use the value in exchange premise (but not all). The key takeaway is that the former premise assumes a transaction whereas the latter does not.

Conclusion

Business valuation has two general premises of value with distinct subcategories used when applicable. If the entity expects to continue operations, the going concern premise of value will typically be used. Companies in or near liquidation will use the liquidation premise of value. If the liquidation value estimate exceeds the going concern value, the highest and best use principle often requires the liquidation value to be used – or at least considered. Finally, the standard of value primarily dictates the particular premise of value used.

SECTION THREE
VALUATION APPROACHES AND METHODS

At this juncture, you've learned quite a bit about business valuation. You've read about its history. You know why companies and individuals have valuations performed and who performs them. No longer apprenticed to the formalities, you understand the nuts and bolts of an engagement letter and what to seek out when reading it. We've even discussed the standards, levels, and premises of valuation.

In Section Three, we move on to the specific valuation approaches business appraisers use to determine company value. Depending on the purpose and scope of the appraisal, some approaches are required (or preferred) by law or legal precedence. Approaches not selected for use in a business appraisal may be required to have been given consideration by the appraiser. Combinations of approaches (and their respective methods) are frequently employed to estimate the final value. Approaches not used to directly value an enterprise often serve as tools to ascertain a reasonableness of the value estimate.

In this section we will investigate the three primary approaches used in business valuation:
1) The Income Approach
2) The Market Approach
3) The Asset Approach

We will also examine some of the methods used under each of the three approaches.

Because this book is intended for closely-held business owners, the discussion will be to the point and relate to concepts you are likely to encounter. I have read tens of thousands of pages of valuation literature on the approaches and methods alone. The information provided in this book is intended to help you understand the approaches used by business appraisers, reasons why appraisers choose particular approaches, and the implied level of value reached under each approach.

To stress that last sentence, pay close attention to the varying levels of value reached under each approach and method.

Finally, we will examine a hybrid approach called the Excess Earnings Method.

The goal of this section is to break down complex information into relatable, readable content. If at first you do not understand a chapter, go back and re-read it. The heart of business valuation lies in the approaches and methods used, and ultimately dictate your company's appraised value.

Chapter Eight

The Income Approach

Introduction

Chapter 8 introduces one of the three primary approaches to valuing closely-held companies. The Income Approach is one of the most prominent valuation approaches. Its prevalence in the valuation of closely-held businesses, however, has not always been favorably adopted by both practitioners and courts. Because the income approach and its many methods require a high degree of finance expertise, the approach was less frequently used when accountants governed the valuation industry. Over the past twenty years, and notably the previous decade, finance professionals have entered the field in greater numbers, bringing with them numerous types of advanced cash flow models.

The income approach, fundamentally, is the value of a company in today's dollars based on future cash flows or tomorrow's dollars. If correctly performed, the income approach is the most customizable approach available to ascertain a closely-held company's value.

Unfortunately, the income approach requires a thorough understanding of finance and economics. Even the simplest cash flow model necessitates sound comprehension of these sciences. Because relatively few appraisers have the requisite depth of knowledge in these areas, mistakes are not unusual in cash flow models. Valuation software has gained popularity for practitioners who lack this knowledge, enabling them to produce an error-free model. As you will learn, however, a model is only as good as its assumptions and the practitioner's understanding of them.

Generally speaking, the income approach contains a numerator and a denominator. This chapter examines the numerator, which is the entity's free cash flow. Chapter 12 dives into the denominator or cost of capital.

The Income Approach

The approach chosen to estimate a company's value will depend on several factors, including the purpose of the appraisal, availability of information, reliability of information, legal reasons (if applicable) and other project-specific variables.

The International Glossary of Business Valuation Terms defines the Income Approach as:

> "The Income (Income-Based) Approach is a general way of determining a value indication of a business, business ownership interest, security, or intangible asset using one or more methods that convert anticipated economic benefits into a present single amount."[14]

The income approach is, perhaps, the most widely used approach in business valuation and its adoption has grown over time. Investment and security analysis posits the income approach as the fundamental approach in determining an investment's intrinsic value. Because security analysis is the examination of investment securities – chiefly publicly traded stocks whose prices and price volatility are observable and measurable – it has a resounding home in closely-held business valuation.

The income approach has grown in popularity over the past few decades. Once an accountant-driven profession, the closely-held business valuation industry has been pushed forward by the influx of highly educated finance professionals. Judges, in turn, are adopting the income approach in greater numbers – with many preferring its use, or at a minimum, its consideration.

With greater adoption comes heightened responsibility by the business appraiser. Valuation models are inherently sensitive to discount rates. A high level of technical aptitude is required to perform complex valuation projects. Business appraisers lacking the expertise of financial valuation theory and application are easy targets for scrutiny. Discount rates used in

---

[14]http://bvfls.aicpa.org/Resources/Business+Valuation/Tools+and+Aids/Definitions+and+Terms/International+Glossary+of+Business+Valuation+Terms.htm.

the denominator are obtained from publicly traded companies, requiring the business appraiser to understand the levels of value and nature of these firms' business operations.

Before diving into the income approach and its methods, I want you to heed the most important adage that applies to any valuation model: **garbage in, garbage out**.

Make sure the cash flows and discount rates are reasonable. Every income approach includes a numerator (the top number) divided by a denominator (the bottom number). The numerator is a cash flow of some extension, or the sum of cash flows while the denominator is the discount or capitalization rate (adjusted for time when appropriate). If the approach doesn't feel right, contact the appraiser and discuss your concerns. Concerns may arise from its application and whether the approach or method should be applied, cash flow projections, discount rates used – any number of factors can produce a reasonable concern. The appraiser should have solid support for the discount and capitalization rates used. Any value estimate can be "backed into" by fudging the numerator, but more easily, by adjusting the denominator. Follow my pointers and prevent becoming a victim of business appraiser ignorance and laziness.

In discussing the income approach and its methods, the focus of this chapter will be on the numerator. In Chapter 12 we will more carefully examine the cost of capital found in the denominator.

Overview

The income approach is a forward-looking means of estimating an enterprise's current value using time value of money concepts. Future cash flows are projected into the future and then discounted back to the present. Cash flows (numerator) represent future cash receipts. The discount or capitalization rate (denominator) accounts for the firm's risk of receiving the projected cash flows. Understanding the basics of each is important.

Time value of money says that a dollar today is worth more than a dollar tomorrow. If the terminology sounds scary, don't let it get the best of you. A dollar is worth more today than tomorrow because of opportunity. You can take a dollar to the bank today, invest it and receive a day's worth of interest by tomorrow. Tomorrow that dollar will be worth more because of the interest earned. In the literal sense, you have more "worth" because of the interest gained from that dollar.

You've likely heard the story from a parent or grandparent about when they were kids, and a candy bar was only a nickel. Yes, that's true; the candy bar did cost five cents. But that was forty years ago. Inflation increased the price of the candy bar along with everything else. Wages earned to pay for that candy bar also increased. After adjusting for inflation, the price is relatively similar today as it was back then. The very same concept applies to cash flow modeling. We estimate what we think cash flows will be in the future. Because the projected cash flows are expected to occur years from now, those future cash flows are worth less today. (Remember, a dollar today is worth more than a dollar tomorrow, so a dollar tomorrow is worth less than a dollar today.) Therefore, we discount, or "bring back" the cash flow projections to what the value is today. That's it! Don't get lost in the technicalities.

Numerator

Business appraisers rely on executive managements' estimates of future growth. Corroborated with industry information obtained through research, the analyst will project a stream of receipts and expenses for a given number of years. Most discounted cash flow models require forecasting discrete cash flow numbers until reaching a sustainable growth rate. Otherwise stated, no additional years are forecasted once a projected stable growth rate has been achieved. In practice, many appraisers predict five to seven years, but no appraiser should be limited to a set number. Also in practice, many do limit themselves to a set number, usually five years. Reasons for this limitation include the inability to forecast beyond five years with precision (a justifiable cause) or "that's how we've always done it here" (an unjustifiable excuse).

Some business appraisers use accounting numbers as the numerator. I see this practice more commonly with accountants who are less versed in finance and economics. Yes, it can be used correctly if the appraiser makes the proper adjustments, but I highly recommend against its use. Business valuation using the income approach seeks the reality of an enterprise's economic value – not its accounting value. Reconciling the two can be complicated and messy. If your appraiser insists on using accounting figures in the numerator (net income, EBITDA or operating income), make sure the denominator matches. Net income serving as an after-tax accounting numerator does not belong in a pre-tax denominator equation.

Denominator

The denominator reflects a company's risk attributes through its cost of capital (or required return). A company's cost of capital is determined by, in principle, the risk of the entity receiving the projected cash flows. Time value of money is incorporated into the denominator to bring the future cash flows back to their present values. The cost of capital reflects the opportunity cost of choosing one investment over another. The cost of capital is (and will be) referred to other names, including the discount rate and the required rate of return. Like the numerator, the cost of capital is also forward-looking.

Opportunity cost is simply the cost of choosing investment X over investment Y. Assume you had money to invest in either stock X or bond Y. Stock X returned 3% over the year whereas bond Y returned 7%. Your opportunity cost – the cost of choosing X over Y – was 4%. In selecting an investment based on its cost of capital, the investor assesses the risks and potential rewards of each.

Riskier firms bear higher costs of capital to entice investment, whereas less risky companies have lower costs of capital. This statement has significant implications.

First, a higher cost of capital implies greater potential returns. Investors seeking higher returns must accept a higher rate of risk (higher discount rate). If you ever wondered why bank CDs pay so little, this is your answer. Bank CDs are safe, low-risk investments. Compare a bank CD to a small biotech firm that has a single product undergoing FDA approval. FDA denial could destroy the company and wipe out the investor's money, whereas approval would bankroll the investor. The bank CD has a low discount rate (low risk/low return) whereas the biotech firm has a high discount rate (high risk/high potential return). It's all about risk versus reward.

The time value of money has decisive persuasion in a cash flow model's valuation estimate. Longer duration cash flow estimates are more difficult to accurately project. Accordingly, time value of money properties reduces the total present value impact from discrete long duration cash flow estimates.

All else equal, the following mathematical rules apply:

- The **lower** the discount rate, the **higher** the present value of the company.
- The **higher** the discount rate, the **lower** the present value of the company.

These rules should make sense. A less risky investment has a lower discount rate. Because there is less risk borne by the investor, he is willing to pay more for it. Inversely, risky investments carry relatively higher discount rates. The investment's price must be less to attract investor dollars because those dollars are at greater risk of loss.

Author's Note: Throughout this book you will see me use the phrase "all else equal." In doing so, I'm saying to hold everything else the same except for the variable of discussion. Assume, for example, the following formula: $Y = A + B + C$, where $A=1$, $B=2$ and $C=3$.

The formula of A+B+C implies that Y is equal to 6 (1+2+3=6). Now assume that A is 5 instead of 1, but B and C are the same. Using these changed assumptions with "all else equal" – that the other variables, B and C, didn't change – the answer to Y has increased (5+2+3=10) relative to the previous value (10 versus 6). That's it. All else equal signifies that the other variables are being held constant, or unchanged.

● ● ●

Free Cash Flow

I promise not to venture into multiple cash flow derivations that years of CFA® studying burned into my brain. I'm also going to avoid accounting projections and the required adjustments needed to morph accounting numbers into economic sense. If your heart desires to learn more about these areas, a library of information is at your fingertips online. Knowing you likely want the core of the matter, let's begin.

(1) Free Cash Flow to Equity (*aka* Net Free Cash Flow)

Free cash flow to equity (FCFE) is the cash flow remaining for common shareholders after a company pays for its current operations and projected growth. Some investors call this the dividend paying capacity of a firm. FCFE accounts for capital expenditures, non-cash expenses (depreciation and amortization), working capital needs, and preferred stock and debt payments. You've probably heard the phrase "pay yourself first." Well, this is the residual after the company pays itself first (in cash). Because you can back into this number several ways, for brevity's sake here's the approach when using net income as the starting point.

Net Income
+ Depreciation & Amortization (and other non-cash charges)
− Capital Expenditures
− Net Working Capital *(needed to support growth)*
− Debt Repayments & Preferred Equity Retirements
+ New Debt Borrowings & Preferred Equity Issued
− Preferred Stock Dividends
= **Free Cash Flow to Equity (FCFE)**

Note: Net Working Capital (NWC) in the FCFE formula can also be positive (i.e. "+") instead of a subtraction as shown above. In most instances, however, NWC represents a cash flow requirement, mandating a subtraction (as shown in the calculation above). Accordingly, we will treat NWC as a subtraction in the FCFE calculation throughout this book. Just understand that NWC can theoretically be an add-back instead of a subtraction.

Again, FCFE is the amount available to *common shareholders*. Follow the equation. Net income is net of debt interest expense, so interest expense for holding debt capital has already been recognized. Common shareholders are last in the food chain, so preferred stockholders also get paid. The FCFE remnant is cash for common shareholders. Common shareholders are residual owners.

(2) Free Cash Flow to the Firm (*aka* Net Cash Flow for Invested Capital)

Free cash flow to the firm (FCFF) is the cash flow available to all suppliers of capital after taking care of a company's internal needs. FCFF is the cash paying ability (not dividend paying ability) of a firm after paying for current operations and projected growth.

Net Income
+ After Tax Interest Expense
+ Depreciation & Amortization (and other non-cash charges)
- Capital Expenditures
- Net Working Capital *(needed to support growth)*
= **Free Cash Flow to the Firm (FCFF)**

Note: Net Working Capital (NWC) in the FCFF formula can also be positive (i.e. "+") instead of a subtraction as shown above. In most instances, however, NWC represents a cash flow requirement, mandating a subtraction (as shown in the calculation above). Accordingly, we will treat NWC as a subtraction in the FCFF calculation throughout this book. Just understand that NWC can theoretically be an add-back instead of a subtraction.

Remember that FCFF is free cash flow to the *firm*. We want to know the free cash flow available to all of the company's capital suppliers. Accordingly, you'll note three differences from FCFE.

1. The first is to remove the impact of debt by adding back the after-tax interest expense. Interest expense is interest on the debt. Interest expense is tax-deductible, providing a tax benefit (cash benefit) to entities using debt. Because we want to know the cash flow ascribed to the firm in its entirety, all capital supplier impacts are removed. To eliminate the effect from using debt, the tax benefit of using debt must be withdrawn. We accomplish this by adding back the cash flow impact since its effect was recognized when deriving net income. This tax benefit add-back erases the cash flow gain from using debt, placing the cash flow stream on even footing among all suppliers of capital.

2. The second difference from FCFE is the removal of the net change in debt and preferred equity. In FCFF we leave these components alone, whereas the changes in FCFE are accounted for (i.e. net additions or subtractions of debt and preferred stock are included in the FCFE formula).

3. Finally, we remove preferred stock dividend payments from the FCFF equation.

Making these adjustments gives the analyst a picture of the gross cash flow available to all suppliers of invested capital – common shareholders, preferred shareholders and debt suppliers. For FCFE, we want to know the residual cash flow to common shareholders only. FCFF, on the other hand, is the gross cash flow to all of the entity's suppliers of capital.

An important caveat to note is that all accounting items (net income, depreciation & amortization) are "normalized." We'll cover normalization adjustments later in this chapter. For now, remember that accounting items for both FCFE and FCFF are normalized and are not "as reported" numbers. The goal is to discern cash flow performance from accounting performance. Cash is cash is cash whereas accounting numbers can be manipulated (Enron is a perfect example).

Which Cash Flow Approach is Better?

If you guessed "it depends," then you are correct. If you're itching for at least one reason now, I'll give you a taste. We touch on more examples and rationales throughout this book.

Both free cash flow multiples are numerators in estimating a firm's value. We must, however, make an apples-to-apples comparison and match the top (numerator) with the bottom (denominator). For this example, assume the appraiser is appraising the invested capital of a company and selects FCFF as the numerator. Many business appraisers refer to published cost of capital studies to choose a discount rate when valuing closely-held companies. Discount rates taken from these cost of capital studies are sourced from publicly traded company stocks. Discount rates are refined by industry and company size, ranging from large to small. Have the discount rates in the discount rate studies been adjusted for taxes? How about leverage (debt)? Companies within the same industry frequently have similar capital structures, but not all. Moreover, their capital structures aren't the same. FCFF is cash left over to all suppliers of invested capital. If unadjusted common stock movement (beta) of these publicly traded stocks is the cost of capital used in the denominator, the equation breaks down – it's theoretically flawed. The numerator includes cash flow to all suppliers of capital, but the denominator accounts for the risk borne only by common shareholders (common shareholders are the last to be repaid, making them the riskiest supplier of capital and bearing the greatest cost of capital). Going this route uses a potentially inflated numerator (FCFF accounts for the gross cash flows of all capital suppliers) divided by a denominator based on common equity variability. The degree of error depends on the ratio differential. Either way, the estimate of value is incorrect. One solution would be to use the weighted average cost of capital, or WACC, as the denominator. We'll discuss WACC in Chapter 12.

This example demonstrates a common flaw in valuation reports, which is the numerator/denominator mismatch. The depth of finance and economics knowledge required to perform a sound cash flow analysis gets challenging, fast. Having the knowledge gained from this one example puts you a leg up when reviewing a business appraisal. Moreover, understanding this concept enables you to uncover critical mistakes that would otherwise go unnoticed.

Two denominator rules apply when discounting cash flows. For FCFE, the discount rate should be the cost of common equity capital. For FCFF, the discount rate should be a firm's weighted average cost of capital. You may be itching to jump ahead and dive into Chapter 12. Don't scratch that itch. This book has been formatted to give you exactly what you need when you need it. Hang with me and I promise to deliver the goods at the right time.

• • •

Modeling 101

Here's where many business owners get lost, which is unfortunate on many levels. As a business owner, you're probably reading this book to gain a better understanding of business valuation. Some of you would like to race to this book's last section and learn about how you can save your business from valuation pitfalls. Understanding the fundamentals of a discounted cash flow model is critical to interpreting how your firm's value may be estimated (if an income approach is used) and how you can increase the value by recognizing and acting upon key value drivers. Cash flow models are the appraiser's primary weapon – used both in peace (gifting) and at war (M&A, divorce, etc.). Knowing how to navigate through a cash flow model is imperative as a business owner. Pushing through to gain an understanding is the largest obstacle many business owners face. Instead of speaking esoteric technical jargon that confuses the most astute individuals, my goal is to simplify the concepts. When you're done reading this book (and when reviewing your company's business valuation report), you will be able to point out the type of cash flow model used, discount rate, cash flow assumptions and whether or not your value estimate makes sense. Hang with me.

Discounting versus Capitalizing

Before getting our feet wet, let's differentiate two terms often misconstrued for one another. The cost of capital, discount rate and required rate of return are all synonymous. Collectively (or interchangeably) they encapsulate the time value of money and risk profile of the expected income stream on a compounded basis in the denominator. In plain-speak, the discount rate represents the total risk, which includes a risk-free rate. In contrast, a capitalization rate is merely a single divisor (denominator) applicable to a single period of cash flow or economic receipts. The capitalization rate subtracts the long-term sustainable growth rate from the discount rate. Don't get too bogged down on this now. The important point to remember is that a discount rate is not the same as a capitalization rate. Many business owners (and appraisers) confuse the two. Defend your position if you find yourself at odds with a business appraiser about the matter – you may be right!

Discounted Cash Flow (DCF) Models

The granddaddy of all cash flow models, the discounted cash flow model is the pinnacle of cash flow forecasting. Future cash flows are projected into the future and discounted back to the present value using an appropriate cost of capital. Projecting cash flows is the practice of predicting the future. Forecast what sales and expense numbers will look like in the future and the model reconciles free cash flow using the projections. The projected free cash flow numbers are then discounted (divided by) the appropriate cost of capital (which incorporates the company's risk, among other variables) to the present value (the denominator also accounts for time). If the concept "time value of money" (TVM) rings a bell, this is TVM at work.

Gordon Growth Model (aka Constant Growth Model)

Here come the formulas that you've been chomping at the bit in anticipation. Don't worry because they aren't as scary as they appear. We are going to start with the basic models and move into more complex, multi-stage models. If you find yourself not understanding a particular concept, go back and re-read the section you didn't comprehend. Each model builds on the previous. Do not skip ahead! Otherwise, you'll be scratching your head and saying I did a poor job of explaining cash flow models. Go in order, read each section and I promise you will get it.

The Gordon Growth Model (GGM) forms the base of cash flow models to come.

$$PV = \frac{FCFo\,(1+g)}{k-g}$$

In this (and other) examples, the term "free cash flow" (FCF) will be used instead of FCFE or FCFF – and for good reason. Because we must always match up (apples-to-apples) the numerator and denominator, each may be used, but their use depends on the circumstance (and therefore, the denominator). The answer of when to use each model is, as you might have guessed, "it depends."

Let's first attack this by defining the notations.
- *PV* is the present value. In this example, it's what your company is worth.
- *FCF with the small zero* is the free cash flow of a previous time (let the phrase "previous time" sink in because many appraisers screw this up). For this to work, the last period's free cash flow must be a normalized number. In other words, if the prior period's free cash flow was off the charts and next year's numbers (and after that) are unlikely to be close, using last year's number would be flawed.
- *g* is the expected long-term sustainable growth rate of free cash flow.
- *k* is the discount rate or cost of capital.

Look at the numerator. In this chapter, you learned that the numerator using the income approach contains a cash flow number. In the GGM, the numerator is a discrete cash flow number (discrete meaning "one period of cash flow") that has been "normalized" to reflect the cash flows expected for eternity. Some appraisers call it the base cash flow because it represents a normalized base cash flow amount that a company would expect to receive under normal circumstances. Forever FCF, as we'll call it, is multiplied by the forever growth rate (g). (It's actually (1 + g) to be mathematically correct.) To sum it up, the numerator is a forever cash flow increased by a forever growth rate.

The denominator used in the GGM is a capitalization rate. Here's where many analysts and owners get confused. As stated before, the discount rate is used to discount a series of cash flows. The GGM, however, is a single-stage model. The model only uses one set of assumptions – one FCF number, one growth rate, one discount rate. Subtracting the long-term sustainable growth rate (g) from the discount rate (k) is the formula for a capitalization rate, also called the cap rate.

Will you see this used? Probably not, at least not as the lone cash flow model to estimate your company's value. It can be used (and is), notably for businesses where the inputs (variables) have been and are expected to remain constant, and neither management nor the appraiser can provide a better estimate. Terminal values in multi-stage cash flow models also use the GGM. You'll learn more about the terminal value later in this chapter.

If an appraiser uses this model, check the following for consistency:
- Does the base free cash flow number make sense?
- Is the appraiser using free cash flow? Many closely-held business appraisers believe EBITDA is the same as free cash flow. Incorrectly calculating free cash flow is the most common flaw I encounter when reviewing appraisals that incorporate single-stage models. Be scrupulous in your review. Chapter 18 will uncover the copious defects of using EBITDA in valuation.
- Does the appraisal use a discount rate instead of a cap rate, or subtract the growth rate from a cap rate? Cost of capital is a concept beholden to economics and finance. Accountants who dabble in valuation tend to confuse the differences.

Capitalized Cash Flow Model

The Capitalized Cash Flow Model rehashes the Gordon Growth Model previously discussed. It is the same formula as the GGM. Because appraisers use terms such as "cap model" or acronyms like "CCM," I gave the capitalized cash flow model its respective section solely for your understanding. The numerator is the expected normalized free cash flow for the next period (period one) divided by a cap rate (discount rate minus expected long-term sustainable growth rate). Or if you wish to take it a step back, the numerator is the previous period's normalized base cash flow multiplied by the expected long-term sustainable growth rate divided by the cap rate.

Two-Stage Model

Break out the popcorn, sit back and relax because two-stage (or multi-stage) models are the weapon of choice for most business appraisers (myself included). The two-stage model mathematically expands the GGM single-stage model. An important detail to keep in mind upon reviewing the model is that I have included three periods in the formula provided. The two-stage formula presented is of three discrete periods (or years, in this example), but the appraiser can use any number of periods. Many appraisers use five to seven years, but the process is the same (the exception would be that additional discrete numerators and denominators would be included to account for the extra time periods forecasted).

$$PV = \frac{FCF1}{(1+k)} + \frac{FCF2}{(1+k)^2} + \frac{FCF3}{(1+k)^3} + \frac{\frac{FCF3\,(1+g)}{k-g}}{(1+k)^3}$$

The notation is the same as that used in the GGM; however, there are important differences to note.

As stated earlier, the formula shown represents a three-year period. Numerators for the first three years represent free cash flow expectations for those particular years and are notated by the numbers "1," "2" and "3" after FCF. The denominator in each of those years is a discount rate, not a cap rate, and is used to discount the numerator (FCF) back to the present value (hence the "power of" notation outside the brackets of each denominator).

Now to that last part – the ugly, yet most influential piece of the formula. It's not ugly when broken into pieces. More importantly, it is imperative (I say that with emphasis) that the appraiser gets this part right. Let's start dissecting.

$$TV = \frac{\frac{FCF3\,(1+g)}{k-g}}{(1+k)^3}$$

Dear reader, meet the Terminal Value (TV).

In most DCF forecasts, the TV represents the majority of a company's total value. If you haven't noticed, this formula is very similar to the GGM. As a business owner, you should make certain the appraiser gets this piece correct. Some of the most common mistakes, moving from top to bottom of the TV ratio, include:

- **Growing the final year's value an extra period, or year.** The DCF model used here is a three-year model. In the complete DCF equation, FCF is grown each year before introducing the TV. Also, note the very top of the TV ratio, where you see a "3" after FCF. Following that we grow (multiply) the 3rd year's FCF by the long-term sustainable growth rate (1+g). Many appraisers fall into the trap of increasing the TV's FCF number an additional period. For example, instead of using FCF3 in the TV, the appraiser will use FCF4 (the 4th year projection) and then grow it by the long-term sustainable growth rate. This step is incorrect and will discredit the valuation. It might seem like double-counting because the 3rd year's FCF is calculated twice – once in the TV and another preceding it in the model. Be assured that this is not double counting.

- **Using a discount rate instead of a cap rate.** On the second level of the TV equation, you see a cap rate (k – g) instead of a discount rate (k). If you haven't noticed yet, this is the GGM we discussed earlier and (k-g) is the cap rate in the GGM. Instead of using a baseline FCF number, we've projected FCF as far as we reliably could and then inserted the GGM to account for remaining growth and risk. Remember that the number of periods used in a DCF analysis is determined by when the company will achieve a sustainable long-term growth rate. At the end of the model we're stating that "we're here." We've reached the point where the rules governing the GGM apply. Beware of appraisers using the discount rate instead of the cap rate on this level. Again, we are talking about the terminal value.

- **Discounting the terminal value by the wrong number of years.** Here we've arrived at the last level of the TV equation, the very bottom part, or (1+k) to the 3rd power. Now that we have computed the terminal value three years into the future, it's time to "bring it home" by discounting the TV back to the present date. Similar to growing FCF an extra year, be sure the appraiser did not make the same mistake here, and the exponent (number "3" outside the brackets) is not increased one too many periods (using "4" instead of "3" would be the crime in this instance).

If you're anything like me, reading books about theory without explanation is painful. Examples help hammer in concepts. Moreover, because I cannot stress enough the importance of understanding how a DCF functions, working through the numbers is a worthy exercise. Assume the following free cash flow projections:

	year 1	year 2	year 3
FCF	$1,000	$1,200	$1,400

Now assume the discount rate (k) is 12%, and the long-term sustainable growth rate (g) is 3%. Mental digestion is more efficient in bite-sized pieces, so let's work through the discrete FCF periods first and then tackle the terminal value (TV).

	year 1	year 2	year 3
FCF =	$1,000	$1,200	$1,400
k = 12%	(1+12%)	$(1+12\%)^2$	$(1+12\%)^3$
PV of CF's	$893	$957	$996
Total Cash Flows (sum)			**$2,846**

Here we just divided each cash flow by the denominator. The denominator is the discount rate (12%) and incorporates each period's time ("bringing it back" to today's values using time value of money). The present values of each period's FCF are added together, totaling $2,846.

Try calculating the formulas on your own. Make sure to add the time value of money subscript. For those familiar with Excel, the notation would be ^2 for the second year, ^3 for the third year and so on. Accountants and those with accounting backgrounds are commonly more familiar with the time value of money factor multipliers. Using them is perfectly acceptable. If you aren't familiar with Excel, use multipliers. You can easily find time value of money multipliers online with a Google search.

Because I want you to understand this, I've created a page that calculates the denominator for you. Go to the website **www.valuationforowners.com** for more information.

Our next step is to calculate the terminal value. To help avoid confusion, I'm going to work through each level individually.

1) <u>Level one of TV:</u> **FCF3 (1 + g)**

	year 3
FCF =	$1,400
g = 3%	x (1+3%)
	$1,442

On the first level, we multiplied year three's FCF by the long-term sustainable growth rate, giving us a value of $1,442.

2) **Level two of TV: k - g**

The second tier instructs us to calculate the cap rate, which is (k – g) or (12% - 3%) = 9%.

At this point, we're merely applying the GGM by dividing the normalized FCF (i.e. long-term sustainable base cash flow) by the cap rate.

$$\frac{\text{FCF TV}}{\text{Cap Rate}} = \frac{\$1{,}442}{9\%} \longrightarrow \text{TV} = \$16{,}022$$

Dividing the free cash flow's terminal value (FCF TV) by the cap rate gives us a TV of $16,022. Using the GGM, this is the company's terminal value as of three years from today. Because we need to know what the value is today, we must discount the TV using the same denominator used when we discounted the discrete free cash flow stream for year three. A discount rate for three years – not a cap rate for four years – is used in the denominator or third level of the terminal value formula.

3) **Level three of TV: $(1 + k)^3$**

We must adjust the discount rate of 12% for three years (we're bringing the year three numerator of $16,022 back to today's value). The following picture shows the steps taken to calculate the discount rate used in the denominator.

k	12%
1+k	1.12
$(1 + k)^3$	1.40

The discount rate is added to 1 and taken to the third power, giving us a denominator of 1.40 (rounded).

4) **Finally, we divide the TV by the denominator.**

Terminal value	$16,022	$\longrightarrow$	$11,404
Denominator	1.40		

The discounted terminal value is $11,404. (If you divide the TV by the rounded denominator of 1.40, the discounted TV is $11,444.) We took the year three TV and incorporated time value of money and risk attributed to the investment, giving us the present day value.

Sum of discrete FCF's	$2,846
Discounted TV +	$11,404
Present value of the company	**$14,250**

Adding the sum of the discrete discounted cash flows to the discounted terminal value gives us a present value conclusion of $14,250.

To summarize, the company's (or investment's) value is worth $14,250 using the aforementioned cash flow projections, discount and growth rates. If you're scratching your head right now, re-read this section and use the tools provided to you at **www.valuationforowners.com** to help you grasp these concepts before moving on.

• • •

Timing of Cash Flows

As a business owner, you love the fact that all of your income comes in on the last day of the year. Isn't it wonderful how easy life is? Oh, and the tooth fairy delivers Christmas presents on Easter. Right...

Remember the exponent outside of the bracket in the denominator? The second year had a "2" and the third year had a "3." We need those numbers to account for the time value of money. Unfortunately, using an absolute, or rounded exponent like we did in the example implicitly assumes the company earns all cash flows at the end of each period. How realistic is that?

In closely-held business valuation, no two companies are alike. When venturing into varying industries, the differences of cash flow timing become greater. Some businesses are seasonal whereas other businesses have relatively even cash flows on a month-to-month basis. I'm not going to dive into the mathematical adjustments because the appraiser should do this after achieving an understanding of your business, which includes knowing the timing of your revenues. Here you can pick apart an appraisal and the appraiser who performed it. If you want to find out if you have a quality business appraiser, this will help.

When valuing companies, I review month to month cash receipts and speak with the company's management to confirm my beliefs. The cash flow models I have created allow me to change the timing of cash flows easily so that the receipts correctly match the timing. Many of the appraisals I work on require a simple midyear convention, implying that cash receipts are received evenly throughout the year.

If your company receives all of its cash at the end of the year, then using a rounded exponent makes sense. I'm going to guess that isn't the case. For that reason, check the discount rate's exponent and see what number is used (a "0.5" would be applied for the first period if using the midyear convention).

Also – and equally important – is consideration of the effective date. If the appraisal's effective date is March 1st and the appraiser forecasts the cash flow receipts on a calendar year basis (meaning each year's cut-off date is December 31st), then the discount rate should be further modified. Using the example of March 1st, two months have already expired in the current year. Even if all of your company's cash receipts occurred on December 31st, using a "1" as the exponent overstates the time by two months (and lowers the value). Every subsequent year will also be incorrect.

If your appraiser makes this mistake, ask why he didn't make the adjustment. If the appraiser can't answer your question or doesn't understand what you're talking about, you have a real problem. Hopefully, you haven't hired that appraiser yet. If not, ask which timing convention the appraiser will employ if he plans on using the income approach to value your company. Asking this question accomplishes two important goals. First, and most important, the answer received will speak volumes about the appraiser's knowledge. Many appraisers collect designations to appear credible, yet lack the fundamental knowledge to carry out the job. If the appraiser doesn't understand what you're asking, this helps you in qualifying a quality appraiser for your job. Second, if the appraiser understands your question, the feedback provided will help you gauge whether or not the appraiser knows your business. Because you're asking this question before engaging an appraiser (do so), the answer may not be correct. Don't penalize the appraiser for not knowing. It's too early in the process to know. You're only interviewing, and the appraiser hasn't reviewed your financial statements or conducted management interviews. Use this opportunity to understand the appraiser's knowledge gap. The appraiser needs to learn your business thoroughly before preparing a cash flow model. Use this as a talking point to expand the discussion about your business.

Normalization and Control Adjustments

A Normalization Adjustment is when an appraiser adjusts or changes a variable to reflect the economic reality of a company. For example, the numerator used in the capitalized cash flow model should reflect an economically valid number. If last year's results blew the top off but aren't expected to continue, the appraiser would normalize the number to one that more accurately reflects the company's expected economic reality. Normalization adjustments are often made to historical financial statements when the appraiser performs a financial analysis of the company's past performance and capitalization trends. The financial analysis is part of the narrative business appraisal and will include a ratio analysis of the normalized financial data. If your company's balance sheet consists of 30% cash whereas your competitors average 5%, the appraiser will remove the excess cash to provide an apples-to-apples ratio analysis comparison.

Control Adjustments, however, alter the appraisal's level of value. The numerator in the income approach determines control, not the denominator. Thus, adjusting the numerator changes the level of value from little or no power (minority level of value) to a control level of value. Remember in Chapter 6 that control, or lack thereof, determines the level of value. Assume the appraisal of a 70% interest in a company for a recently deceased business owner. For this valuation, the fair market value standard is used. Under the fair market value standard, the "hypothetical buyer and seller" presumption is made. Now assume that the subject entity is paying its employees 70% of sales whereas companies in the same industry and of similar size only pay their employees 40% of sales. According to the premise of value maximization and that human labor can be replaced, a hypothetical buyer would – to increase value – align the company's labor expense more closely with that of the industry's labor expense ratio. Reducing wages that generously exceeds the industry norm to one that more closely resembles that of the industry will improve the company's bottom line and value, all else equal. The appraiser, using industry statistics, compensation studies, and trade journals as support, will reduce expected labor expenses to more closely align the company's expense with that of the industry. Recall that the subject interest is a controlling interest and a hypothetical owner with control could make such changes. Remember, the fair market value standard requires a hypothetical buyer and seller. The economically sound decision (strictly economics here) would require a reduction in labor expense. Making a control reduction converts the level of value from a minority level (can't enforce change) to a controlling level.

Be careful not to confuse the two. Normalization adjustments are not control adjustments and vice versa. Control adjustments alter the level of value whereas normalization adjustments do not. Control adjustments are changes made from the controlling owners' vantage point. Normalization adjustments make no such claim, but instead, try to "clean up" the noise to improve comparability. Control adjustments change future cash flows. Normalization adjustments do not (unless accounted for elsewhere in the appraisal).

Conclusion

The objective of this chapter was to introduce you to the income approach and the primary methods used when an appraiser decides to use an income approach. If using the income approach, a discounted cash flow of some sort will almost always be the appraiser's tool of choice. We walked through an example of how a cash flow model works. You learned that the discount rate and capitalization rate are not the same (and why). I have also included the common flaws appraisers make and how to find them. Most of the chapter focused on the numerator, free cash flow. Chapter 12 provides greater insight into the denominator, cost of capital. Don't skip chapters. To fully comprehend the cost of capital concept and its importance in business valuation, you need to understand the other valuation approaches

Chapter Nine

The Market Approach

Introduction

The market approach is arguably the most empirically supportable approach to estimate an entity's value as of a particular date. Securing adequate and reliable information, however, constrains its use in the ability to apply it when appraising closely-held companies. Revenue Ruling 59-60 advises the appraiser to consider the market approach when performing an appraisal that falls under the ruling's scope.

Business appraisers seek to determine a company's value as of a specific date. The market approach provides an observable avenue to extract pricing information as of that particular time and apply it to the closely-held company. Multiples obtained from publicly traded companies, for example, are used as a proxy to determine what a closely-held business is worth. Transaction multiples of companies in similar industries are also used to establish a closely-held company's value. Reliability and comparability of information between businesses are crucial in the application of the market approach.

The Market Approach

The International Glossary of Business Valuation Terms defines the Market Approach as:

> "The Market Approach is a general way of determining a value indication of a business, business ownership interest, security, or intangible asset by using one or more methods that compare the

subject to similar businesses, business ownership interests, securities, or intangible assets that have been sold."[15]

The two methods most commonly used under the market approach are:
1) The Guideline Public Company Method
2) The Guideline Company Transaction Method

The underlying principle of the market approach is to use either publicly traded companies similar to the closely-held company *or* transaction multiples of private companies within the closely-held company's industry to determine a price. Publicly traded company prices are observable since their stocks trade on national exchanges. Information for these companies is widely available for free either through the U.S. Securities and Exchange Commission (SEC) or third party vendors. An active market is necessary when using the guideline public company method. As a result, companies trading on the major exchanges are typically used (NYSE, NASDAQ). Under the guideline company transaction method, transaction multiples and other financial metrics are procured from subscription-based vendors. (Pratt's Stats is a popular subscription-based provider of transaction multiples.)

A key benefit of using the guideline public company method is that information is abundant for publicly traded companies. The drawbacks, however, can be considerable. The relative size difference between the publicly traded businesses and the subject closely-held entity is often significant. Also, many publicly traded companies have numerous product or service lines and earn diversified revenue streams, whereas the concentration of product or service offerings for closely-held companies is common. Consequently, distortions in the similarity between the closely-held company and the larger publicly traded peer group companies can disqualify the market approach entirely.

You can't beat the market approach as a method of estimating company value as of a specific date when sufficient reliable and relevant information is available. Extrapolating publicly traded company information and using that information as the foundation for a closely-held entity, if soundly performed, provides a reliable statistic on what the current price of the closely-held company should be by proxy of observable prices. If transaction multiples are used instead, sorting out

---

[15]http://bvfls.aicpa.org/Resources/Business+Valuation/Tools+and+Aids/Definitions+and+Terms/International+Glossary+of+Business+Valuation+Terms.htm.

similar entities and using observable data multiples also supports the notion of a "real" price as opposed to a hypothetical estimate. The income approach, while strong in theory, cannot surpass the market approach in tangible proof. Whether publicly traded company price multiples or private company transaction multiples are used to determine a price conclusion, the reasonableness factor supporting the value estimate is improved by using the market approach.

When appropriate, the market approach may be combined with the income approach, with each approach weighted by the appraiser's best judgment. If the market approach is decided not to be an appropriate method, it still may be used – and often is – as a sanity check on the value conclusion.

Method One: The Guideline Public Company Method

The International Glossary of Business Valuation Terms defines the Guideline Public Company Method as:

> "A method within the market approach whereby market multiples are derived from market prices of stocks of companies that are engaged in the same or similar lines of business and that are actively traded on a free and open market."[16]

The guideline public company method (GPCM) is widely used to value medium to large closely-held companies when the appraiser can locate publicly traded comparable companies (called "comps"). Smaller businesses can also be appraised using this approach given the substantive number of micro-capitalization stocks traded on the NASDAQ exchange. Pink sheet stocks (unregulated markets), or the exchange they transact on, is not considered to be an "active market." The appraiser should avoid using pink sheet stocks as comparable companies under this method.

When It's Used

Valuations for tax-related purposes must at least consider the market approach. Fair market value is the standard used for tax-related appraisals. As the adoption of the fair market value standard has flourished and Revenue Ruling 59-60's prescription has increased as a guiding light for other appraisal purposes; today the market approach is widely considered

---

[16] Ibid.

and applied in many business valuations that extend beyond tax-related engagements.

Revenue Ruling 59-60 requires "careful analysis in each case"[17] and defines eight factors to consider when performing an appraisal under the guise of Revenue Ruling 59-60, with the market approach being one and noted as:

> "The market price of stocks of corporations engaged in the same or a similar line of business having their stocks actively traded in a free and open market, either on an exchange or over-the-counter."[18]

Revenue Ruling 59-60's interpretation understands that not every appraisal will use all factors. The ruling insists, however, that all factors should be considered in tax-related appraisals using the fair market value standard. Again, because this standard and the ruling have been adopted for several other purposes, the language is frequently applicable to non-tax-related appraisals as well.

When considered a candidate for the market approach, the appraiser will search for publicly traded companies that are similar to the subject closely-held entity. Many "mom and pop" enterprises quickly disqualify from using this method due to the inadequacy of similar publicly traded companies. In addition to matching companies within a similar industry, size discrepancies can render a guideline company impractical. For example, using Google as a comparable company under the GPCM to estimate the value of a small online advertising company would be impractical due to the relative size discrepancy. Another problem is aligning revenue streams. Closely-held companies are not only concentrated in sources of revenue, but also in customers. Having two or three customers representing half of an entity's total sales base is not unusual. On the flipside, many publicly traded companies diversify their revenue streams in both lines of business and customers. United Technologies (UTX) earns revenue from industries ranging from aerospace and defense to commercial refrigeration. Despite having one of the largest commercial refrigeration operations in the world, sales from the division are only a part of total revenue, which collectively includes defense, aerospace, elevators, HVAC, etc. Using UTX as a comparable company without division of segment lines in the valuation of a closely-

---

[17] Rev. Rul. 59-60, 1959-1 CB 237 -- IRC Sec. 2031.
[18] Ibid.

held commercial refrigeration company would be difficult to justify as appropriate. These are a few reasons why the guideline public company method is not always deemed proper.

The appraiser must also consider factors other than the industry when using the market approach. Tax courts have affirmed value conclusions using the market approach when the business appraiser used companies with similar economic characteristics that operated in differing industries. Companies with similar customer targets, seasonality, brand awareness and the like could be (and have been) used as successful comparable companies. The key determinant is that the comparable companies selected using the GPCM make economic sense.

Information Problems

If the appraiser can find a sufficient number of publicly traded comparable companies, information gathering is straightforward under this method. First, the analyst should select an adequate number of entities. What constitutes adequacy? (I bet you guessed the answer!) "It depends" is the industry answer, although fewer than three is probably too scarce. The appraiser should find an adequate number of companies to avoid significant variances in valuation multiples. In practice, five or more should be selected if using the guideline public company method.

Information on publicly traded companies is the bonus of this method because it's plentiful, easily retrievable and (best of all) free. The SEC requires publicly traded companies to file quarterly reports (10-Q filings) and annual reports (10-K filings). Quarterly reports are "reviewed" (not audited) and can easily be downloaded into Excel. Annual reports are "audited" and are also easily transported into Excel. Finally, third party data resources are available, for a fee, to retrieve information in a more efficient manner. The downfall of using third party providers is the efficiency gain can result in a loss in quality. Most third party data providers download the SEC information and categorize it into pre-determined categories, resulting in the loss of discrete items which may be relevant to the appraiser. Third party data services are invaluable in saving time, but the appraiser should review the raw data to ensure he did not unintentionally ignore any material items.

How It Works

After importing the data (into Excel, for example), the appraiser calculates financial ratios of the comparable companies. The ratios are then converted into multiples, and these multiples are then applied to the closely-held company's financial statistics. We'll go through an example in a minute, but don't gloss over the previous two sentences. Through this application, the appraiser is extracting pricing multiples from the publicly traded companies and applying those multiples to the subject closely-held company.

Let's walk through an example using the "price to sales per share" ratio. Assume the comparable publicly traded company's stock price was trading at $10 and the company had sales per share of $8. The price to sales per share ratio would then be 1.25 ($10 ÷ $8). Now assume the closely-held company had sales of $20 million for the most recent year. To extract the "market price" based on the price to sales per share ratio, the appraiser multiplies the publicly traded company multiple of 1.25 by the closely-held company's sales figure of $20 million. Therefore, the value of the closely-held company's equity using this assumption is $25 million. Notice how this is the value of the company's common equity and not the company's total value. By using per share amounts, we separate common equity from other suppliers of capital. We'll address that differential soon, but keep it fresh in your mind as you read through this chapter.

Common Multiples

Remember two seconds ago when I told you to keep something fresh in your mind? We're here (see, that didn't take long).

The following multiples are equity multiples – also referred to as pricing multiples – and are used to value the common equity (and only common equity) of a closely-held company.
- Price to sales per share (P/SPS)
- Price to book value per share (P/BVPS)
- Price to earnings per share (P/EPS)
- Price to cash flow per share (P/CFPS) (Cash flow, as you know, is more than a single calculation. It can take many forms. The appraiser should ensure that the calculation is consistent.)

Appraisers also use other ratios, but these are the most common in calculating equity values. Notice how each ratio contains "price" as the numerator. Using "price" in the numerator is an important concept and key to why these ratios are used to calculate common equity and not total capital. Price, as employed in the multiple, is the price of common shares of the publicly traded company's common equity capital. Common stock represents the value of the company's common equity. If valuing common equity, the price per common share is the correct numerator to use. Also, note that the denominators are all "per share" amounts. Again, we're valuing the common equity of the closely-held company. As such, we need the relevant numerator value applicable to common shareholders, requiring the use of per share numbers (of common stock) in the denominator.

Using multiples with price as the numerator has some drawbacks, the most important being the failure to recognize a company's capital structure. Price is attributed to common equity shareholders and ignores debt and preferred equity suppliers of capital. Companies with vastly different capital structures (and hence, financial risk differences) can yield similar common equity multiples that may be baseless when compared with each other. Invested capital multiples are used to correct this problem.

The following multiples are invested capital multiples used to value the company as a whole with consideration of all suppliers of capital. Because we want the market value of invested capital (the current value of all capital), the notation for the market value of a company's invested capital is MVIC.

- MVIC to sales (MVIC/S)
- MVIC to book value of invested capital (MVIC/BVIC)
- MVIC to earnings before interest and tax expense (MVIC/EBIT)
- MVIC to earnings before interest, tax, depreciation and amortization expense (MVIC/EBITDA)

In addition to the change in the numerator (using MVIC instead of P), the denominators have also changed when compared to the equity multiples. Gone is the "per share" verbiage following each multiple's denominators. All invested capital is accounted for when using MVIC as the numerator. Remember that ratios should be on an apples-to-apples comparison. To match the numerator with the denominator, we need to find denominators that include information pertinent to all suppliers of capital.

Business appraisals customarily focus on appraising a closely-held company's common equity value, so the MVIC multiples require an additional step to extract the common equity component. If we include all suppliers of capital (usually just debt for many small to medium-sized closely-held companies), then we must remove the non-common equity components.

Assume, for example, that the appraiser selects a comparable company's MVIC/sales multiple of 1.10 to apply to the subject closely-held business. Annual sales for the closely-held company's most recent year were $20 million. Finally, presume the closely-held company carries an interest-bearing debt amount of $5 million.

To calculate the equity value of the closely-held company based on the publicly traded guideline company multiple, we first multiply the MVIC/sales multiple of 1.10 by the closely-held company's sales of $20 million. The product of $22 million yields the closely-held company's total capital estimate, not common equity. By using a total capital numerator (MVIC) and denominator (total company sales), we account for all suppliers of capital. The closely-held company's debt of $5 million is then subtracted from the total capital value of $22 million, giving us a common equity value of $17 million. The preferred stock would also be subtracted from the value if the closely-held company had preferred equity.

As a business owner reviewing an appraisal, you should be aware of a particular area of concern. Having reviewed other business appraisals and noting the erroneous application of market multiples (making apples-to-bananas ratio comparisons), I would be amiss for not mentioning it. Make sure the appraiser uses time periods that align with the valuation. If an appraisal has an April 1st effective date, for example, the guideline public company data should also be as of April 1st. Many publicly traded companies use a calendar year as their fiscal year (therefore, December 31st is the year-end). Year-end financial statements (10-K filings) retrieved from the SEC's website incorporate a full year. An easy (lazy) method is to ignore the quarter-end financial statements (ending March 31st) and only use the most recent year-end financial statement information. The SEC doesn't require trailing twelve-month data to be included in quarterly income statements (10-Q filings). Incorporating the latest quarter requires work, which requires time, which increases cost, which is why cheap appraisers produce inferior products. The dates won't always align, perhaps because the appraisal's effective date is in-between quarters of the publicly traded guideline companies. If the appraisal's effective date is in-between quarters, the appraiser should, at a minimum, use the most recent quarter prior to the effective date.

Another approach is to use the quarterly financial statements that are substantially closer to the effective date – even if the quarter-end date occurs after the closely-held business appraisal's effective date. I know this goes against what you learned earlier in this book about how the appraiser can only use information "known or knowable" as of the effective date. My rebuttal is that most information for publicly traded companies is perceptible because of information transparency in equity markets. Therefore, it passes the "knowable" test in many situations. I use this method only when the effective date and publicly traded company period-end dates are very close.

Normalization Adjustments

The appraiser should make normalization adjustments to financial statistics of the guideline public companies and the subject closely-held company when necessary. Valuation is the discovery, or pursuit, of a company's true economic value. Non-recurring items and other normalization adjustments are made to ensure comparability between the publicly traded guideline companies and the subject closely-held entity. Without normalizing the guideline companies' financial information, erratic multiples with little significance to the economic operations of the company are introduced. Fortunately, many publicly traded companies operate efficiently enough where necessary normalization adjustments are minimal (if made at all).

Level of Value

When valuing the common equity of a minority interest in a closely-held company, most appraisers will use equity or pricing multiples. Common stocks traded on a stock exchange are assumed to transact at a marketable minority level of value. Buyers of these shares are (assumed to be, and in most instances are) minority investors who lack control of the company's operations. The shares trade on a liquid, marketable exchange.

For control valuations, invested capital multiples – where MVIC is the numerator – should be used. The premise behind this recommended application is that the controlling owner of a closely-held company has the wherewithal to change the company's financial structure. A controlling owner can make operational decisions and dictate the firm's debt to equity balance. Using a pricing multiple (price as the numerator) assumes the interest is a common shareholder with the voting powers of a minority shareholder. A minority shareholder lacks the control to impact capital structure decisions. On the other hand, controlling interest owners possess these traits that minority shareholders lack. Accordingly, the application of pricing multiples (minority level multiples) for a controlling interest, without further adjustments, would produce an incorrect level of value conclusion.

Method Two: The Guideline Company Transaction Method

The guideline company transaction method (GCTM) is the other commonly used method under the market approach. Instead of relying on publicly traded company multiples to determine value, the GCTM uses multiples derived from actual transactions that have occurred. The appraiser then applies those multiples to the subject closely-held company. Estimating a closely-held company's value using merger and acquisition multiples (otherwise known as transaction multiples), this method is also known as the Merger and Acquisition Method.

The International Glossary of Business Valuation Terms defines the Merger and Acquisition Method as:

> "A method within the market approach whereby pricing multiples are derived from transactions of significant interests in companies engaged in the same or similar lines of business."[19]

When It's Used

Valuations for tax-related purposes must at least consider the market approach. The same standards and considerations noted in the guideline public company method apply. As previously discussed in the guideline public company method, one of the principal impediments of using the guideline public company method is securing an adequate number of comparable publicly traded companies. Revenue Ruling 59-60 requires consideration of the market approach. Here's where the GCTM becomes especially advantageous.

Closely-held companies, notably smaller firms, are typically single product or service focused businesses. Despite the company's industry, these businesses are usually fragmented. Many fall in the small to medium-size value range. Think of the local dentist, insurance agency, auto-repair center – any product or service offering that requires a local presence. Economies of scale afforded to multinational conglomerates are not possible for these types of firms. I'm not claiming that economies of scale aren't realizable at a smaller level – they are – but the level of scale is much lower on a comparable dollar level. Economies of scale are cost savings (advantages) received from increased size, whether size is defined as output or scale of operations.

---

[19] http://bvfls.aicpa.org/Resources/Business+Valuation/Tools+and+Aids/Definitions+and+Terms/International+Glossary+of+Business+Valuation+Terms.htm.

Unlike the guideline public company method where information is abundant and free to access, closely-held company transaction information can be difficult and costly to obtain. Closely-held business owners of private businesses are not usually ecstatic about opening up their company's financial statements to third parties (and rightfully so). Some, however, agree to disclose information to service providers, especially if the transaction took place through a business broker. The extent of information provided by the business brokers often depends on the transacting parties' willingness to disclose information. Sometimes the entire "deal" (so to speak) is provided, whereas other times only particular multiples are given without full disclosure of owner compensation or other financial details. Hence, a degree of reporting bias is introduced into the data.

By subscribing to one of the available databases, appraisers can search for transactions applicable to the subject closely-held company. Industry, geography and financial relativity (sales, for example) are used to narrow down deal multiples that best "fit" the subject entity.

The benefit of using transaction multiples is that they are frequently more relatable to the closely-held company. Appraising the local dentist's office is nearly impossible to do using the guideline public company method. Dentistry is a fragmented industry, meaning dental offices are spread throughout the country, in both ownership and geography. Most dental practices consist of three or fewer practitioners per building, with many having just one. Database transaction information provides a more comparable level of value. Moreover, the transactions reported are real deals. They provide a direct indication of value.

Finally, the guideline company transaction method can be used as a test of reasonableness. Using dentistry as an example, we know that the guideline public company method is highly unlikely to be used under the market approach. Assume the closely-held business being appraised is a specialty dentistry practice and few, if any, transactions are available for this particular niche. The income approach is deemed appropriate, but the market approach has been determined as not being reliable enough to provide a sound value estimate. Using the income approach to value the entity directly, the appraiser can "check" to see if the value estimate is reasonable using private transaction market multiples. In this case, the appraiser would find transactions similar to the specialty – perhaps general dentistry if the economic demand factors were congruent – and use those multiples as a test of reasonableness on the value conclusion derived from the income approach.

The force propelling the GCTM as a test of reasonableness lies in the understanding that while the transaction data failed to be reliable enough to calculate the closely-held entity's value directly, the data is good enough to help ensure the value estimate isn't illogical. Business appraisals should read like a thesis paper with all appropriate support included. In many circumstances, the GCTM can aid the appraiser in supporting the argument, or conclusion of value.

Information Problems

We already discussed the difficulties of information retrieval, so now we'll address the information used. As a business owner, you want the appraiser to use the most reliable and relevant statistical multiples to estimate your firm's value. Business appraisers have considerable subjectivity in deciding the search components when filtering for transaction multiples.

The period used to filter transactions should be proper. Transaction multiples for most technology firms during the late 1990s would not apply to technology companies in the late 2000s. Because you know the industry better than the appraiser, feel free (trust me, we appreciate the information) to divulge your industry's trend information. An insufficient number of transaction multiples may influence the period used. For example, the appraiser may expand the time horizon and include more years to obtain an adequate number of transactions. By casting a wider net to "catch" more transaction multiples, the data may include non-normal time periods. The impact on your firm's value could be better or worse, but in either case, it will be incorrect if significant non-normal and non-current trends have occurred within the period that would bias the value one way or another.

After filtering for transaction multiples, the database provides a summary of transactions included in the search population. A series of multiples – which we will address shortly – are listed, along with each multiples' respective dispersion metrics. Dispersion measures differ by the database provider, but a range, mean (average), median and coefficient of variation (CV) are common for most database vendors. The range is simply the lowest and highest transaction multiples. The mean and median multiples are the average and middle multiples, respectively. Finally, the coefficient of variation indicates the extent of the population's variance in relation to the population's mean multiple for all transactions included in the search (i.e. the population).

Many appraisals include the summary information in the report. If so, identify which transaction multiples the business appraiser used to value your company. Of the multiples selected, see what their respective CVs are compared to the multiples not selected. All else equal, you should prefer a multiple with a lower CV. The lower variation (lower CV) indicates that transactions are occurring at multiples closer to the population's average transaction multiple (i.e. the data is more reliable). Think of it like a target that's been shot several times. A target with a tight cluster around the middle indicates a good shot and is analogous to a low CV. On the other hand, a target with shots scattered all around suggests a comparatively poor shot and is analogous to a high CV. Some business appraisers, especially when valuing a company using both the market approach and the income approach, will select and apply the multiple that best "fits" their value estimate. Don't fall prey to this lazy scheme. At times, the higher CV multiples will make sense. If so, the appraiser should provide a sound justification for support. Also, determine whether the appraiser used the mean or median multiple. Averages (mean) can provide significantly varying indications of value if outliers exist, whereas the median more ably ignores outliers by selecting the middle multiple. More often than not, the median multiple should be used.

Assume, for example, that you have ten transaction multiples. Eight transaction multiples are the same at 0.5; one multiple is at 0.3 and the last at 5.0. The variation may appear dubious, but in practice, it's not uncommon. The mean and median of this data set is 0.93 (rounded to 0.9) and 0.5, respectively. Here's a tabular view of the data.

Mean	0.9
Standard Deviation	1.4
Min	0.3
25th Percentile	0.5
Median	0.5
75th Percentile	0.5
Max	5.0

Obviously, the median multiple is more reflective of the population and should be used. The mean is 86% greater than the median – and that's a lot! The median, however, lies within a standard deviation of the mean. In other words, the difference is not statistically different. Using the mean could be justified when viewing it from a purely statistical viewpoint, especially if the dataset included twenty or more transactions. The point is, you know which transaction multiples are more likely to be relevant based on the modes (frequency of a multiple's occurrence) of the transactions in the dataset. But what if the appraiser's income approach estimate was on the high side? It's much easier to select the mean and justify an inappropriate multiple than it is to perform additional research on market multiples. A reasonable approach under this circumstance – after additional information was selected, tested, and continued to conclude that the market approach was correct – is to rethink the income approach's assumptions. Let me tell you; that's a lot of work. What if the appraiser works for a firm that uses billable hours to price valuation engagements and account for employee productivity? Overages are frowned upon as a lack of planning on the appraiser's account or indicates that the appraiser is taking too long to complete a project. Either way, the appraiser is pressured to get your project done as soon as possible. Knowing that, which route do you think the appraiser will take? Plugging in the mean multiple can save days of the appraiser's time whereas a thorough search for the truth will penalize the appraiser under most of these firms' cultures. It's worth your time to review the transaction multiples selected if the appraiser uses the guideline company transaction method.

A final point that I want you to be aware of is the use of multiple transaction databases to extract valuation multiples. Procuring private company transaction data is difficult. Many of the databases obtain transaction information from the same sources, so overlap of multiples is not unusual. Business appraisers should eliminate any overlapping multiples found in the dataset when multiple database providers are used to acquire transaction multiples. Reviewing tens or hundreds of multiples takes time and effort, both characteristics of a quality appraiser. Another "tell" to help determine if your appraiser has quality components is to request the data (if not provided) and search the information yourself to see if overlapping multiples exist in the dataset. The appraiser may or may not be cooperative with your request, and CPAs are typically not required to release it since the data isn't client-provided information. Overlapping transaction data nullifies the statistical validity of the multiples by double-counting transactions. Whether the effect is up or down depends on the search. No matter the directional impact, the price estimate will be statistically flawed.

How It Works

Appraisers usually select more than one multiple to provide greater assurance of accuracy. Transaction multiples are then applied (multiplied) to the closely-held company's financial statistic. In a perfect world, the multiples would all provide identical outcomes. In reality, the multiples will differ, but the differences are often manageable if the data is reliable and statistically valid. Depending on the variance of results and circumstances, the appraiser may eliminate certain multiples and average the results or weight multiples by a weighting factor based upon subjective reliability and calculate a weighted average. Or the appraiser might use an entirely different method to determine the multiple. The key takeaway here is that selecting multiples is a subjective process. Although the information may be statistically sound, the appraiser has considerable latitude in which multiple to apply. Many appraisers are familiar with the average, or mean, and use that. What if the dataset has significant variability and the median or harmonic mean (a definition beyond the scope of this book) are more reasonable multiples? Having reliable information is one thing. Applying the correct statistic and supporting its application is where quality appraisers shine from the pack.

Before we get to common transaction multiples that you can expect to see, let's walk through the practice of applying multiples to a closely-held company's financial data. Assume the transaction database's median MVIC/sales multiple is 0.45. To extract the company's total invested capital multiple (MVIC represents all invested capital), the appraiser multiplies the transaction multiple of 0.45 by the closely-held company's sales. Using $20 million as sales, the company's MVIC is $9 million (0.45 x $20 million = $9 million). Subtract invested capital other than common equity – interest bearing debt and preferred stock – to calculate the closely-held company's common equity value.

Common Multiples

Private closely-held companies lack observable prices. Unlike the guideline public company method where prices and financial multiples are easy to access, the same information cannot be easily found for closely-held private companies. Aside from the lack of transparency, most of the transactions included in the databases when using the guideline company transaction method are asset sales as opposed to stock sales. Where a stock sale would have a single price, an asset sale has many "prices" that are allocated to pieces of the transaction. I don't want to confuse you too much here. You're reading this book to understand an appraisal report better, not to learn about purchase price allocation and tax treatment of goodwill. The key takeaway is that most of the transactions within the databases used to select multiples under the guideline company transaction method are asset sales. If not filtered, the mixture can include both asset and stock sales. Your appraiser should scrub each transaction to determine its merit, and the inclusion or exclusion of a transaction will vary depending on the subject closely-held company.

Some of the more common multiples used are:
- MVIC/sales (or net sales)
- MVIC/gross profit
- MVIC/EBIT
- MVIC/EBITDA
- MVIC/discretionary earnings
- MVIC/book value

At face value, these appear digestible – and they are if you know the full extent of information included in each numerator and denominator. I first had this under "information problems," but I think it fits better here so you can visualize the multiples. Each transaction database provider has its respective formula for defining the numerator and denominator. Most of the attention is on the denominator as the numerator is calculated similarly by most data vendors and valuation textbooks. Denominators, on the other hand, differ. The difference depends on the service providers used to obtain the multiples. Recall the transaction overlap that occurs when appraisers use multiple database providers and fail to eliminate duplicates. An added problem of using multiple transaction database providers is the definition of multiples. Even after eliminating duplicate transactions, the appraiser must further adjust for formulaic differences in the multiples. Formulaic differences are typically focused on the denominator. Adjusting for differences takes time, effort and knowledge. Contact your appraiser for the definition if you would like to know which database the appraiser used and the applicable definition of each variable.

Normalization Adjustments

Normalization adjustments, if necessary, are made to the closely-held company's historical financial statements. The purpose is to provide comparability for ratio analysis. Unlike the guideline public company method, however, there are no peer group companies to compare to the subject closely-held company. Industry data providers fill this void, providing common-size financial information and ratios. Normalization adjustments to the closely-held company's financial information will be made to place the company on an apples-to-apples comparison to companies within the industry. Caution must be taken because a normalization adjustment becomes a control adjustment if improperly administered. Adjustments made by the appraiser will depend on the appraisal's level of value. The appraiser, especially if valuing a minority interest, may not make any normalization adjustments. Minority shareholders lack the influence to impact operations or change the company's capital structure. Accordingly, appraisers operating under this guise believe that no adjustments should be made for minority interest appraisals. On the other hand, normalizing financial information is customarily done to gain critical insight into the actual performance of the company's operations. I see the merits in both camps. Normalization adjustments depend on the subject interest. Whether or not adjustments should be applied cannot be elucidated in one guideline paragraph.

Level of Value

Merger and acquisition transaction multiples imply one party has gained control and another has relinquished it. Transaction multiples, therefore, produce a control level of value. Whether the control level is marketable or nonmarketable is a matter of debate in the valuation community. I'll leave it up to your business appraiser to make that decision, but here's how I approach the issue.

For control valuations (where the calculated estimate yields a controlling level of value) a discount for lack of marketability is applied on a case-by-case basis. In my appraisals I refer to this as an illiquidity discount, reflecting a discount for lack of liquidity. Marketability is achieved through the transaction. As such, the value of marketability is already embedded into the transaction multiple. However, I'm not valuing the transaction multiples. I'm valuing a closely-held company that would incur transaction costs to achieve liquidity. Selling a company is not a costless activity. Transaction costs, including legal, brokerage, accounting and administrative expenses are incurred during the transaction. Be cautious of illiquidity discounts painted as discounts for lack of marketability. Anything higher than 15% is beyond my comfort level. I get uncomfortable at 10%, but the actual discount taken depends on the size and nature of the company. Applying the same 15% lack of liquidity discount to a company with a balance sheet holding 80% cash and liquid investments to another company whose assets consist primarily of machinery and equipment is likely not reasonable. Again, however, the discount depends on the subject interest and this example should not be used as a boilerplate discount determinant for all appraisals.

Discounts for lack of control (DLOC) and lack of marketability (DLOM) are frequently applied in minority level of value appraisals. Moreover, the discounts are implemented in that order, sequentially (Chapter 13 examines valuation discounts). Minority shareholders lack the ability to control company operations and are limited in liquidity and marketability of their interest. Unlike a controlling shareholder that can affect change, a minority shareholder is at the mercy of controlling shareholders and governing documents. Discounts for lack of marketability for minority interest appraisals are nearly always much larger than those for control-level valuations.

• • •

Rules of Thumb

Rules of thumb populate every industry. Closely-held business owners like to have a sense of what their company is worth. In many cases, rules of thumb provide a semi-accurate value estimate. Throughout my career, I've witnessed some industries to have (surprisingly) relatively accurate rule of thumb valuation estimates. What I've also gleaned is that annual sales figures tend to be the most reliable rule of thumb value indicator. An example would be to use two times sales (multiply two by last year's sales) to calculate the rule of thumb value estimate (again, this is very much driven by industry). EBITDA, on the other hand, is what most business owners like to suggest when discussing value. EBITDA serves a purpose in some industries when using a rule of thumb approach. Those industries are those that:

1) Have the same capital structure (same debt to equity mix),
2) Have the same working capital requirements,
3) Have the same tax rate, legal structure, and depreciate fixed assets the same,
4) Spend the same amount on capital expenditures (Cap-Ex), and
5) Operate in an industry with zero real growth (the multiple never changes).

Companies within a handful of industries have comparable attributes. For these industries, EBITDA can be applied as a rule of thumb to provide a semblance of value. EBITDA, however, is one of the crudest proxy cash flow multiples. It serves a purpose, especially in financial analysis, but EBITDA's use in the valuation of closely-held companies can be cancerous. Chapter 18 discusses the many pitfalls of using EBITDA as a valuation tool, and why you should be weary of the use of EBITDA in closely-held business appraisals.

When Rules of Thumb Are Used

Here we're talking about using rules of thumb in valuations of closely-held businesses. Rules of thumb fall under the market approach because each industry tends to have them. First, rules of thumb should not be used as a direct method to estimate a company's value. Unless each company in an industry is exactly the same and sells for the same pricing multiples, rules of thumb are useless for direct application in valuing companies.

However, (yes, there's a catch) rules of thumb can be useful when performing a test of reasonableness, which is a "sanity check" on the value conclusion. If a rule of thumb is used to perform a sanity check, the appraiser must perform enough research to assure that a statistical relationship exists between the rule of thumb and the value conclusion.

Let me give you an example of a beverage distributor business valuation I performed. The rule of thumb used in this particular industry was a price per case of beverages. Management and ownership were unyielding in their belief that a particular distributor's value was based solely on the volume of cases sold multiplied by a per-case price. Using any other approach, according to management's perspective, was akin to cursing industry scripture. The company had acquired other distributors throughout the years, and the prices paid for these distributors were based on this rule of thumb. After considerable research, interviews with management, speaking with other industry executives and direct customers, I learned that their understanding of price and value were not in harmony.

The company sold several brands of beverages, mostly to retail outlets. Some brands had existed for decades while others were relatively new. The one common denominator was that all of the company's products were consumable beverages – and that was the only similarity. Each brand carried a different growth rate (some brands were growing while others were fading away), price point (consumers paid a premium for some and much less for others) and sales volume. Using management's rule of thumb multiple, about two-thirds of the values were correct. A large quantity (about one-third), however, were premium beverages carrying multiples of 30-60% higher than the rule of thumb used. Ownership and management, accustomed to buying entire distributors, failed to dig deeper into the growth potential and price trends of the individual brands. Cognizant of what distributors were selling for as a whole, they ignored the portfolio of individual beverages in each of the distributors. Ownership and management also knew that some brands carried a higher multiple than others. What they failed to recognize was that the industry they operated in was undergoing a seismic shift in consumer tastes – and it had been doing so for the previous five years. Instead of addressing the underlying problem, ownership, operating under the rule of thumb principle, acquired other distributors to increase the company's gross sales. Mathematically this should make sense if the multiples were correct. Greater volume multiplied by a rule of thumb price multiple equates to a larger bottom line dollar margin (with the expectation that margin percentages would remain static). It didn't happen.

Flaws

The beverage company example is characteristic of businesses and industries that are married to rules of thumb. Some are – most aren't. Let's discuss why rules of thumb are best reserved for sanity checks, when appropriate, and should never be used as a primary method for valuing a closely-held company.

Are you unique (your business, that is)? If you're better than your competitor, and you have similar sales, margins, etc., then why is your company worth more than your competitor? On paper, you two are more or less same. Why would an investor pay more for you than your competitor?

Forgive me for being direct. When meeting with clients I don't engage the topic in this manner (unless we're friends, then I absolutely do!). I can count the number of times on my elbow that a business owner said his company's direct competitors were "better than" or "worth more than" the business owner's company. Business owners are proud of their heritage, their business, its products or services, and naturally believe their company's value is superior. When speaking to you, the business owner, the business appraiser needs to understand why your company is more valuable than your competition. If your firm's financial performance lines up with competing firms in your industry, why would anybody pay a dime more for your company than your competitor?

An entire chapter could be devoted to the responses alone! Most include something to do with a particular process, a specialized tool, history of operations, key individuals in the company, reputation and the like. All are excellent answers, too.

And all are reasons why rules of thumb don't work. Using a rule of thumb puts your company on the same valuation playing field as every other company in your industry. Intangible value – all the characteristics listed above (and there are more) – is a real value. Why would anybody pay $1,000 for an iPhone when a $300 Samsung smartphone provides similar utility? Both companies operate in the same space. Both sell similar products. How about a Chevy compared to a Honda? Quality between the two has never been closer. GM has recently exceeded its foreign competition in many categories – yet foreign cars carry a higher price tag. Why?

The answers to these questions are numerous, and nearly all are correct. "Value" identifies itself in many shapes and forms. But one thing is clear: no two companies are exactly alike. As a result, rules of thumb should not be used to value a closely-held company directly.

Conclusion

Appraisers using the market approach have two general methods at their disposal. The guideline public company method extracts financial multiples of publicly traded companies that are similar or have similar attributes to the closely-held company. Once extracted, the multiples are applied to the closely-held company's financial data, providing a market value estimate. The level of value is a marketable minority level if unadjusted for control.

The guideline company transaction method pulls transaction multiples from deals that have transpired within the closely-held company's industry. These multiples are then applied to the subject closely-held company's financial data. Because these transactions indicate a transfer of ownership, the level of value under this method is that of control.

Rules of thumb have been used for generations as a rough means to determine value. Today's advanced valuation approaches and methods disqualify using a rule of thumb to estimate a firm's value directly. Using a rule of thumb approach can, however, serve as a test of reasonableness of the value conclusion.

Chapter Ten

The Asset Approach

Introduction

Unlike the income and market approaches which are frequently used to value operating entities, the asset approach is reserved for specific valuation engagements. Years ago I viewed the asset approach as a liquidation method. That is, I saw it as the value of the subject operating entity as if the company was dead. A "floor" value of the company. My view today is much different. A rigorously applied asset approach can be one of the most thorough ways to valuing an operating entity (when appropriate).

The asset approach is customarily applied when the premise of value is a liquidation premise, or when the highest and best use of the subject interest calls for the asset approach. Before diving into the asset approach, however, I would be amiss without briefly touching on a hybrid approach called the Excess Earnings Method (EEM). The excess earnings method incorporates both the asset approach and the income approach. The EEM is often used when the standard of value is fair value (especially with financial reporting and marital dissolution). Chapter 11 discusses the excess earnings method.

Most owners (and appraisers) view the asset approach as the floor value of a company. As previously mentioned, I too believed this to be true early in my career. Many appraisers continue to use it as a sanity check on the value of a company, or test of reasonableness.

As opposed to the income and market approaches to value, the asset approach is relatively straightforward in its application. The appraiser "writes up" the assets of the company to their current values and subtracts the debt from the written up asset values. The residual amount is the fair value of the company's equity.

One common problem in the asset approach is the mismatch of the premises of value. Under the asset approach, the business appraiser focuses on the firm's aggregate net assets to provide an estimate of value. Either the going concern or liquidation premise of value is used. The individual assets themselves are often subject to different appraisal premises of value. Instead of two premises of value used in business valuation, real estate appraisers have several premises of value that may conflict with the business appraisal's premise of value. When added up, the premises of value for the underlying assets of the company may differ, subverting the business appraisal's efficacy.

The Asset Approach (The Adjusted Net Asset Approach)

The asset approach is also known as the adjusted net asset approach, cost approach, net asset approach or asset accumulation approach. No matter the terminology, the asset approach – which I refer to as the adjusted net asset approach – is a simple formula that is often misunderstood.

The International Glossary of Business Valuation Terms defines the Asset Approach as:

> "A general way of determining a value indication of a business, business ownership interest, or security using one or more methods based on the value of the assets net of liabilities."[20]

Revenue Ruling 59-60 provides instruction for business appraisers to review the asset approach. When discussing weight to be accorded to various factors, the ruling states:

> "Earnings may be the most important criterion of value in some cases whereas asset value will receive primary consideration in others. In general, the appraiser will accord primary consideration to earnings when valuing stocks of companies which sell products or services to the public; conversely, in the investment or holding

---

[20] http://bvfls.aicpa.org/Resources/Business+Valuation/Tools+and+Aids/Definitions+and+Terms/International+Glossary+of+Business+Valuation+Terms.htm.

> type of company, the appraiser may accord the greatest weight to the assets underlying the security to be valued."[21]

The ruling is saying that for businesses that make and sell goods and services, the income approach should be afforded greater weight. Holding company values, on the other hand, are often closely tied to the values of the holding company's underlying assets. As stated, for these enterprises the appraiser is advised to consider giving "the greatest weight to the assets underlying the security to be valued." Most operating entities sell goods and services. For these companies, the income approach will be considered. Many Real Estate Investment Trusts (REITs) and Family Limited Partnerships (FLPs) are not in the business of selling products and services. REITs that hold commercial or substantial income producing real estate properties are an exception. These entities offer a service, and the approach (or approaches) used to value companies that fall within this area will usually consist of both the income and asset approaches (and possibly the market approach as well).

Regardless, many of these non-operating holding companies own valuable assets, usually securities and real estate (numerous asset classes and types can be held within these holding company structures), highlighting the relevance of using the asset approach.

The second section in Revenue-Ruling 59-60 applicable to the asset approach is as follows:

> "The value of the stock of a closely held investment or real estate holding company, whether or not family owned, is closely related to the value of the assets underlying the stock. For companies of this type, the appraiser should determine the fair market values of the assets of the company. Operating expenses of such a company and the cost of liquidating it, if any, merit consideration when appraising the relative values of the stock and the underlying assets. The market values of the underlying assets give due weight to potential earnings and dividends of the particular items of property underlying the stock, capitalized at rates deemed proper by the investing public at the date of appraisal. A current appraisal by the investing public should be superior to the retrospective opinion of an individual. For these reasons, adjusted net worth should be accorded greater weight in valuing the stock of a closely held investment or real estate holding company,

---

[21] Rev. Rul. 59-60, 1959-1 CB 237 -- IRC Sec. 2031.

whether or not family owned, than any of the other customary yardsticks of appraisal, such as earnings and dividend paying capacity."

Here the IRS is drilling down into real estate holding companies, in addition to other similarly structured entities. Other important factors to note is the consideration of expenses, including liquidation expenses. Capitalization rates are mentioned. Appraisals of the assets are said to be preferred over the retrospective opinion of individuals. To end the paragraph, the IRS tells the appraiser when the adjusted net worth (asset approach) should be considered over other approaches to valuation.

When It's Used

The asset approach is customarily employed per the direction of Revenue Ruling 59-60 (pushing aside the excess earnings method for now). Holding companies or entities whose values are embodied in their underlying assets as opposed to their earnings capability are usually appraised using the asset approach. Again, examples here include real estate holding companies (REITs) and family limited partnerships (FLPs) where the entity's value is more directly aligned with the value of the company's underlying assets as opposed to its earnings ability.

My specialty as a valuation practitioner lies primarily in estate planning and gift tax valuations. FLPs are commonly used as instruments to pass wealth from one generation to the next (known as "gifting"). Many FLPs consist of liquid securities (stocks and bonds) and real estate (hunting properties, farm land, just about everything). Appraising the liquid securities is straightforward. Stocks and bonds are publicly traded. Price information is non-disputable and easy to obtain. On the other hand, real estate requires real estate appraisals. For these FLPs, the client orders appraisals for the real estate held in the FLP and the real estate appraisal is valued to match the "effective date" of the FLP appraisal. Combined, the liquid securities and real estate rarely possess much, if any, earnings power. Using the income approach would be futile with little income to discount or capitalize. We're trying to uncover the entity's value. An entity (or investment) with significant asset-level values but low-income generation is analogous to valuing your home based on the income stream you receive. You likely receive no income, and probably pay a mortgage. Nonetheless, the home has value. Appraising a holding company using the asset approach is similar. Depending on the underlying assets, the value could be (and often is) significant. Accordingly, the IRS states that attention should be given to the values of the underlying assets. Valuation discounts are then applied to the value of the entity, lowering the value of the partnership interest. A lower value of the partnership interest means less tax is paid on the gift of the partnership interest. The size of valuation discounts applied depends on the size of the interest gifted, the restrictive guidance in the partnership agreement, underlying assets and other entity-specific facts.

Information Problems

In my experience, most holding companies that business owners invest in hold little (if any) closely-held stock. As such, let's focus on what you're likely to encounter. Again, this is from my experience, and some owners will have holding companies with significant positions in closely-held company stock. First, if the appraiser is performing an appraisal using the asset approach, you're likely either gifting or facing liquidation. Assuming (and hoping) the former is the case; I'll address the information problems prevalent when appraising a holding company for gifting purposes.

Note: *A holding company can be structured in several ways. Limited Partnerships (or Family Limited Partnerships) – FLPs – are just one common way. Limited Liability Companies (LLCs) and other structures are also used for holding companies.*

Underlying asset values are either very easy or tough to obtain – and there's usually no middle ground. Pricing for stocks and bonds can be found online with ease. Real estate or fixed assets (tractors, large pieces of machinery) require an appraiser skilled in appraising that particular asset type. Once a real estate or real property appraiser is selected, the appraiser must be informed of the correct "effective date" that matches the business appraisal (FLP appraisal and business appraisal are used interchangeably here). Moreover, the premise of value must be in harmony with the business appraisal. Here's where real estate and business appraisal standards vary. Remember from Chapter 7 that there are two premises of value in business appraisal: going concern and liquidation. Real estate appraisers have additional premises of value. Because this is a book on business valuation and not real estate, I'll spare you the differing premises of value and reasons each is used. As a business owner, know that the premise of value for the real estate or real property appraisal must align with that of the business appraisal. If you have chosen a quality business appraiser and real estate appraiser, each will understand what you mean. The important point is to make sure the premise of value and the effective date of the real estate or real property appraisal matches the business appraisal.

Another problem I encounter is the subject interest's size. I take issue with the business appraiser or attorney advising on the transaction here, yet it's the business owner who pays the cost of the aforementioned parties lack of attention. Here's how it usually works: the real estate appraiser will be contacted by the owner's attorney or the business appraiser (or the owner). The real estate appraiser is told to value a property, using an explicit premise for a defined effective date. No problems yet. What the informant fails to tell the real estate appraiser – and what the real estate appraiser will infer – is the size of the subject interest. Gifting customarily transpires over many years, with gifts made annually. Therefore, the interest is a minority interest (which as you know, is worth less than a controlling interest). One thing that doesn't vary between business and real estate (in principle) is control versus minority value. A parcel of indivisible property is worth much less than the entirety, especially for real estate. Implying the appraisal is for the entire property, the real estate appraiser proceeds and completes the appraisal. The appraisal is then sent to the business appraiser to complete the valuation. A quality business appraiser will read through the real estate appraisal to make sure everything matches (if not, the IRS will – and here's another circumstance where cheap becomes expensive). While reading through the real estate appraisal, the business appraiser notes the real estate appraisal's value is of the entire piece of land, not the small percentage included in the business appraisal.

Now somebody – whoever is willing to own up to the mistake – is faced with a costly and reputation-damaging scenario. The cost will be borne by the business owner even though in most cases the error has been caused by the attorney or the business appraiser. I have yet to encounter a real estate appraiser blunder the subject interest valuation as long as the information was communicated correctly before the real estate appraiser began the appraisal process. With a relatively worthless appraisal, the real estate appraiser must re-appraise a certain percentage of the property (not the whole). Procrastination amplifies the cost. Gift tax valuations aren't usually on the top of business owners' minds. Employee-owners are more concerned with running the daily operations of their firms. Not until an attorney contacts them about "doing the annual gift" does it come into play. With a last minute valuation performed to begin with, now the real estate appraiser must re-appraise the property with the newfound information – that the interest is a minority interest and not the entire divisible piece.

Fortunately, despite the mistake, most of the real estate appraiser's work has already been done for the new minority interest appraisal since the appraiser has already performed a complete property appraisal. Determining a minority interest from the controlling value usually takes a comparatively less amount of time. Nonetheless, the real estate appraiser is also conducting appraisals for other clients, all wich are time sensitive. Do not think the appraiser will not charge a premium for this added value. Regardless of the time spent making adjustments, you need a correct appraisal and the value of having it being correct is substantial. No matter what the added expense is, it's an added expense that could have been avoided at the onset by communicating to the real estate appraiser what percentage was to be appraised.

While discussed earlier in the book, I need to emphasize again that a real estate appraisal will save you money in the end. (This is particularly the case when the property's value is significant.) Saving time and money are necessary, but if you want the appraisal done right, spend the money now and sleep easy. Or you can roll the dice and pay multiples later in tax penalties and endure an IRS audit. Don't use values pulled from a county assessor's website. Tax districts assess properties differently according to the tax code unique to that county. Moreover, the date of the valuation, percentage interest of the subject property appraised, and premise of value will all differ from the county's assessment. Imagine an IRS engineer opening up your file where real estate is a quarter or more of the entity's total value and the engineer can't find a real estate appraisal. The lack of support introduces an immediate red flag and possible cause for an audit. Save yourself a headache and do it right the first time.

One final information problem that exists more often with operating entities versus FLPs and other holding companies is the existence of intangible value. Under the asset approach, each asset is appraised individually and then summed together as a collective group of assets. Intangible values such as management excellence and superior succession planning (to name a few) are left out of the valuation. The excess earnings method, which incorporates the asset approach as part of its valuation procedures, attempts to capture the intangible value of an entity. You'll learn about the excess earnings method in the next chapter.

How It Works

Of the many names given to the asset approach, I like the adjusted net asset approach best because it accurately reflects the processes required. As a business owner, you're not likely to encounter the asset approach being used in your company's valuation unless it's a holding company. The asset approach is often performed for gifting strategies that business owners use to reduce their taxable estates and for family succession planning. To keep things simple, I'm not going to get into the complexities involved in adjusting operating-entity values. If you find yourself reading an operating entity valuation where the appraiser used the asset approach, know that more adjustments than those noted below will likely be made. Off-balance sheet arrangements, inventory, prepaid items – these are traits of operating entities and rarely apply to FLPs.

The calculation at its basic form is as follows:

1) Assets are written up to their fair market values. Any assets on the balance sheet that do not reflect their actual values require an appraisal (e.g. real estate).

2) Liabilities – usually long-term debt for holding companies – are measured at cost (the amount of debt remaining). The theoretically correct method is to have an appraisal of the debt. Interest-bearing debt is similar to a bond. Market values (prices) of publicly traded bonds (debt) change daily, depending on interest rates, duration, and other factors. Accordingly, the debt should be adjusted to reflect the true economic value of debt on the books. Separately valuing the debt would be especially important if the debt's interest rate varied significantly from the interest rate of similar instruments as of the effective date. In practice, most FLPs carry minimal debt, and this isn't a concern. Off-balance sheet debt, such as operating leases, should also be included as debt when computing the adjusted net asset value of a company.

3) Now that the asset and liability values have been written up to their current values, subtract the debt from the assets. The result is the current value of the entity's equity value.

Level of Value

The net asset value resulting from the asset approach assumes the owner has full access to the assets. As a result, the level of value is that of control. Marketability is also assumed because the liquid assets (marketable) and real estate appraisal values (marketable) align. Together, the adjusted net asset approach concludes a control, marketable level of value.

Accounting Book Value is Incorrect

Accounting book value and economic book value are different concepts that usually provide radically different values – and this fact cannot be truer when an entity owns real estate. Book value, or accounting equity, is the subtraction of liabilities from total assets on a company's accounting balance sheet. Accounting and economic principles are not the same. Because FLPs often hold real estate, we'll focus on this particular line item.

United States accounting rules (GAAP) requires most companies to hold real estate at cost. The definition of "cost" includes items in addition to the cost of the actual real estate, but the principle is that the cost number initially recorded stays the same. Note that I'm not talking about improvements (e.g. buildings) – just real estate. A purchase of land in 1955 registered at $5,000 will be listed on a 2016 balance sheet at $5,000. The accounting value is unrealistic compared to the economic value. You can imagine scenarios where the real estate's value could be between $10,000 and millions of dollars.

Not much else needs to be said here. Don't use accounting book value as an estimate of value under the asset approach if the entity owns real estate.

• • •

FLPs – Tell Me More

You purchased this book to increase your understanding of business valuation and business appraisals. Nowhere in the title or chapters did I mention tax strategies to legally minimize taxes and retain business ownership in a tax-efficient manner. I felt, however, that you should be aware of these plans. Family limited partnerships (FLPs) usually require the application of the asset approach. Accordingly, I felt this section belonged here while it was fresh in your mind.

FLPs and other asset holding companies structured to accomplish the same purpose are collectively referred to as Investment Partnerships. For this chapter, however, we'll use the FLP nomenclature – but both represent the same strategy or investment vehicle.

Many owners of small and medium-sized businesses believe these are strategies of the ultra-rich. Yes, the ultra-rich use these strategies – but there's no reason why you can't or shouldn't either.

Gifting strategies encompass entire books in the legal, accounting and valuation worlds. I'm going to provide an example and if you find yourself interested in gifting, contact your trusted attorney. If your attorney doesn't know, contact one who practices in estate planning. Don't knock your attorney for not knowing – estate planning is a niche practice. Any practitioner (legal, accounting or valuation) who practices in all fields is an expert in none. Also, don't fall into the trap of believing that one attorney can solve all of your legal concerns. Many business owners have a lawyer they conduct their business affairs through. Because you trust your attorney (I'm assuming so), seek referrals for estate planning attorneys. Beware of blindly accepting a referral, though, because the referral may be a "that's the only estate planning attorney I know" type of scenario. Get a good one.

In this example, we're going to discuss a family limited partnership (FLP) comprised of liquid securities (publicly traded stocks) and a parcel of real estate. The depth and breadth of this example are microscopic. Gifting shares of closely-held company stock to transition a business in a tax-efficient manner (not covered here) is one of my favorite types of valuation engagements – and the strategies in just that scenario vary widely. Don't succumb to the notion that "trusts" and "estate-planning" are solely for the ultra-rich. Business owners sometimes get caught up in the negative connotation of spoiled trust fund children without understanding the legal protection and tax savings these tools provide. I'm not an attorney and do not offer legal advice. That point cannot be stressed enough. I can, however, give you a simple example that may open your eyes to what you might be missing out on.

Chapter 13 covers valuation discounts, so don't yet concern yourself about how the discounts are calculated. It isn't necessary for this example.

The following strategy is under intense IRS scrutiny. In late 2015, the IRS almost amended IRC 2704(b) under Chapter 14. Chapter 14 of the Internal Revenue Code establishes rules for making transfers of an estate to family members. Moreover, Chapter 14 allows a family business owner to lower the owner's taxable estate by transferring appreciating assets to other family members. The owner retains an interest in the asset but removes appreciation potential from the owner's estate. Because the standard of value is fair market value, valuation discounts are used to further reduce the value transferred. While the intended breadth or depth of the pending IRS action is unknown, one thing is for certain: the IRS isn't letting down. Furthermore, there are a number of tests that this type of transaction must meet to be allowable (IRC Sections 2701-2704, which makes up Chapter 14). If not allowed, the underlying assets are written up to their values (no valuation discounts), and the tax is applied to the undiscounted value. Do not blindly enter such transactions without the counsel of a good (emphasis added) estate planning attorney.

Assume you have a portfolio of $10 million. The portfolio consists of publicly traded stocks and a parcel of land. At the suggestion of your estate planning attorney, you create a family limited partnership and place the assets in the partnership. You have three children that you wish to gift interests of the partnership to over an extended period. Limited partnerships consist of both general and limited partners. General partners make decisions whereas limited partners are economic participants. General partners usually own a fraction of the entire partnership, yet have control of the partnership's actions. General partners are the management of a company (or FLP, in this case). Limited partners have little say, if any, in business operations. Per your attorney's advice, you create a separate entity (an LLC) which is the general partner. Under the LLC's operating agreement, you are the general partner and make all partnership decisions.

As of 2016, the IRS allowed tax-free gifts of $14,000 per recipient. In this case, for example, you could gift each child $14,000 tax-free, for a total of $42,000, and pay no tax (for one year, in 2016). Gifting strategies established well in advance can provide incredible tax savings. The annual gift exclusion is reviewed annually and adjusted for inflation.

Five years later you start making gifts to your children. Each child will receive a 3% minority limited partner interest in the partnership. You have an appraisal performed on the real estate, and the remaining assets are liquid securities. After summing the assets together, over the past five years, the partnership has grown from $10 million to $15 million in value. Each child will receive a 3% interest or $450,000 in the value of the underlying assets via the partnership.

A business appraiser is retained to value each of the gifted interests. After reading the restrictive language in the partnership agreement that severely restricts transfers of partnership interests, lack of meaningful voting power, etc. – the business appraiser determines a 30% total valuation discount is reasonable. A total valuation discount includes a discount for lack of control (DLOC) to account for the minority level of value, and is combined with a discount for lack of marketability (DLOM) because the interests are not freely marketable (can't trade them on an active market and receive proceeds in a reasonable period). Together these discounts total 30%. In Chapter 13 you'll learn about valuation discounts, but note that DLOCs and DLOMs are not summed together because they're multiplicative. You do not add a 15% DLOC to a 15% DLOM to reach a 30% total discount.

With a 30% discount, the taxable values of each gift declines from $450,000 to $315,000. Instead of paying gift tax on $1.35 million, you're taxed on $945,000. The tax savings alone are worth six figures.

The example above ignores built-in capital gains taxes. A hypothetical buyer would surely consider the tax consequences incurred for buying an investment that had an embedded tax liability of $5 million (or $150,000 per 3% recipient). Previous tax court rulings have allowed dollar-for-dollar reductions in value to account for the implied tax liability, increasing the dollar size of the gift while retaining the percentage transferred. Other rulings have supported the present value of a contingent tax liability. The structure of the entity (C-corporations versus a pass-through entity, such as an LP) is also an important factor to consider in handling the built-in capital gains. The point of the built-in capital gains tax reduction is that the taxable amount of the interest is reduced, lowering the tax paid on a pre-discounted basis (e.g. the value is reduced before applying valuation discounts). Built-in gains apply to the asset approach only. Assets are taxed when sold. Income is taxed when earned. Because we're discussing assets and not income, the built-in gains tax reduction only applies when using the asset approach.

To wrap this chapter up, I'm going to list some of the benefits of gifting, followed by some pointers to note when making gifts.

Why would somebody follow through with a gifting strategy like the one given in the example?
- Tax avoidance (not evasion) provides for the transfer of assets with minimal tax incurred. Valuation discounts amplify the amount transferred and minimize taxes.
- Removing assets from a higher tax bracket and placing them in a lower tax bracket creates a tax alpha. Of course, this assumes your

children are in a lower tax bracket. Alpha is merely beating another alternative (outperforming a specified benchmark). You could keep the assets and pay a higher tax, or you could pass them to your children, pay the gift tax now and let the incremental tax savings grow. Over time, and incorporating time value of money properties, the value of the tax savings (including gift tax paid when the gift was made) will exceed the "do nothing now" strategy. Tax savings are attributed to the incremental differences in tax brackets and taxes paid by you and the recipients, which in this example are your children.

- Asset retention. The real estate you wanted to stay within your family will remain with your family.
- Lower estate taxes upon death. In 2016, the taxable estate threshold per person is $5.45 million, or $10.9 million per married couple. Amounts exceeding this rate are taxed at 40% (max rate). Gifting reduces your taxable estate. Ignore this if you would rather pay the government estate tax instead of passing your wealth on to loved ones.

Contact your attorney for guidance, but here are some pointers you should note when making taxable gifts:

- Gifting interests upon formation of the FLP, or soon after, will draw the IRS's ire. Wait months (or years) before gifting FLP interests. Immediate gifts signify that the FLP's sole purpose is to avoid taxes. Details were left out for brevity's sake, but the purpose of an FLP should not be entirely to avoid taxes. Contact an attorney before acting or face the IRS voiding the gift transactions, leaving you with a hefty tax bill and possible fines.
- If you haven't learned by now, the IRS doesn't like cheap. Document and support your values. Don't just use the book value of a company to define its worth. Use real estate appraisals to secure values for FLP valuations when real estate is held in the entity.
- Don't fall for appraisers promising exaggerated discounts. This tactic is becoming more commonplace as nefarious appraisers compete on price (they don't have quality, so they're price competitors). Despite the competition, any appraiser must be able to stand behind the business valuation performed. Appraisers promising substantial valuation discounts before reviewing FLP documents are unethical. Some appraisers become known as "aggressive" and position their firms accordingly. Good luck fighting the IRS with those guys.
- Finally, make sure the gifts are denominated in dollars. Appraisers come from differing backgrounds, and many seem to have a difficult

time understanding why this is important. Ask an attorney or appraiser who has had to perform a valuation rebuttal and you'll be quick to learn. We (business appraisers) like to work in percentages and units. Make it clear to the IRS what you are doing. Spell it out in plain English. Confusing them can only worsen the problem.

Conclusion

The asset approach, or adjusted net asset approach, yields the economic equity of a closely-held company. Balance sheet assets and liabilities are written up to their current values. Present value liabilities are subtracted from the current value of assets, producing the current value of the closely-held company's equity. Because economic and accounting values often differ, accounting values should not be used as proxies for current values. Accordingly, a company's accounting book value of equity should not be mistaken for its actual economic value.

You also learned how family limited partnerships can be used to transfer wealth in a tax-efficient manner. I hope this added material injected a glimpse into how succession planning works — especially if you don't currently have a succession planning strategy in place. The example provided was just one of several opportunities available to help you transition ownership of your business (or other assets/wealth) from one generation to the next. Strategies can be customized to meet your needs and desires. If you don't currently participate in a succession planning strategy, I encourage you to speak with an estate planning attorney and determine whether a succession planning strategy is right for you.

Chapter Eleven

The Excess Earnings Method

Introduction
The Excess Earnings Method, also called the Formula Approach, is a hybrid between the asset and income approaches. Application of the method has evolved over time, and its breadth has increased. One of the implicit shortfalls of using the asset approach when valuing operating entities is the inability to capture the intangible value of a going concern or collective group of assets. The excess earnings method attempts to capture the intangible portion by adding another approach to the asset approach.

The Excess Earnings Method
Prohibition helped to establish the excess earnings method. In 1920, the IRS published the Appeals and Revenue Memorandum 34 (ARM 34) in response to Congress amending the Constitution by passing the 18th Amendment and implementing Prohibition. Businesses involved in the alcohol trade were suddenly worthless due to the ban on spirit production and consumption. ARM 34 created a basic equation to determine the intangible value of alcohol distilleries to compensate alcohol brewers for their losses resulting from Prohibition. Known as the excess earnings method, or the formula method, it lives on today. Because many of these companies negatively impacted by Prohibition had little value regarding tangible assets (things that can be touched) but were otherwise very profitable, the excess earnings method provided a formulaic way to

measure the intangible value (a value that's there, but can't be touched). While born in 1920, the excess earnings method would later be mentioned in IRS Revenue Ruling 68-609.

The excess earnings method is the most inappropriately applied method in valuation today. To give you a full understanding why it's inappropriately used – and because you may encounter an appraiser using this approach for your valuation – you need to understand what the method was meant to accomplish. According to Revenue Ruling 68-609, the "formula" approach should be used as follows (emphasis added):

> "A percentage return on the average annual value of the tangible assets used in a business is determined, using a period of years (preferably not less than five) immediately prior to the valuation date. The amount of the percentage return on tangible assets, thus determined, is deducted from the average earnings of the business for such period and the remainder, if any, is considered to be the amount of the average annual earnings from the intangible assets of the business for the period. This amount (considered as the average annual earnings from intangibles), capitalized at a percentage of, say, 15 to 20 percent, is the value of the intangible assets of the business determined under the "formula" approach.
>
> The percentage of return on the average annual value of the tangible assets used should be the percentage prevailing in the industry involved at the date of valuation, or (when the industry percentage is not available) a percentage of 8 to 10 percent may be used.
>
> The 8 percent rate of return and the 15 percent rate of capitalization are applied to tangibles and intangibles, respectively, of businesses with a small risk factor and stable and regular earnings; the 10 percent rate of return and 20 percent rate of capitalization are applied to businesses in which the hazards of business are relatively high.
>
> The above rates are used as examples and are not appropriate in all cases. In applying the "formula" approach, the average earnings period and the capitalization rates are dependent upon the facts pertinent thereto in each case.
>
> The past earnings to which the formula is applied should fairly reflect the probable future earnings. Ordinarily, the period should not be less than five years, and abnormal years, whether above or

below the average, should be eliminated. If the business is a sole proprietorship or partnership, there should be deducted from the earnings of the business a reasonable amount for services performed by the owner or partners engaged in the business. See Lloyd B. Sanderson Estate v. Commissioner, 42 F.2d 160 (1930). Further, only the tangible assets entering into net worth, including accounts and bills receivable in excess of accounts and bills payable, are used for determining earnings on the tangible assets. Factors that influence the capitalization rate include (1) the nature of the business, (2) the risk involved, and (3) the stability or irregularity of earnings.

The "formula" approach **should not be used if there is better evidence available** from which the value of intangibles can be determined. If the assets of a going business are sold upon the basis of a rate of capitalization that can be substantiated as being realistic, though it is not within the range of figures indicated here as the ones ordinarily to be adopted, the same rate of capitalization should be used in determining the value of intangibles.

Accordingly, the "formula" approach may be used for determining the fair market value **of intangible assets of a business only if there is no better basis therefore available.**

See also Revenue Ruling 59-60, C.B. 1959-1, 237, as modified by Revenue Ruling 65-193, C.B. 1965-2, 370, which sets forth the proper approach to use in the valuation of closely held corporate stocks for estate and gift tax purposes. The general approach, methods, and factors, outlined in Revenue Ruling 59-60, as modified, are equally applicable to valuations of corporate stocks for income and other tax purposes as well as for estate and gift tax purposes. They apply also to problems involving the determination of the fair market value of business interests of any type, including partnerships and proprietorships, and of intangible assets for all tax purposes."[22]

The IRS lists two critical points in Revenue Ruling 68-609 – points that many business appraisers ignore.

First, the method "should not be used if there is better evidence available from which the value of intangibles can be determined." In other words,

---

[22] Rev. Rul. 68-609, 1968-2 C.B. 327 IRC Sec. 1001.

the excess earnings method is a method of last resort. Nonetheless, many business appraisers are often quick to pull the excess earnings method valuation model as their weapon of choice.

Second, the method may be used for determining the fair market value "of intangible assets of a business only if there is no better basis therefore available." The IRS is now emphasizing that the method should be used to value a business's intangible assets – not the business as a whole. The ruling states again that even when used to value intangible assets of a business (not the entire business), that it should be used "if there is no better basis therefore available." The IRS is making the point clear: only use this method for intangible asset valuations as a last resort when no other methods are available.

Before jumping the gun, let's get better acquainted with the excess earnings method.

The International Glossary of Business Valuation Terms defines the Excess Earnings Method as:

> "A specific way of determining a value indication of a business, business ownership interest, or security determined as the sum of a) the value of the assets derived by capitalizing excess earnings and b) the value of the selected asset base. Also frequently used to value intangible assets."[23]

Excess earnings are an important element embedded within the definition. The terminology is important enough to require its own definition.

The International Glossary of Business Valuation Terms further defines Excess Earnings as:

> "That amount of anticipated economic benefits that exceeds an appropriate rate of return on the value of a selected asset base (often net tangible assets) used to generate those anticipated economic benefits."[24]

According to the definition of the excess earnings method, the price is determined in two steps. First, excess earnings are divided by a capitalization rate – referred to as "capitalizing excess earnings" in the

---

[23] http://bvfls.aicpa.org/Resources/Business+Valuation/Tools+and+Aids/Definitions+and+Terms/International+Glossary+of+Business+Valuation+Terms.htm.
[24] Ibid.

definition. Recall that a capitalization rate is the discount rate minus a long-term sustainable growth rate. Second, the value of the net tangible assets is added to the capitalized excess earnings value to obtain the estimate of value for the subject interest.

When It's Used

The method is widely used by business brokers when valuing private practices and small businesses. Business appraisers not in the business of brokering companies also use (read: misuse) the method. In other words, it's frequently used by various practitioners, but in many cases should not. Knowing its prevalence and abuse, let's review some areas where the excess earnings method has greater acceptance.

Intangible asset valuation is theoretically the most useful area for the excess earnings method. While no capitalization rates can be empirically supported, business appraisers can "back in" to a company's overall cost of capital to ensure the rate makes sense. Large corporations, many who are publicly traded, often require appraisals of intangible assets. Business appraisers are often left with no other sound method to appraise a particular intangible asset (emphasis on "intangible asset" and not an entire business).

Marital dissolution (divorce) valuations often employ the excess earnings method when valuing a business. Theoretically unsound as applied, the method does solve a few quandaries. Divorce courts are concerned with equitable resolutions. Small business owners and private practices often have a considerable intangible value component that cannot be separated. Think of a newly minted physician whose wife worked three jobs to support her husband's dream of becoming a doctor. After completing residency and securing a job, the husband files for divorce. How does a court determine equitable distribution? In this case, the doctor has value in expected earnings that his wife helped create by working multiple jobs to finance his education. The "value" in this case is called goodwill. You can't see or touch it, but it clearly exists. Divorce courts seek to split the value equitably.

The excess earnings method helps solve that problem by identifying the goodwill component in total value. Goodwill value in this circumstance has two variants: personal goodwill and business goodwill. Personal goodwill value is attached to the owner whereas business goodwill value (also called enterprise goodwill) is appended to the business or private practice. State law dictates the separation of goodwill. If you're a business owner approaching a divorce, discuss this matter with your attorney. Not only is the treatment of goodwill obscure, but laws governing separation of goodwill vary from state to state.

How It Works

The method is relatively easy to implement. Its ease of understanding is another reason divorce courts like it so much.

1) Estimate normalized future expected earnings of the company.
2) Appraise the firm's tangible assets and liabilities at their fair market values and subtract the appraised liabilities from appraised assets (adjusted net asset approach). The residual is the firm's net tangible asset value.
3) Select a required rate of return attributed to the net tangible assets and multiply this rate by the net tangible asset value derived from step two. The resulting product is the earnings value assigned to the net tangible assets of the company.
4) Subtract earnings attributed to the net tangible assets in step three from normalized future expected earnings in step one. The difference is the "excess earnings" of the company ascribed to the intangible value of the entity.
5) Select a required capitalization rate attributed to the intangible value of the corporation and divide excess earnings by the capitalization rate. The resulting value is the company's intangible value.
6) Add the net tangible asset value (step 2) to the intangible value (step 5). The resulting number is the firm's value.

As an example, assume a business appraiser selected the excess earnings method to value a closely-held business. The normalized future expected earnings of the company were determined to be $2 million. Appraisals were performed on the company's assets and liabilities, leaving an adjusted net asset value of $1 million. The appraiser selected 13% as an appropriate required rate of return on the net tangible assets. A 35% capitalization rate for the excess earnings was deemed appropriate by the appraiser. (Note that these rates were selected by the appraiser – the rate selection is subjective.)

| Step 1 | Normalized Estimated Future Income | $2,000,000 |

| Step 2 | Fair Market Value of Net Tangible Assets | $1,000,000 |

Step 3	Fair Market Value of Net Tangible Assets	$1,000,000
	x Rate of Return on Net Tangible Assets	13%
	Earnings Attributed to Net Tangible Assets	$130,000

Step 4	Normalized Estimated Future Income	$2,000,000
	− Earnings Attributed to Net Tangible Assets	$130,000
	Excess Earnings	$1,870,000

Step 5	Excess Earnings	$1,870,000
	÷ Capitalization Rate	35%
	Intangible Value	$5,342,857

Step 6	Fair Market Value of Net Tangible Assets	$1,000,000
	+ Intangible Value	$5,342,857
	Total Value of the Entity	**$6,342,857**

Using the excess earnings method (and the values and rates previously mentioned) produces a total entity value of approximately $6.34 million.

Level of Value

Because an asset approach is used to determine value, the excess earnings method yields a control level of value. The reasons bestowing the control level of value are the same as discussed in Chapter 10.

Problems Associated with Using the Excess Earnings Method

The excess earnings method carries an implied assumption that the company's earnings can be correctly divided and assigned to intangible and tangible parts of the enterprise. No empirical evidence exists to support this hypothesis. Without evidence, the business appraiser is given complete discretion to assign what is, and what is not, tangible and intangible (on the allocation of earnings). Business valuations should read like a thesis. Quality appraisals are written so that no other conclusion appears reasonable. The excess earnings method fails in many aspects of a sound business appraisal, with little to no empirical support available for the reader to rely upon. Subjectivity is required in business valuation. However, the less subjective an appraisal is to human manipulation, the more reliable the value estimate will be.

A capitalization rate for excess earnings is required, which leads to an enormous problem. Empirical data for cost of capital (discount rates) used to calculate the intangible value in the excess earnings method doesn't exist. Appraising operating entities using observable data is tough enough as-is, but at least we have access to transaction data and publicly traded company information. Choosing a capitalization rate with little to guide the appraiser and support the value conclusion opens the door to increased scrutiny.

Finally, the IRS clearly states that the method is to be used as a method of last resort. Furthermore, this method of last resort should be used only for intangible assets. Applying the excess earnings method to operating entities as a general approach defies Revenue Ruling 59-60.

Other problems exist – such as using the capitalization rate verbatim as stated in the ruling (e.g. inserting 8% because the number is listed in the ruling), despite the ruling instructing not to do so – but I'll forge on and save you the ranting. My goal in this chapter was to introduce you to the excess earnings method, provide you an overview of how it's applied, and nail down why it has little use as a method in the valuation of many closely-held businesses. Despite my ranting, the method is accepted in many divorce cases because it's easier for judges to understand, and judges aren't in the business of valuation. Also, because personal and corporate goodwill (beyond the scope of this book) are boiling points in divorce proceedings when illiquid corporate equity is involved, the method allows for goodwill value to be separated from the business. State law dictates goodwill treatment in divorce appraisals.

The excess earnings method is commonly used in fair value accounting for financial reporting purposes. Variants of the model are also commonly used in healthcare valuation. Goodwill impairment testing and many intangible asset valuations have no better options than the excess earnings method. Because I do not value companies or assets for such purposes, I disclaim any scrutiny of the excess earnings method for financial reporting purposes. (The same disclaimer applies to many healthcare engagements as well.) Closely-held companies that I value, and appraisals that I review, would almost always be neglected by using the excess earnings method. Nonetheless, the method is justifiably used for a handful of purposes where no better option is available.

Conclusion

The excess earnings method was created during Prohibition, but it is used today for a variety of purposes. The IRS has since come out against the method, instructing appraisers to use it as a method of last resort – and only for intangible assets. Despite these instructions, appraisers continue to use – and misuse – the excess earnings method. Its simplicity in use and understanding allows appraisers who lack sound knowledge in finance and economics to employ it. Courts of equity have also used the method because of its simplicity and ability to divide tangible and intangible value. Nonetheless, the flaws of the excess earnings method are pronounced. The level of value resulting from the excess earnings method is that of control.

Finally, some appraisers legitimately use the approach for intangible asset valuation and goodwill value because no better methods exist. Most of the legitimate uses are for financial reporting purposes under the fair value standard or fair market value standard for healthcare valuations.

SECTION FOUR
THE APPRAISER'S TOOLKIT

If you aren't a bit overwhelmed after reading Section Three, consider yourself astute in having a sound grip on closely-held business valuation. Most people, let alone business owners, require a second passing of the approaches and methods discussed in Section Three. Trust me; I did my best to make the material as digestible as possible without altering the technical points you need to know.

Caution – do not proceed to Section Four if the material in any of the previous sections does not sit well. This book is designed to build upon itself. Comprehension of each chapter is imperative to grasping the concepts in subsequent chapters. I want you to get this! Now is the time to go back and re-read anything that didn't quite make sense.

Section Four discusses the "as we will discuss in Chapter ..." material that you've already seen. If you found yourself thinking "why wasn't that covered before this part" while reading Sections Two and Three, you'll soon understand why. I didn't say this material was uncomplicated, but I've broken it down in relatable terms and provided examples that you can easily understand.

Section Four is the culmination of a business valuation appraisal. First, we examine the cost of capital. You've seen it referred to as the denominator in the income approach. Due to the inherent sensitivity of valuation models used in the income approach, the cost of capital, in my opinion, is the most vital element of a discounted cash flow valuation estimate. Projections, naturally, are subjective. Differing cash flow projections produce different value conclusions, but a differing discount or capitalization rate will impact the valuation more profoundly.

Cost of capital separates finance professionals from the general business valuation practitioners or accountants who dabble in valuation. In this section, you will learn the fundamentals enabling you to read and understand an appraisal report. You will also be given tips and target points to look for, notably in areas where I see appraisers frequently mess up. What you will not receive is a section filled with finance lingo and the alternative measures, models, formulas and theories that help derive the cost of capital. If you hold the CFA® charter or have a Ph.D. in finance or economics, this section's contents will be more than familiar. None of my clients have either of those. Assuming you fall in the same boat, it's imperative that you pay close attention and follow along while reading.

We'll then discuss valuation discounts and control premiums. Business owners frequently misunderstand valuation discounts. My goal is to eradicate any misunderstanding you may have about them. The most frustrating questions I receive from business owners and attorneys alike come from valuation discounts. Read and understand this section thoroughly. Unlike the cost of capital, valuation discounts and control premiums are not difficult to comprehend. This book is written to help business owners understand business valuation. Because many owners gift interests in their company to succeeding family members or have taxable estates upon death, valuation discounts and control premiums are important instruments in the closely-held business appraiser's toolkit. You will learn how valuation discounts and control premiums are applied, when they apply, how large the discounts should or should not be, control premiums and when they're used, and the logic underpinning discounts and premiums. The standards, premises, and levels of value become important when deciding valuation discounts and control premiums. Because I know you didn't skip chapters (right?!), this will make perfect sense.

Finally, this section ends with a walkthrough of a business valuation report. When you reach Chapter 14, you will have the know-how to understand what's happening as you navigate through a business appraisal. Remember that business valuation encompasses many scopes and purposes, and that appraisal reports may vary based on the intent of the valuation. Nonetheless, the format we cover is that which is typically found in most business valuation appraisals regardless of the purpose of the report.

Chapter Twelve

Cost of Capital

Introduction

Cost of capital, as a term, both frightens and confuses people not accustomed to hearing it. The name itself sounds like technical jargon, and it isn't something casually mentioned at social events. In addition to cost of capital, there are subtleties that define exactly what's being discussed. Are we talking about equity capital, debt capital or total capital? In this chapter, we dig into the types of capital, how cost of capital is determined (from a high-level view), and what exactly is included in the cost of capital.

From years of working with business owners who excel in their profession and leave the financial part to their CFOs or accountants, I know the wording can be initially tough to swallow. To alleviate any concern, let me break down what each word means. *Cost* is just that – a cost. Why would anybody be confused about that? Well, because cost in this sense is defined as a percentage. Most people think of "cost" as a dollar amount. Fixed equipment costs $XXX or your attorney bills $YYY per hour. Yes, the cost element is measured in dollar terms in cost of capital – but to capture the true "cost" we use percentages (which are derived from dollars). Hang in there if you're still confused. This is complicated stuff. *Capital* means money. No real ambiguity there. We will further define the types of capital, or money, as we go along. Debt capital (borrowing) is almost always cheaper than equity capital (stock). Calculating debt capital is different than equity capital. A company's total cost of capital is a mix of the debt and equity held by the enterprise.

Cost of Capital

The International Glossary of Business Valuation Terms defines Cost of Capital as:

> "The expected rate of return that the market requires in order to attract funds to a particular investment."[25]

An easier way to understand cost of capital is that investors will not invest in an asset (stock, company) if there is a more enticing substitute available at the same price. If two products provide identical utility and have the same risk attributes, why pay more for one than the other? Cost of capital helps explain this concept. More accurately stated (in economic terms), the cost of capital for an investment is the opportunity cost or cost of giving up an investment in lieu of another. The "what might have been" of economics, if you will, when considering two investments and choosing one over another.

First Things First

You already know what "capital" means in cost of capital. It's the sum of your company's balance sheet (debt, common and preferred equity). If your firm doesn't have corporate "stock" (LLC, LP, and others), the "equity" component is the net of debt residual. When determining the cost of capital, business appraisers ascribe a specific cost to each element of capital (debt and equity). If the entire business is valued, a blended rate incorporating all costs of capital will be used.

Cost of capital is forward-looking. It is based on the future, not the past. This should make sense to you. Think of the income approach and how projected cash flows are used in the numerator. The denominator – cost of capital – must also be forward-looking to match the expected cash flows in the numerator. Remember the numerator/denominator combination must always be apples-to-apples, and that mismatching the two is a frequent source of appraiser error.

Cost of capital includes two main components. The first component is the Risk-Free Rate, which itself includes three compensatory elements. Of these three, the first is a Rental Rate that compensates an investor for foregoing risk-free lending. The second element compensates investors for inflation and is referred to as the Inflation Premium. The final risk-

---

[25]http://bvfls.aicpa.org/Resources/Business+Valuation/Tools+and+Aids/Definitions+and+Terms/International+Glossary+of+Business+Valuation+Terms.htm.

free element, Maturity Risk, compensates for the possibility of the investment's market value changing.

Risk-Free Rate Components

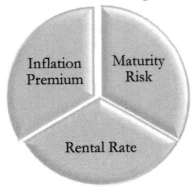

The second cost of capital component is the Risk Premium. While the risk-free rate is readily determined, the risk premium is much harder to compute. Furthermore, the risk premium can be – and usually is – subjectively adjusted to account for firm-specific factors, otherwise known as unsystematic risk. We'll talk more about the equity risk premium later in this chapter.

Another characteristic of the cost of capital is that it's a function of the investment and not the investor. Investment prices are acquired from marketplaces where large groups of investors dictate prices. Prices of shares traded on the stock market, for example, are determined by investors' buying and selling. If more investors are buying instead of selling, stock prices increase. When considering all buyers and sellers, the investment's characteristics are what account for its performance – not the investor's. Additionally, the cost of capital is based on market values (i.e. stock prices) and not book, par or other accounting values.

Investors build inflation projections into investment decisions. Therefore, the cost of capital, determined by market values, is stated in nominal terms. "Nominal" means the rate includes inflation. Its counterpart is real terms. "Real" is the value after subtracting inflation. A quick and straightforward method that isn't precisely correct (but close enough) is to consider an 8% investment return where inflation is 3%. The nominal rate is 8% (includes inflation) whereas the real rate of 5% removes inflation (8% - 3% = 5%). Investors seek higher real returns because the real component is what increases relative wealth and purchasing power. Nonetheless, the cost of capital is more often than not stated in nominal terms.

The final characteristic I want to hit on is that the cost of capital and discount rate are the same. In Chapter 8 (Income Approach) you learned to project future cash flows and then "bring them back" to the present using a discount rate and time value of money. The discount rate, or cost of capital, is the expected return of the investment that reflects the risk profile of the investment (company). The denominator includes the cost of capital, adjusted for the time value of money.

Discounting and Capitalizing

In Chapter 8 you learned the following: "The cost of capital, discount rate and required rate of return are all synonymous. Collectively (or interchangeably) they encapsulate the time value of money and risk profile of the expected income stream on a compounded basis in the denominator. In plain-speak, the discount rate represents the total risk, which includes a risk-free rate. In contrast, a capitalization rate is merely a divisor (denominator) applicable to a single period of cash flow or economic receipts. The capitalization rate subtracts the long-term sustainable growth rate from the discount rate. Don't get too bogged down on this now. The important point to remember is that a discount rate is not the same as a capitalization rate."

Examples helped demonstrate when to use a discount rate or a capitalization rate. Remember that a capitalization rate is the discount rate net of the long-term sustainable growth rate. If 8% was the discount rate and 3% was the long-term growth rate, then the cap rate would be 5%.

Another significant difference between the two is that a discount rate is a denominator applicable to a series of cash flow streams whereas a cap rate applies to a discrete (i.e. one period) cash flow. Many discounted cash flow models use both a discount rate and a cap rate. The discount rate is used for each period's cash flow, and the cap rate is used to capitalize the terminal value. Both discount rates and cap rates are used in the denominator for a specified benefit stream serving as the numerator (usually free cash flow).

Cost of Capital Methods – An Introduction

This book examines the more widely used approaches in determining the cost of capital for closely-held companies. I love reading and writing about cost of capital. A cash flow model's denominator contains a wealth of information that defines the company's value. Here's where non-finance professionals often get flustered. Calculating the appropriate cost of capital, along with the processes, methods, models and fundamentals behind it, is taught in the CFA curriculum and Ph.D. programs. I'm fortunate to have gone through both the CPA and CFA® programs because I have a clear understanding of what is and isn't taught in each. The former hardly brushes on the concept while the latter fries your brain ensuring you know it cold. You, the owner, could probably care less about calculating cost of capital. Nonetheless, you should be aware of the basics behind the cost of capital approaches because appraisers tend to neglect this area more than others. A lack of knowledge is mostly to blame, although appraisers can get around this lack of knowledge by using third party sources (e.g. valuation software). The focus on cash flow projections usually takes precedence over cost of capital because both the owner and appraiser understand observable numbers such as projected revenue, cost of goods sold, etc. This creates a significant problem. The investment's risk and growth potential are captured in the denominator or cost of capital. Focusing on the numerator at the expense of the denominator impairs the value estimate. An appraiser can be spot-on with the cash flow projections, but the denominator carries greater relative importance in calculating the entity's value. I would much rather prefer a good (less than spot-on) cash flow forecast and a stellar cost of capital derivation. Cash flow projections are incredibly subjective whereas the cost of capital can be estimated more objectively.

Let me demonstrate how significant cost of capital is in valuing a company. For this example, we'll use a capitalization rate (discount rate – long-term sustainable growth rate = capitalization rate). The normalized free cash flow number is $100,000; the discount rate is 8%, and the long-term sustainable growth rate (LTSGR) is 3% - thus the cap rate is 5%. Capitalizing the single period cash flow by the cap rate gives us a value of $2 million for the company.

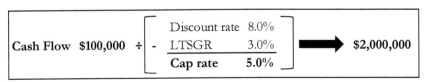

To illustrate the relative impact of the denominator versus the numerator, we're going to make two iterations.

1) The first iteration will be to increase the numerator (cash flow) by 10% to $110,000. Everything else remains the same.
2) The second iteration keeps cash flow at $100,000, but increases the discount rate by 10% (from 8.0% to 8.8%).

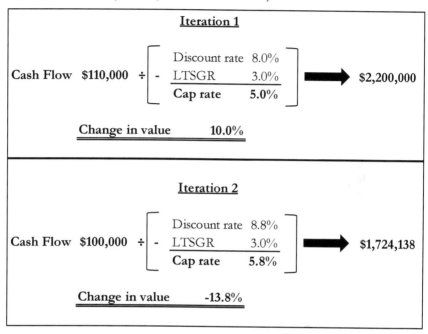

As shown in the example, changing the denominator by 10% created a much larger value disparity versus the 10% change in cash flow. The absolute change (ignoring the minus signs) may not appear significant at face value. I can see the logic there. What's problematic is a lack of knowledge of the two. You understand the cash flow projections and can argue with the business appraiser all day about how your company will perform for the next five years. The denominator, however, is not familiar territory. How are you going to argue that? It's not something you know much about. Guess what; chances are your appraiser doesn't know much about it either. What many appraisers do know is the art of acquiescing to your demands.

Assume, for example; an appraiser is valuing this entity using both a market approach and an income approach. After performing the market approach, the appraiser needs the value estimate provided by the income approach to be $2 million for the market approach calculation to make sense. The problem is that you know the cash flow stream should be $130,000, not $100,000. Let me show you how the appraiser is going to back into his number without you batting an eye.

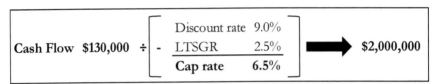

Both sides win their personal battles. However, the value estimate – the most important item at hand – is wrong. The appraiser needs the value to be $2 million. He also needs to get you off the phone, so his billable hour tally doesn't spiral out of control. Using your cash flow number, he adjusts the denominator, slightly increasing the discount rate (from 8% to 9%) while decreasing the growth rate (from 3% to 2.5%). The net result is an increase in the cap rate from 5% to 6.5%. Increasing the cap rate lowers the value, and therefore, he's able to achieve the $2 million value.

While you were arguing about cash flow projections, the appraiser took advantage of the denominator – the most important number in the ratio, yet the least observed by business owners. Don't fall prey to these tactics. As we go through the cost of capital methods, I'll point out how business appraisers tweak cost of capital multiples to fit their estimates, discrediting the value.

Cost of Capital Methods

This book provides the need-to-know points of the following three methods:
1) Build-Up Method
2) Capital Asset Pricing Method (CAPM)
3) Modified Capital Asset Pricing Method (MCAPM)

Other methods exist and are used by appraisers. New methods have been introduced over the last decade. These new methods, however, have yet to gain enough traction or popularity to merit inclusion in this book, which seeks to provide a high-level view of what a business owner should look for in a business valuation. Adoption of newer and more sophisticated models will inevitably increase as more highly skilled finance professionals enter the closely-held business valuation field.

(1) The Build-Up Method (BUM)

A standard method often used for smaller companies, the BUM uses historical discount rates from publicly traded companies as the "base rate" in deriving a company's cost of capital. Duff & Phelps (D&P) publishes its annual Risk Premium Report that many appraisers use to determine the cost of capital for closely-held companies. In the D&P report, companies are broken into deciles based on size. Smaller companies usually have a higher cost of capital (more risk) than larger companies and vice versa. Under the BUM, the appraiser uses the following equation to determine the closely-held company's cost of capital:

> **BUM Cost of Capital Formula**
>
> Cost of Capital (Discount Rate) = RfR + RPe + RPs ± RPu

The D&P report is used to determine the cost of common equity capital of the subject company when using the build-up method. It is not the cost of debt or preferred equity capital. Discount rates for common equity are higher than debt because of the greater risk of receiving only the residual economic benefits (whereas debt is senior to common equity shareholders in the event of a liquidation) coupled with the tax benefits of debt (interest expense is tax deductible). In the case of liquidation, debt is safer than common equity. As such, debt investors require a lower return – incurring the company a lower cost – than common equity investors. If you're unfamiliar with that last sentence, here's the general approach of liquidation when considering common equity, debt, and preferred equity capital. When a company is forced (or chooses) to liquidate, suppliers of debt capital are paid first among the three. Next in line are preferred equity (stock) owners. If anything is left over – and there rarely is – common equity (stock) owners collect the remnants. Because they are last in line, common equity holders require the greatest return, and thus, incur the highest cost of capital to an enterprise. Preferred equity is the second most expensive capital component, and debt is the least costly (of the three).

The Risk-Free Rate (RfR) is the 20-year yield of U.S. Treasury securities. Because the United States has halted the issuance of 20-year securities, appraisers look to the 30-year bond with 20 years remaining as the referenced yield or calculate the implied yield by algebraically bootstrapping the rates. Most data providers use the nominal rate versus the real rate, so inflation is included in the risk-free rate.

The Equity Risk Premium (RPe) is the discount rate observed in the study (e.g. Duff & Phelps) and represents the discount rate in excess of the 20-year risk-free rate. Duff & Phelps calculates the RPe by taking the historical market rate of return and subtracting the historical 20-year risk-free rate. This excess return is what one should expect to receive by holding the investment and includes market variability. Beta, a variable we will discuss shortly, is "built into" the premium when using the BUM. Beta is a measure of volatility or risk. Publishers calculate total common equity market returns when determining the risk premiums used in the BUM studies. Since total returns are calculated, the volatility (beta) is captured in the premium. Therefore, no beta adjustment is made when using the BUM. Furthermore, the RPe is broken down by industry and size. Accordingly, industry risk attributes are included in the premium as are risk factors associated with company size operating within the respective industry.

The Size Risk Premium (RPs) incorporates the company's size into the cost of capital equation. Empirical data supports a negative relationship between a company's size and its cost of capital. All else equal, large companies carry lower risk premiums whereas smaller companies have greater risk premiums. Historical market performance supports this relationship as small stocks have tended to outperform large stocks over time. Smaller stocks have the propensity to fluctuate more than larger stocks, incurring a higher beta or risk variable. Furthermore, smaller companies are associated with greater risk for a host of factors (less access to capital, higher failure rate and higher cost of borrowing – among others). Collectively, smaller companies have a higher cost of common equity. The RPs allows the business appraiser to compensate for the size (risk) of the subject company.

Leading cost of capital publications – Duff & Phelps, for example – divide company size into deciles. Once the closely-held company's industry is selected, the appraiser chooses the D&P cost of capital applicable to that particular industry. D&P then displays the industry cost of capital by company size, broken into ten categories (deciles). Next, the appraiser finds the company's size and selects the appropriate risk premium. The selected premium is the equity risk premium for the closely-held company and, when using D&P, includes the size premium.

Did you catch that? I hope you're engaged in this stuff because I love it and want you to at least not fall asleep on me. A gaping hole exists here. How can the appraiser select the correct company size before valuing the company? It's like a dog chasing its tail. The answer involves an iterative process and several calculations to determine an agreeable value. Do you think appraisers (many who lack thorough knowledge on this matter) know how to choose the right number? It took me countless hours to create the models needed to perform this process. Do you think the accountant who dabbles in business valuation on the side knows any of this, let alone has created the statistical models required to accurately select the appropriate cost of capital (or have the know-how to do so)? If your firm is small, the D&P publication provides a regression formula that helps improve the cost of capital calculation's accuracy. Again, does the local CPA know regression? I'm poking a bit of fun at my CPA brethren because I know from experience how much valuation, finance, econometrics, and statistics are covered in the CPA program – including the business valuation credential programs. Approximately none is included in the former while only the basics are taught (i.e. mentioned) in the latter.

Unsystematic Risk (RPu) is risk unique to the firm. Up until this point, we've covered three of the four inputs of the BUM. The previous three are observable and supportable. They aren't made up or pulled from the sky. Unsystematic risk, however, is purely subjective and can take many forms, both qualitative and quantitative. Unsystematic risk could include lack of management depth, concentrated sales to a handful of customers (or supplier concentration), poor succession planning – anything firm-specific that the appraiser believes warrants an adjustment to the firm's risk that is different than the companies included in the risk premium study. A note of caution: appraisers often use this variable to "back into" a desired value. The unsystematic risk adjustment must make sense and be firmly supported in the valuation report.

Earlier in this chapter, I demonstrated how a small change in the denominator, the cost of capital, can significantly impact the entity's value estimate. I also showed how an appraiser can adjust the denominator to fit a desired value estimate. While reviewing your appraisal, pay particular attention to the firm-specific adjustments of your company's cost of capital. Appraisers sometimes arbitrarily increase or decrease the unsystematic component according to subjective notions. Perhaps the assumptions are correct and deserve adjusting. Maybe the appraiser failed to understand your company fully and ascribed a benefit (decrease in the rate) or penalty (increase in the rate) out of a preconceived impression or misunderstanding. Or maybe the appraiser used this area to back into the number sought after. Whatever the case, you need to pay particular attention to cost of capital adjustments specific to your firm. If they don't make sense, ask the appraiser why he made the changes. The appraiser must not only convince you that the adjustments are correct, but the business appraisal itself must be convincing to the reader (IRS, judge or other) so that the adjustments can withstand professional scrutiny.

Business valuation is both an art and a science. The previous three components illustrated the science of valuation whereas this final part, the RPu, encapsulates the art. Professional judgment is required to be exercised by the appraiser. Subjective judgment by a low-quality appraiser void of a thorough understanding of these concepts can – and will – lead to a poor appraisal. Your job as a business owner (or trusted adviser to a business owner) is to scour the cost of capital section of the valuation report. Look for adjustments made to the cost of capital. Appraisers rushing through projects (the billable hour clock is ticking) often include a sentence or two in the report explaining why an adjustment was made. Do not settle with an appraisal report short of being complete and convincing. All adjustments must be supported in the business appraisal. After years of reviewing business valuations, I know the hotspots where appraisers cut corners. If the BUM is used in the valuation, one of the first sections I examine is the cost of capital. You don't want to know how many fail to pass muster after just this section's review.

Also, be cognizant of which adjustments have been made. In the BUM, the size premium (RPs) is included as part of the equity risk premium (RPe) for the leading cost of capital data provider Duff & Phelps. Regression equations are provided in the D&P report, allowing the appraiser to incorporate your firm's variables and produce a more robust cost of capital figure. Thus, adjusting size under the RPu variables would be highly suspect, especially if the regression equation is used. Some appraisers adjust for industry risk without providing a thorough explanation supporting the adjustment. Duff & Phelps divides cost of capital by industry in its report. If the companies used to determine your firm's cost of capital operate in the same industry as you do, why would an adjustment be made? Perhaps your business is small, and the appraiser adjusts for having concentrated sales to a select number of customers. If that's the case, did the appraiser review the companies included in the smallest decile – the same decile from which your cost of capital was chosen from? Do those companies also have concentrated sales? If so, why adjust for concentrated sales when the companies included in determining your equity risk premium suffer the same dilemma?

If you haven't guessed by now, business valuation consumes an extraordinary amount of time. Even the most experienced appraisers well educated in finance and economics get stumped with complex valuation projects. Every variable must be interrogated. I do not understand how valuation practitioners have for years flown under the radar unscathed, unknowingly making fundamental mistakes without question. My hope – and belief – is that as more highly skilled valuation professionals enter the field, lower-skilled practitioners and generalists who currently permeate the industry will move on to other areas, fall back into public accounting, or increase their finance and econometric knowledge. Unfortunately, these changes will take time. You, however, are now better equipped to protect your company's business valuation from succumbing to flawed valuation practices.

(2) The Capital Asset Pricing Model (CAPM)

The International Glossary of Business Valuation Terms defines the Capital Asset Pricing Model as:

> "A model in which the cost of capital for any stock or portfolio of stocks equals a risk-free rate plus a risk premium that is proportionate to the systematic risk of the stock or portfolio."[26]

Under the CAPM, a company's equity risk premium – the total rate of return minus the risk-free rate – is a linear function of a company's beta. When using the word "company," the more correct term is "common stock." CAPM is a function of publicly traded common equities or stocks. Okay, what does that mean? Linear means just that – a line. Beta is synonymous with risk. Perhaps that technical-laden explanation doesn't help much. I'm more of a visual learner, so let's look at a picture to help us conquer the technicalities. But before introducing the picture here's the CAPM equation followed with an explanation of the model's inputs.

Capital Asset Pricing Model (CAPM)
$E(R_i) = RfR + \beta(MR - RfR)$

The Expected Return (E(Ri)) for security "i" – where "i" is the security being valued – is the discount rate, expected return or cost of capital. All mean the same thing.

---

[26] Ibid.

The Risk-Free Rate (RfR) is a U.S. Treasury rate, although the duration can vary depending on the appraiser or the subject interest. The 20-year rate is widely used in calculating CAPM for closely-held companies, but I've also seen the 10-year rate used as well. The rate should match the expected time horizon of the entity being valued. A company near liquidation would use a shorter rate whereas a longer rate would be appropriate for a company projected to operate into perpetuity. In practice, and as you will soon learn, a modified approach to CAPM is typically used instead of the classic CAPM. As a result, the 20-year rate is most often the duration of choice to maintain congruence with the data from which size premiums are taken from.

The Beta (β) is a measure of volatility or risk. A high beta will increase the expected return (discount rate) whereas a low beta will decrease the discount rate and lower the expected return – all else equal. In other words, a riskier asset, as measured by its beta or stock volatility, requires a greater return to entice investment and vice versa. A beta of 1.0 implies that the stock's volatility equals the benchmark's volatility. A beta greater than 1.0 means the company is riskier than the market. Finally, a beta of less than 1.0 indicates lower volatility and infers a safer company or investment when compared to the benchmark's volatility. The reference from which the beta is calculated against varies by service provider. Most providers calculate beta based on movement relative to the S&P 500 index using the monthly change for the previous five years. Betas can also be customized to reflect a particular strategy or index.

The Expected Market Return (MR) is a consensus of how the broad market is expected to behave. Calculating the MR is disputed by virtue of subjectivity. Because the MR is a forward-looking return, the precision of accuracy is unknown. Duration is another consideration worthy of attention. If the company is expected to exist into perpetuity, a long-term expected market rate of return should be used.

The Market Risk Premium ((MR – RfR)), or market return in excess of the risk-free rate, is multiplied by the beta to yield the equity risk premium. The market risk premium and equity risk premium are not the same. The market risk premium is the market return in excess of the risk-free rate. The equity risk premium includes the company's risk by applying the beta – or relative volatility of the company's (stock) compared to the overall market – to the market risk premium. In other words, the equity risk premium is the market risk premium multiplied by the beta.

Adding the risk-free rate to the equity risk premium solves for the total discount rate or expected return of the company's common equity capital.

Because we're talking about a single security (hence the notation "i" indicating a particular stock), the CAPM model predicts where a security should lie on the security market line (SML). The SML is the linear part mentioned earlier and is illustrated in the following graph.

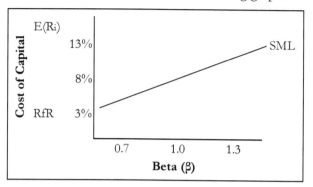

Let's work through this picture because if you can grasp the concepts here, you're well on your way to understanding CAPM. For full disclosure, you should know that nine critical assumptions underlie CAPM. These assumptions are beyond the scope of this book. Regardless, I felt obligated to provide them to you outside of this book. You can find the nine CAPM assumptions on the website **www.valuationforowners.com**.

The left side of the picture (Y axis/vertical) represents the cost of capital, and the bottom (X axis/horizontal) accounts for the beta. According to CAPM, the cost of capital is the risk-free rate (noted by RfR) plus the product of the beta and market risk premium (the equity risk premium). On the left side, you can see that the cost of capital increases from top to bottom (3% to 13%). On the underside you'll note that risk – as measured by beta – increases from left to right (0.7 to 1.3). The SML is the linear part or line that moves upward from left to right within the picture.

CAPM tells us that a security will lie somewhere on the SML, given its beta and equity risk premium. Securities plotting below the SML should be purchased and those positioned above the SML should be sold. You can see that a security with a lower beta rewards investors less – and costs companies less – by virtue of a lower cost of capital. On the other hand, investors demand that companies with high betas or businesses with greater relative risk provide a higher rate of return. A higher return for equity investors equates to a more significant cost of capital for the enterprise.

Working through an example should hammer this concept down. It looks scary, but it really is quite simple.

Assume the risk-free rate (RfR) is 3%, the expected market return (MR) is 12%, and the stock's beta (β) is 1.2. With just these three inputs, using the CAPM equation we can determine the stock's cost of capital to the company or expected return to the investor. Both imply the same and are used interchangeably.

$$E(Ri) = RfR + \beta(MR - RfR)$$
$$E(Ri) = 3\% + 1.2(12\% - 3\%)$$
$$E(Ri) = 3\% + 10.8\%$$
$$\mathbf{E(Ri) = 13.8\%}$$

The cost of capital in this example according to the CAPM is 13.8%. Recall that the equity risk premium is a "linear function of a company's beta." What this means is that risk – beta – drives the company's equity risk premium. Going back to the SML picture, you see that the SML moves linearly. In other words, the cost of capital increases as the beta increases, and vice versa. In practical terms, this makes complete sense. You expect to be compensated more for a risky asset (high tech company stock) compared to a low-risk investment (bank CD).

Continuing with our example, instead of using 1.2 as the beta let's use 0.7. CAPM says that the equity risk premium is a linear function of a company's beta; thus, a lower beta (0.7 vs. 1.2) should produce a lower cost of capital, all else equal. Lower risk implies a lower return.

$$E(Ri) = RfR + \beta(MR - RfR)$$
$$E(Ri) = 3\% + 0.7(12\% - 3\%)$$
$$E(Ri) = 3\% + 6.3\%$$
$$\mathbf{E(Ri) = 9.3\%}$$

As expected, the cost of capital decreased. Lowering the beta reduced the required rate of return, or cost of capital, from 13.8% to 9.3%, all else equal. For all securities, the risk-free rate (RfR) and expected market return (MR) are the same. Therefore, the sole variable driving the cost of capital is the beta.

To wrap up beta when used in the CAPM, remember the following:
- Higher beta = more risk = higher cost of capital
- Lower beta = less risk = lower cost of capital

I'm off the technical podium. Yes, that was more technical than most would like (including me). Trust me, though; I had to do it. Everything will make sense in the end. As Steve Jobs once said (I'm paraphrasing here), "You can't connect the dots looking forward; you can only connect them looking backward." To get to the end and connect the dots, however, you must move forward.

CAPM has its critics, and many of the bullets are aimed at CAPM's assumptions. Many studies attack beta as being a statistically poor measure of risk. The goal of CAPM is to extract systematic risk or market risk. Systematic risk is the risk that cannot be diversified away by holding alternative investments in the market (e.g. a diversified portfolio). Accordingly, systematic risk reflects the pure risk of the overall market and has a beta of 1.0.

The other risk component, unsystematic risk, is not addressed in CAPM. Unsystematic risk can be diversified away by holding a greater number of equities in a portfolio, with the equities having different correlation coefficients (stocks that don't move in the same direction all the time). We know that capital structures of publicly traded companies differ. Additionally, we are aware that your business differs – perhaps considerably – to publicly traded companies in the market. Closely-held business valuation is concerned with appraising the value of the closely-held company. Qualities of the closely-held company must be addressed and cannot be left to the discernment of a broad-market based calculation such as the CAPM. Because your business differs from those in the market, a modification to CAPM is necessary. The modification, or inclusion of additional factors, incorporates the firm-specific elements of your company. Fortunately, the modifications are small, and we've already covered most of the extra variables in the build-up method (BUM).

Dear reader, meet the Modified CAPM.

(3) The Modified Capital Asset Pricing Model (MCAPM)

The MCAPM builds on the original CAPM. Additional variables to account for company size and unsystematic risk – risk unique to the company – are introduced.

> **Modified Capital Asset Pricing Model (MCAPM)**
>
> $E(R_i) = RfR + \beta(MR - RfR) + R_s + R_u$

Several variables – RfR, β, MR – are the same as in the CAPM formula previously discussed. MCAPM's additional variables include:

The Risk Premium for Size (Rs) is used to compensate investors for size. Because company size and risk have a corollary, this additional premium adjustment allows the appraiser to match the closely-held company's risk premium with companies of similar size. Duff & Phelps (among others) provides size data for MCAPM adjustments.

The BUM also has a size premium component, but the adjustment is different so don't get these two confused. Under the BUM, the cost of capital is broken into deciles based on company size. The appraiser, therefore, includes the size risk premium by selecting the equity risk premium applicable to the appraisal company's size. Because CAPM does not discern size (MR includes all market securities), a size adjustment is needed when using the MCAPM. Duff & Phelps includes size premiums in its annual risk premium report. To sum it up – rarely is a size adjustment made when using the BUM, but a size adjustment is warranted in the MCAPM.

Unsystematic Risk (Ru), or firm-specific risk, is congruent to unsystematic risk previously defined in the build-up method. If you don't remember that part, or you skimmed through it, go back and re-read it before moving on. The same rules apply here as they did under the BUM. Moreover, business appraisers use the same tricks, adjusting the multiple to reach a value in their comfort zone. As a business owner or adviser to an owner, you must scrutinize this section carefully. The other variables of the MCAPM are empirically supported, meaning the appraiser has little to no wiggle room in the numbers. Unsystematic risk is where an appraiser can manipulate the value.

For closely-held companies, the MCAPM allows the appraiser to calculate a company-specific discount rate. The CAPM extracts a pure market risk premium that fails to account fully for the subject closely-held company's risk profile. Unlike the CAPM, the MCAPM adjusts for the size of the company and firm-specific attributes or the closely-held company's unsystematic risk. Similar to the BUM, however, subjectivity is introduced in the unsystematic risk adjustment. Be cautious of appraisers adjusting the "Ru" to back-in to a desired value estimate. Also, make sure the adjustment is firmly supported in the narrative portion of the appraisal.

• • •

Beta Adjustments

Beta has its problems as-is. Aside from highlighting some key points you should know, we're not going to jump very deep into beta adjustments. Data providers of beta define the measurement periods differently, which alone can make beta adjustments tricky. If your appraiser uses CAPM or MCAPM where the equation includes beta, you're probably going to see two beta adjustments which require a three step process.

Beta, as you recall, is defined as market movement. A higher beta implies increased risk whereas a lower beta signifies lower risk. You might be asking "higher than what?" Beta is a relative statistic, meaning its measurement is compared to something else (because the beta is larger or smaller than some other investment or benchmark). Most betas are measured against a broad market index, typically the S&P 500. Some data publishers use other broad market indices, and specialized betas can be calculated for specific strategies. The point of calculating beta is to determine how risky an asset (company's stock) is relative to a broad-based benchmark (e.g. the overall stock market).

Nearly all publicly traded companies carry long-term debt on their balance sheets as part of their overall capital structure. In finance-speak, debt is called "leverage." I prefer England's term for debt, referred to as "gearing." It makes more sense from a practical view, but I digress. If the definition of leverage as being a form of debt is new to you, keep in mind that we'll be using the term throughout this section. Leverage means nothing more than debt. Any business owner knows that having more debt on a company's balance sheet implicitly increases its financial risk. Beta is a measure of market risk, priced by market participants, who are buyers and sellers of stocks. These stocks are of companies with differing capital structures, but most having a degree of leverage. Therefore, betas obtained from the market are referred to as levered betas.

When valuing a company, the business appraiser must match apples with apples, and beta is no exception. If using the MCAPM to value a business, applying a levered beta to a company with no debt would be erroneous. The beta value must either match the capital structure of the company being appraised or that of a hypothetical capital structure. This beta value "match" depends on the purpose of the appraisal and level of value desired. For this chapter assume the appraiser is seeking to match the closely-held company's current capital structure unless stated otherwise.

To match betas, appraisers will go through an "un-levering" and subsequent "re-levering" process that adjusts the beta to fit the company's capital structure. The objective of un-levering the beta is to strip out the impact of the publicly traded companies' leverage from the beta. The un-levered beta (also called the "asset beta") is then re-levered to incorporate the capital structure of the subject closely-held company.

In principle, the processes are similar for all of the beta adjustment methods. You don't need to know the methods or formulas. A quick tutorial on the fundamentals, however, will help you navigate through a business appraisal more efficiently.

Again, several methods are available to adjust beta, and all have benefits and limitations. Nonetheless, the principle remains the same.

1) Once a group of publicly traded companies in your industry is found, each of the company's betas is un-levered using one of the beta adjustment formulas (which we'll discuss later). The publicly traded companies' unadjusted betas are levered. As a result, the appraiser needs to strip out the impact of debt financing from the beta statistic, resulting in an asset beta (un-levered beta). An asset beta implies the firm is financed with 100% equity and zero debt.

2) Next, the appraiser will select an un-levered beta from the publicly traded companies. Professional judgment is required as to which beta statistic is used. The median beta, a weighted average of the betas, simple average or some other technique may be applied to determine the applicable beta ultimately selected.

3) Using the beta statistic selected, the appraiser will re-lever the beta to incorporate your firm's capital structure or expected capital structure. The re-levered beta will be used in the MCAPM formula to determine your company's total cost of capital. Because the publicly traded companies selected are from your industry, the resulting beta statistic

(in theory) should be the most representative beta statistic for your firm.

One important note on the third point: if the appraiser is valuing a minority interest level of your company, check to see if the appraiser modified your firm's capital structure. Adjusting the actual capital structure to a hypothetical structure requires control. Only a controlling interest owner can alter a company's capital structure. If the appraiser makes an adjustment that doesn't match your firm's current or expected capital structure and the appraisal's level of value is a minority level, you have a problem. Similar to cash flow adjustments in the income approach, the appraiser must handle denominator changes with caution. Taking a firm with a debt-to-equity split of 10%-90% to 50%-50% is significant, and only a controlling owner could make such an adjustment. This guideline goes back to the apples-to-apples rule that the numerator and denominator must always match. If the interest being appraised is a minority interest, the appraiser should not make control adjustments to the capital structure when re-levering the beta.

As promised, the approaches commonly used for beta adjustments are:
- Hamada
- Fernandez
- Harris-Pringle
- Miles-Ezzell
- Practitioners'
- Other methods

In my experience of reviewing business valuations performed by other appraisers, I've noticed that general practitioners tend to favor the Hamada approach more than specialized business appraisers. That's not to say Hamada is the most widely used approach by all generalists – it very well may not be. I'm merely communicating information based on my experience so that you have a better understanding of the business valuation industry from a practitioner's perspective who also reviews appraisals. I have also noticed that those who use the Hamada approach tend to be CPA firms that offer business valuation as an ancillary service. Coincidentally enough, the Hamada approach is the simplest approach to implement and easiest to understand. It's also the approach taught and tested on the ABV examination (or so when I took it), so its use by these CPAs makes sense.

Hamada is also the last approach I would use in the group. The other methods alleviate many of the critical flaws embedded in the Hamada approach. (I'm a CPA with the ABV, so don't think I'm making personal accusations or trying to belittle a particular group of practitioners. That isn't my intent. No sane person would disrepute their professional credentials. I'm just telling you what I see so that you are better equipped to make an informed decision.)

When reviewing an appraisal, here's what I look for if the MCAPM is used and the beta has been adjusted. No single method should be seen as a go-to for all valuation engagements. I prefer the Harris-Pringle, Miles-Ezzell and Fernandez approaches. Nonetheless, each should be employed according to the case at hand (except the Hamada approach – there are too many flaws in Hamada, and better methods are available to justify using Hamada).

The general guidelines a valuation practitioner should adhere to when selecting the appropriate beta adjustment method are as follows:
- If the company being appraised is expected to maintain a constant capital structure in accounting terms (a fixed debt-to-equity value), I prefer to use the Fernandez approach. Explaining why is beyond the scope of this book but it is the most appropriate given the assumptions and limitations of the model compared to the other approaches.
- If the company being appraised is expected to maintain a constant capital structure in market values (debt-to-equity ratio), the appraiser should use either the Harris-Pringle or Miles-Ezzell approaches. The difference between this and the previous bullet point is that the capital structure must be measured in market values – not book values (accounting values). A company's book value of equity (accounting equity) will almost always differ from its economic, or market value of equity. Market values should be used when using either the Harris-Pringle or Miles-Ezzell approaches.

Selecting the most appropriate method is important as the resulting beta statistics can vary extensively. According to the CAPM, the equity risk premium is a linear function of the beta. Your firm's value will be driven one way or the other by the beta, so getting it as precise as possible is crucial.

I just scratched the surface on some very complex material. You should have a general understanding of the beta approaches used in a business valuation, how the approaches are applied (in principle) when certain approaches should be favored over others, and that the Hamada approach is a method of last resort. Hopefully, you're starting to see that business valuation – if done right – requires a highly skilled professional.

The Weighted Average Cost of Capital (WACC)

Up to this point (in this chapter), we've discussed the cost of capital for common equity only. Most closely-held companies incorporate some portion of debt into their capital structures. Like equity, debt also has a "cost" and this chapter is about the cost of capital, not just cost of common equity capital. The weighted average cost of capital, or "WACC," is also referred to as a blended rate because it includes all components of a company's capital structure.

The International Glossary of Business Valuation Terms defines the Weighted Average Cost of Capital as:

> "The cost of capital (discount rate) determined by the weighted average, at market value, of the cost of all financing sources in the business enterprise's capital structure."[27]

The previous three approaches compute the cost of common equity capital only. The WACC incorporates the company's debt, preferred and common equity when calculating the total discount rate. WACC accounts for all suppliers of capital and is, therefore, appropriate for appraisals of a company's total invested capital.

Weighted Average Cost of Capital (WACC)

$$WACC = (K_e * W_e) + (K_d [1-t] * W_d) + (K_p * W_p)$$

The Cost of Common Equity (Ke) is calculated using the cost of equity models (BUM, CAPM, MCAPM).

The Weight of Common Equity (We) is the percent of equity capital to total capital.

The Cost of Debt (Kd) is the pre-tax cost of debt. Multiplying Kd by one minus the tax rate yields the after-tax cost of debt. This adjustment is

---

[27] Ibid.

made because interest expense is a tax-deductible expense. Therefore, we must account for the tax savings of debt capital.

The Weight of Debt (Wd) is the percent of debt capital to total capital.

The Cost of Preferred Equity (Kp) is the cost of preferred stock.

The Weight of Preferred Equity (Wp) is the percent of the preferred stock to total capital.

Cost of capital approaches/calculations are used for debt and preferred equity (in addition to the common equity approaches discussed in this chapter). Procedures for calculating the cost of capital for debt and preferred equity are beyond the scope of this book. Preferred equity is less commonly used as a source of capital for small to medium-sized closely-held businesses (relative to larger entities and publicly traded firms). Some have preferred equity shares outstanding, but on a relative basis most don't. Debt, however, is commonplace. Computing the cost of debt capital, and the adjustments needed to accurately calculate the cost (inclusion of off-balance sheet leases, for example), is beyond what this book is trying to accomplish. Many appraisers use the interest rate of debt. Others use interest rates derived from publicly traded corporate debt (corporate bond yields with a Baa-quality grade are often used as an interest rate proxy on debt for closely-held business valuations).

Nonetheless, WACC requires the appraiser to use market values, not book or accounting values, which leads us to a problem. The WACC is needed to compute the market value of the company, but the WACC formula requires the appraiser to know what the market value of the company is to determine the WACC. Furthermore, we must know the cost and value of each capital component to calculate the overall WACC.

We know that the cost of equity can be calculated using one of the methods covered earlier in this chapter. Determining the cost of debt, in practice, tends to be more subjective in its application. We briefly covered a few approaches business appraisers use to estimate the cost of debt. The most theoretically correct approach would be to perform a rigorous debt capital appraisal to determine the cost of debt capital. Depending on the interest being appraised, this approach may be required. Using the interest rate (cost) of the loan will sometimes suffice – notably for smaller firms with no/few off-balance sheet debt financing agreements and low balance, short duration debt capital.

Having the costs of debt and equity capital, we now need to know the weights of each. Not only the weights but specifically the market value weights (not the book value or accounting statement value weights). Knowing the market value weights with exact precision is impossible. Mathematical computations (and lots of them) can aid the practitioner to determine a close guess of what the weights should be.

More advanced practitioners have Excel models to help solve this "dog chasing its tail" problem. An iterative process is used to determine the estimated market value weights of each component. The models I've created (and use) simplify this process. Microsoft may have lost its coolness factor with the masses years ago, but I remain a glowing fan of Excel (this might help explain why my kids don't think I'm cool). Describing the processes of the computational iterations is, again, beyond the scope of this book.

Numerator/Denominator Matching

In Chapter 8 we focused on the numerator. After reading this chapter, you've learned about the denominator. The question now becomes which numerator applies to which denominator, and vice versa. While alternative approaches exist, let's address the primary rules of matching the numerator (free cash flow) with the denominator (cost of capital).

FCFF/WACC

WACC is used when valuing an entire company (not just equity) – although it can be used to value equity. Remember that the numerator (free cash flow) and denominator (WACC) need to match. If using WACC as the denominator, cash flows to all suppliers of capital that are associated with the denominator must be included in the numerator. In other words, using free cash flow to equity as the numerator and WACC as the denominator would produce an apples-to-pears comparison. It's wrong because the two don't match. Free cash flow to the firm (FCFF) should be used as the numerator if WACC is the denominator (generally speaking).

If WACC is used to value your company and you would like to know the equity value, the process is relatively straightforward. Subtract the market value (not book value) of debt from the total value of the enterprise. The residual is the market value of total equity. If preferred equity is in the capital structure, subtract the market value of preferred equity from total equity to discern the value of common equity. In Chapter 8 we examined cash flow models. When valuing invested capital, and the numerator includes free cash flow to the firm, WACC should be the denominator.

This discussion on WACC was high-level. Nearly every formula has implied assumptions, and WACC is no exception. If the WACC assumptions are broken, the discount rate is flawed. Levels of value can be mistakenly violated (using hypothetical control weights when valuing a minority interest, for example). Taxes are another important determinant in the WACC computation (tax-related items are some of the chief weaknesses when using the WACC). Your understanding of WACC as a business owner, or an adviser to an owner, is to know how it's applied and what it consists of – both of which have been covered.

FCFE/Ke

Free cash flow to equity (FCFE) should be used as the numerator when the denominator contains a cost of common equity discount or capitalization rate. The build-up method (BUM), CAPM and MCAPM all provide minority interest cost of equity capital levels of value as long as the numerator – FCFE – has not been adjusted for control. Any of these cost of equity capital rates can be used in the denominator in the models discussed in Chapter 8. The rate applies solely to common equity, or its equivalent (e.g. limited partnership equity) if the interest being appraised is structured as a pass-through entity. Cost of equity capital rates are discount rates and not capitalization rates. Long-term sustainable growth must be subtracted from the discount rate to yield a capitalization rate. Because the cost of common equity applies solely to common equity, do not subtract debt or preferred equity when valuing common equity. This is in contrast to the FCFF/WACC formula that includes all suppliers of equity capital. Unlike FCFF/WACC, the FCFE/Ke includes cash flow and stock variability representing only that of common stock and not that of the entire company's capital structure.

Taxes and Corporate Structure

If we're going to keep everything apples-to-apples, then taxes need to be addressed. Public companies, whose stocks are used to derive cost of capital, are structured as C-corporations. Most small to medium-sized private closely-held companies, however, are organized as pass-through entities (S-corps, LLC, LPs, etc.). A disparity, therefore, exists between the enterprise being valued (assuming it's a pass-through entity) and the cost of capital which the closely-held company's cash flows are being discounted at. Do you tax the projected earnings of the closely-held company at the C-corporation level to maintain an apples-to-apples comparison with the tax rates of the publicly traded C-corporations from which the cost of capital is obtained? The answer is, "it depends." Tax courts and the IRS have changed positions on this issue, so I'm going to abstain from the argument. If you're a business owner of a pass-through entity, be aware that the appraiser may or may not impute a corporate tax, despite the fact your entity pays no tax at the company level.

Conclusion

The income approach's denominator includes the cost of capital. Determining an accurate cost of capital is one of the most complex challenges in closely-held business valuation. Cost of capital represents the opportunity cost of investing in one investment instead of another. The primary approaches business appraisers use to estimate a closely-held company's cost of capital for common equity are: (1) the build-up method (BUM), (2) the capital asset pricing model (CAPM), and (3) the modified capital asset pricing model (MCAPM). The CAPM and MCAPM include beta as an equation component while the BUM already includes beta. Therefore, practitioners using the BUM should not make a beta adjustment.

Beta adjustments are made to account for your company's capital structure. Several methods are used to make these adjustments, and you learned when each method should be employed.

The weighted average cost of capital (WACC) is the blended cost of capital for an entire company. Unlike the BUM, CAPM, and MCAPM, which account for common stock, the WACC considers all suppliers of capital.

Finally, numerators and denominators should always agree. Mismatching the two is a frequent error made by business valuation practitioners. Incorrectly coupling the two invalidates the value conclusion.

Chapter Thirteen

Valuation Discounts and Control Premiums

Introduction

Valuation discounts and control premiums are used to match the estimate of value conclusion with the level of value desired. In Chapter 6 you learned about the levels of value. In subsequent chapters, we examined how the various valuation approaches and methods resulted in different level of value conclusions. Adjustments are needed to either bring down the value (discount) to match the level or increase the value (premium) because of control attributes.

In this chapter, we'll cover the two most common valuation discounts used in closely-held business valuation. A discussion of control premiums and their usage will then follow. Remember that discounts and premiums are used to move down or up the Levels of Value Hierarchy as shown below:

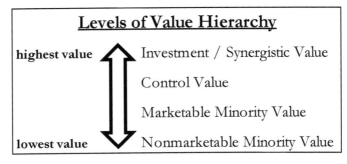

Valuation Discounts

When adjusting for levels of value – and notably for nonmarketable minority interests – two types of valuation discounts are used in the adjustment. The first adjustment is called a Discount for Lack of Control and is also known as a Minority Discount. The second adjustment is a Discount for Lack of Marketability and is referred to as a Marketability Discount.

The following picture depicts how the appraiser uses valuation discounts to achieve the desired level of value from a control level of value to a nonmarketable minority level of value. On the other hand, a control premium is needed to elevate the interest from a minority level of value to a control level.

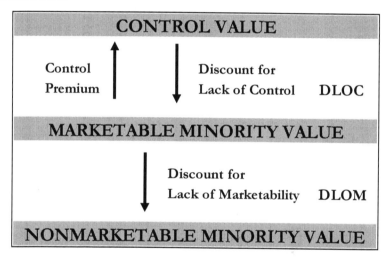

Discount for Lack of Control (DLOC)

The International Glossary of Business Valuation Terms defines Discount for Lack of Control as:

> "An amount or percentage deducted from the pro rata share of value of 100% of an equity interest in a business to reflect the absence of some or all of the powers of control."[28]

---

[28] http://bvfls.aicpa.org/Resources/Business+Valuation/Tools+and+Aids/Definitions+and+Terms/International+Glossary+of+Business+Valuation+Terms.htm.

A discount for lack of control is embedded in shares traded on national stock exchanges. An investor who owns 1,000 shares of Apple's common stock owns minority level shares of Apple. As a common shareholder, the owner has the right to vote on certain matters. As of January 8, 2016, however, Apple had more than 5.5 billion shares outstanding. With 1,000 shares, the shareholder's vote is essentially meaningless.

This exact concept is what accounts for a discount for lack of control (DLOC). If the valuation approach used in the business appraisal provides a control value estimate and the appraiser is valuing a minority interest – one without control – then a DLOC must be applied to the control value calculation to account for the lack of control. On the other hand, if the approach used in the appraisal provides a minority interest value estimate then no DLOC should be applied if the engagement is to appraise a minority interest.

Calculating the DLOC

Continuing with the example of owning 1,000 shares of Apple, the predicament now becomes quantifying the discount embedded in the minority shares. Investors cannot readily observe a discount in the stock price. Unfortunately, no direct information source provides minority discounts. Therefore, business appraisers turn to the minority discount's counterpart – control premiums.

Because evidence directly supporting minority discounts is non-existent, control level transaction data is used to calculate an implied discount for lack of control. When a company acquires another entity, a premium is often paid in the acquisition. Control transactions can be statistically measured and are observable. Like transaction multiples, implied minority discount data is offered through subscription services. FactSet Mergerstat's Control Premium Study is what I use, and it's also prominently used by other appraisers. Knowing the control premium, the appraiser calculates the DLOC using the following equation.

$$DLOC = 1 - \frac{1}{1 + \text{Control Premium}}$$

Walking through an example, assume that a business appraiser is valuing the common equity of a closely-held minority interest. Using the guideline company transaction method, the appraiser arrives at a control level of value. Because the subject appraisal interest is a minority interest, the appraiser must adjust the control level to a minority level of value. Using

FactSet Mergerstat's subscription service, the appraiser filters by industry and size (among other criteria), selects a time period of transaction data, and receives a control premium. Mergerstat also computes the implied DLOC, so the mathematical conversion isn't required. For our sake, we'll work through the calculation.

Before calculating the discount, it's important to note that the appraiser is given a range of discounts. Mergerstat, for example, provides a list of each transaction within the filtered group, including pricing information, date, etc. At this point, we're concerned with the premium, or implied discount (we'll address the other pieces later). The range, mean and median of premiums are provided, as are the implied discounts pertaining to each measure of dispersion. The term "implied" is crucial because the discounts are derived using the previous equation. Minority discounts aren't observable, and thus, an implied discount must be calculated through control transaction premiums. A wide range of discounts can cause the mean (average) and median's difference to be statistically significant (e.g. unreliable). In other words, the business appraiser has subjectivity, which can be used to support the appraiser's agenda. Business appraisers aggressive with valuation discounts will use these broad ranges to support substantial valuation discounts without supporting why the massive discount was selected (instead of the median, mean, or some other measure of central tendency).

Continuing with our example, assume we choose the median control premium of 10.2%. The control premium, using the previous equation, is converted to an implied minority discount as shown below.

$$DLOC = 1 - \frac{1}{1 + 10.2\%}$$

$$DLOC = 1 - 0.907441$$

$$\mathbf{DLOC = 9.26\%}$$

The control premium of 10.2% is converted into an implied minority discount of 9.26% (rounded). Further assume that the pre-discounted control value of the company's equity is $20 million. The appraiser needs to adjust the value from control to minority. This process is shown as follows.

Control Value of the Entity $20,000,000	× DLOC (%) 9.26% =	DLOC ($) $1,852,000
Control Value of the Entity $20,000,000	− DLOC ($) $1,852,000 ➡	Marketable Minority Value of the Entity $18,148,000

The marketable minority value of the company is $18,148,000. Like the Apple stock, this is the value of the company if owned by minority shareholders and traded on an active market. Marketable implies (generally speaking) that the interest is liquid. Knowing the closely-held company is not readily marketable (traded on an exchange), an additional adjustment – a discount for lack of marketability – will be subsequently applied (marketability discounts are covered later in this chapter).

DLOC Information Problems

A fundamental problem exists when using transaction multiples to calculate minority discounts. Each transaction's intent is unclear, despite knowing the financial attributes for most. In other words, we can see what was paid for the company acquired, but we do not know why it was purchased. As discussed in Chapter 6, investors/owners who possess control will pay more for synergistic benefits that add value to their firm. Financial investors, on the other hand, are less involved and seek higher returns from more passive investing. As a result, a mixture of intents populates the transaction multiples. Qualitative information cannot be reliably measured, and consequently, becomes problematic when relied upon from a statistical analysis framework.

Another problem is how the industries themselves are defined. For example, a company that specializes in technological services may not have a specific identifiable industry code (either SIC or NAICS code) with which to search for in Mergerstat. If one is located, transaction data for the industry code may not be available. However, the business appraiser, when valuing a minority interest, must apply a DLOC to a control level of value. Professional judgment is required to get the data. Many appraisers search for industries that are similar to the entity and use these related industries when selecting an industry code. Other appraisers examine multiple industries and average, for example, the median discounts from each industry. No matter the method selected, the information will not be entirely objective. Depending on the industry and the entity being appraised, the multiple may not make sense. If the appraiser fails to gain a complete understanding of your company and its key business drivers, the lack of knowledge could become especially problematic when selecting "similar" industries.

A statistical error I witness all too often is the removal of all discounts from the control transaction data set. Remember that control premiums are used to calculate the implied minority discount. Minority discounts themselves are not observable – they're calculated by referencing control premiums. Yes, the appraiser is seeking a discount to adjust for the lack of control. Removing discounts, however, distorts reality because observable transaction discounts have occurred. The impact of removing discounts increases the control premium multiple, and concurrently, the implied DLOC. One method I've seen – and have used on occasion – is the removal of outliers when a sufficient amount of data exists. The removal must occur on both ends to protect the data set's statistical validity. If the search provides 80 relevant transactions, for example, elimination of the bottom and top ten percent may provide a more statistically valid measure of central tendency. Removing only one side (discounts) and leaving in premiums artificially distorts the data upwards, procuring a higher implied minority discount. Arguing this position to the IRS or court would be a tough sell, and one I don't recommend.

Not including enough transactions may also invalidate the information. Having three or four transactions that significantly vary is hardly an indication of market pricing. No magic number exists for how many transactions an appraiser should select, and much of the reliability depends on the dispersion of multiples. If the range is significant, the business appraiser should include as many multiples as possible. On the other hand, if the data is clustered, fewer multiples may suffice. Again, this is a judgment call, and the position taken should be well supported in the business appraisal.

Including a search date or time horizon that is too long or too narrow can provide erroneous data. Transaction multiples during recessions infrequently reflect the reality of an economic upswing. Thus, using transaction data from recessionary economic periods may depress the DLOC as investors seek liquidity (and sell at lower multiples). Professional judgment is required to select the appropriate time frame. Many appraisers use a full economic cycle – typically seven years – to provide a smoothed variable. Because the future is unknown as of the effective date, a smoothed multiple helps capture all phases of an economic cycle in the statistic.

Finally, matching the numerator and denominator must be assured to maintain the appropriate level of value. If the guideline public company method is used, the level of value is already that of a minority interest investor. No DLOC should be applied if the engagement is to appraise a minority interest. Accordingly, no control adjustments should be made to the numerator. Normalization adjustments do not change the level of value from minority to control, but control adjustments do. The two are sometimes confused by practitioners, and the business appraiser should be careful when making any prospective changes to cash flow projections. In practice, business appraisers rarely adjust prospective cash flows when appraising a minority interest because the interest would have no ability to enforce business decisions (and concomitantly, cash flows).

Closed-End Investment Fund Studies

When valuing holding companies whose underlying assets consist of publicly traded securities, closed-end fund studies are frequently used to determine the DLOC. Closed-end funds are issued by fund companies and trade like stocks on active exchanges. Unlike open-end funds, whose shares are redeemed at their underlying net asset values following the close of daily exchange trading, closed-end funds trade throughout the day. Also unlike open-end funds, closed-end fund values typically vary from their net asset values.

For example, assume an open-end fund contained three stocks within the fund. Each stock closes at $100 per share at the end of trading for the day. Fund transactions would occur at $300 (3 stocks times $100 per share). Closed-end funds will (and usually do) vary from their underlying holdings' values. A closed-end fund holding the same shares as the open-end fund previously mentioned may trade at $270, or at a 10% discount from its net asset value (NAV). The discount is thought to reflect the DLOC. Remember, closed-end fund shares enjoy liquidity so a discount for lack of marketability would be inapplicable. Fund managers make the investment decisions, leaving owners of closed-end funds at a marketable minority level of value (no voice on decisions or control).

The Wall Street Journal and other financial data providers publish discounts on a weekly or other periodic basis. Bloomberg terminals can be used to customize studies that "fit" the subject interest. Whatever approach is taken, the discounts are typically divided into equities, municipal bonds, corporate bonds, and government bonds. Discounts observed from each class are then used as the discount for the subject interest.

Using CEIC (closed-end investment company) studies is commonplace when appraising asset or investment holding companies, notably family limited partnerships where the underlying assets consist of liquid securities. Like any other statistic, judgment comes into play when deciding which CEIC discount to apply. The obvious choice is that the DLOC for equities should be applied to the closely-held company's equities, corporate bond DLOC to the closely-held company's bonds, and so on. Aside from the obvious, there are two additional points you should note when reviewing an appraisal regarding CEIC studies and the DLOC used.

First, every array of data will have a range. Within the equity discounts, the range may include a premium. Moreover, an average, median and other measures of central tendency should be observed. Median discounts usually reflect a more accurate picture of the actual economic discount as opposed to the average, which is more sensitive to the impact of outliers. This sensitivity becomes considerable as the range increases (larger dispersion in the data set). Moreover, some appraisers will remove the premiums from the data set which artificially increases the DLOC. If discounts are being sought, excluding premiums to achieve a larger discount is statistically incorrect. If the dispersion is large, equally removing outliers from both the top and bottom may help provide a more reliable data set. Professional judgment is required as to what modifications are made (if any).

Second, applying a single DLOC to an entity's mixture of underlying assets is akin to matching apples with kiwi fruit. The most common area I see this is the valuation of holding companies, especially family limited partnerships where the underlying assets are liquid securities of equities and fixed income (bonds). Courts have scrutinized business appraisers for being lazy in practice. The criticism here focuses on the appraiser's lack of attention for relevancy of the dataset from which discounts are procured from. It appears that no amount of court scrutiny will alter the practice of these appraisers. Here, instead of applying equity DLOCs to equity securities, corporate debt DLOCs to corporate bonds and so on, the appraisers will select a single closed-end fund and apply its discounts (or an average discount of multiple funds), and apply the chosen discount to the entire FLP interest (a single rate for all asset classes). Sometimes the business appraiser will perform a rough analysis about the percentage of equity and debt components held in the CEIC, but that's about the extent of effort applied. Going this route saves the appraiser considerable time, but invalidates the analysis because it ignores the underlying holdings and strategy of the CEIC. This nefarious practice results in the erroneous practice of discounting cash at the same level of equities and bonds (corporate, government and municipal). However, each asset class carries discrepant risk profiles which impact investor demand, and consequently, the DLOC.

Non-Voting Share Discounts for Lack of Control

I want to address a common misperception about non-voting shares and lack of control discounts for minority interests. It's important to note that I'm addressing minority interests and not controlling interests. The percentage difference in value between minority interest voting and non-voting shares is small if any (~5%). Even with the right to vote, a minority investor's vote is relatively meaningless – and empirical data of publicly traded stocks supports the marginal discount. If both the voting and non-voting minority interests enjoy equal economic benefits aside from voting power, the difference in value is minimal – if not absent – because the minority interest has no operative control in decision making. As long as the economic benefits are the same for the two classes, the minority discount will be small or inapplicable.

Discount for Lack of Marketability (DLOM)

Discounts for lack of control (DLOC) are usually much lower, and although implied through control premiums, are more objective than discounts for lack of marketability. Collectively, DLOCs are more supportable than discounts for lack of marketability (DLOM). Closely-held businesses and investments without access to public markets or other governance mechanisms providing liquidity suffer in value compared to exchange traded securities, all else equal. Unlike publicly traded shares where cash can be received three days following a stock's sale, closely-held businesses and investments lack such liquidity. Even when governance documents provide liquidity mechanisms, the timing of the transaction and amount of proceeds received is much more opaque than publicly traded securities. Compensating for these marketability and illiquidity features, business appraisers apply discounts for lack of marketability (DLOMs).

The International Glossary of Business Valuation Terms defines Discount for Lack of Marketability as:

> "An amount or percentage deducted from the value of an ownership interest to reflect the relative absence of marketability."[29]

The "relative absence of marketability" in the definition refers to the absence of marketability and liquidity features of closely-held business interests that exist in active markets (securities exchanges). Closely-held business interests – notably minority interests – are restricted from an active securities exchange and are also subject to the restrictive language of the entity's governing document. Partnership and operating agreements (e.g. governing documents) limit the transfer of interests, some being more restrictive than others. DLOMs help compensate investors for these restrictions.

To reinforce the concept, assume the business appraiser is valuing a minority interest and has arrived at a minority level of value. More correctly stated – the level is a marketable minority level of value. It is assumed marketable because it's at the same level as marketable securities (publicly traded stocks). A hypothetical investor in the closely-held minority interest, however, understands the interest is not liquid. To entice investment – and compensate for the lack of marketability – the interest's value must be further reduced by applying a DLOM. After the lack of marketability discount has been implemented, the interest is at a nonmarketable minority interest level of value. At this level, all discounts have been incorporated to include a lack of control (minority shareholders have no say in corporate decision making) and a lack of marketability (due to the lack of liquidity, sale or hypothecation of the investment). The inability to transfer the shares, inhibited by the interest's governing documents, also contribute to the DLOM. The lack of marketability discount encapsulates both liquidity and transferability restrictions.

Sources of Information for DLOMs

An enormous amount of information, mostly through academic and professional studies, is available to peruse at your convenience. Instead of teaching you about the studies used to help quantify DLOMs, I'm going to hit on the parts that you should be aware of as a business owner.

---

[29] Ibid.

Two primary schools of thought are used to quantify DLOMs:
1) Restricted Stock Studies, and
2) Pre-IPO Studies

Other studies exist, but these two are by far the most widely used and recognized by the IRS and courts to support lack of marketability discounts.

Restricted Stock Studies

Restricted stocks are stocks of publicly traded companies, with a caveat. These restricted stocks carry marketability restrictions, disallowing the owner from selling the restricted shares on an active securities exchange where the company's publicly traded shares are listed. SEC Rule 144 guidelines govern the required minimum holding period or time restriction on sales. Again, these shares cannot be traded on a public exchange.

Investment companies often purchase shares of restricted stock at a discount from investors who desire immediate liquidity. The difference between the publicly traded stock price and the price paid "off market" is the quantifiable discount reflecting the lack of marketability. The IRS recognizes the concept of marketability discounts and has provided guidance in revenue rulings for restricted stock studies throughout the years (notably Revenue Ruling 77-287).

A simple example should help drill in the concept. Company X is a public company with shares traded on the New York Stock Exchange. The most recent stock price was $50 per share. Company X issues restricted shares to an investor (restricted stock is common with companies who go public via an IPO). Rather than wait for the time restriction to lapse, the investor sells the shares directly to an investment company for $35 per share. The difference of $15 represents a 30% discount from the stock's publicly traded equivalent price. To obtain instant liquidity, the investor gave up 30% of the publicly traded value. On the other hand, the investment company is now at risk of the stock's value declining. The investment company must wait for the time restriction to lapse to sell the shares on the NYSE. If Company X's share price tumbles, the investment company is at risk of losing money. The discount compensates the investment company for taking on both time and market risk. Accordingly, the discount represents the difference between a company's shares that are marketable on an exchange and those that are otherwise similar but not marketable.

Now that you understand what restricted stocks are and how they provide insight into marketability discounts, here's where the water gets murky. First, a plethora of discount studies exist. Many are more than forty to fifty years old, yet they are still used in valuation reports today. Second, the minimum time restriction under SEC Rule 144 changed from several years to six months in early 2008. As you might expect, discounts fell when the minimum holding restriction was reduced. A shorter holding period would, understandably, reduce the marketability discount as investors sidelined for only six months before having the option to realize liquidity.

Here's what you should be on the hunt for when reviewing an appraisal. Business appraisers should not include every restricted stock study applicable to DLOMs as being relevant in the appraisal unless the study is pertinent to the subject interest (e.g. your company or the appraisal interest). Only relevant studies should be used to support the discount. Courts have been very stern in their scorn of business appraisers inserting boilerplate language of studies, and then magically selecting a marketability discount without rhyme or reason. Many of the studies available to business appraisers today (nearly all) pre-date the 2008 decreased time holding restriction, and therefore, likely overstate the appropriate DLOM. Also, consideration of the particular securities included in the studies should be addressed in the business appraisal. A bundle of high-growth, low-dividend stocks trading in 1979 with an extensive holding restriction does not compare well to a basket of moderate growth, high-dividend stocks trading today with a six-month holding constraint. Using one to support the other is statistical blasphemy – yet, it occurs all too often.

Another factor that I believe influences the DLOM is price volatility. To help demonstrate, refer to the earlier example where an investment company purchased restricted stock from an investor at a 30% discount from the company's publicly traded stock price. The required holding period is an essential component of the discount. A lower holding period would, understandably, decrease the duration of market exposure (i.e. less market risk) the investment company is subject to. My research, however, indicates a meaningful correlation exists between marketability discounts and stock price volatility. A highly volatile market subjects the restricted stock owner to greater market risk. All else equal, an investor purchasing restricted stock will pay a lower discount when market volatility is low, and vice versa. Low market volatility partially reduces the market risk of the required holding period. While time is a significant element impacting the overall DLOM, I believe price volatility also plays a pivotal role, and my research supports this hypothesis. In summary, I believe higher volatility translates into a larger DLOM, and vice versa. The statistical data (since 2008) supports my belief, but a larger sample size is needed to make a concrete affirmation.

Pre-IPO Studies

Pre-IPO studies are the other source of DLOM studies business appraisers use to quantify marketability discounts. An IPO, or initial public offering, is when a company begins trading on a secondary exchange (e.g. NYSE, NASDAQ). Pre-IPO studies attempt to capture the price differential of a stock's non-publicly traded price before the stock trades on an exchange from the stock's publicly traded price following an IPO. In other words, the stock's price differential before trading on an exchange (nonmarketable) to after it begins trading (marketable). The time differential of when the "pre" date is measured varies from study to study. Each study's objective is to partition the marketability element from the stock's price.

In theory, the concept is sensible. Assume Company Y is a private company with several shareholders, and its stock has traded through private transactions at $15 per share. A few months later the company announces that it's going public, and its shares will be listed on the New York Stock Exchange. Six months after that, the shares begin trading on the NYSE at $22 per share. According to Pre-IPO studies, the difference of $7 – a 32% discount – is a reflection of the stock's marketability or lack thereof.

Like everything else discussed in this book, business appraisers cannot blindly assign a value, discount or adjustment without applying professional judgment and providing adequate support. Historical studies may not be relevant today. Think of the dot-com boom of the late 1990s and the comparatively different world we live in now. Another fault with these studies sits with the source and intent of information. Many buyers of pre-IPO stocks are insiders having non-public information.
Convertible preferred shares have become increasingly transacted instead of common shares. Nonetheless, convertible preferred stock transactions are included in these pre-IPO studies despite being an inherently different type of security.

Companies that file for IPOs can also remove the filing if the market isn't conducive to an offering. In other words, the number of IPOs tends to fall when markets decline in value. Conversely, when stock markets rise, companies are more willing to file for IPOs. A statistical prejudice called sample selection bias invades the study. By choosing population samples of distinctly different time frames, the sample does not fairly represent the total population.

Similar to the restricted stock studies, be on the lookout for the boilerplate inclusion of every pre-IPO study published. Comparing dates, companies, security types and industries fundamentally different than the subject closely-held business is not preferred. Restricted stock studies and pre-IPO studies merit inclusion in determining marketability discounts of closely-held companies. The argument begins when these discounts are applied arbitrarily without virtue or proper support.

• • •

Appraiser Mistakes

To give you an idea of what to look for, I'll run through an example of an appraisal I reviewed while writing this book. Because I've seen many like it, the case serves as an excellent illustration of what a business appraiser should not do (yet many seem to do it). Remember, a fundamental concern for appraisers is time. Quality work requires time, yet time is the antithesis of the billable hour.

The appraisal I reviewed was for a minority interest in an operating company. In the valuation discounts section, notably the DLOM part, the appraisal included every major study ever published. The report listed the names and results of each study. After reading through boilerplate language (13 pages of it) I got to the analysis section where the appraiser attempted to justify which discount to apply. In a mere paragraph, the appraiser concluded that a 35% discount was appropriate because the subject interest was "more risky than X study, less marketable than Y study" and so on. No discussion comparing specific attributes of the closely-held company interest to any of the studies was provided. Instead, I was left to read 13 pages of boilerplate text and a short paragraph of weak support attempting to justify a discount that had no quantitative or qualitative merit. Why did the appraiser choose 35%? The IRS wants to know — and after reading it, so did I. You can't blame the IRS, court or any reader who faults such lack of discussion. As I've stated before, a business appraisal should read like a thesis with every adjustment explained so that no other possibility appears reasonable. At a minimum

163

the discount should be supported with something other than "stronger, weaker, more restrictive – therefore, a 35% appears reasonable."

As you've heard several times by now, business valuation is both an art and a science. The objective is to use as much science (observable, quantifiable data) as possible. When applying subjectivity (i.e. "art") to data, a rigorous examination supporting the appraiser's decisions should be included in the report. There is no perfect answer – that's just the nature of the business. Nonetheless, business appraisers can support their value estimate in the business appraisal by supporting each adjustment made. An explanation that includes relatable data supporting the modification is necessary. In reality, very few do. Business appraisers that apply aggressive valuation discounts are notorious for this practice. Sometimes it works. When it doesn't, however, the price tag can be considerable (and include hefty fines). We, as business appraisers, are ethically bound to support our value estimates. We are not biased advocates of our clients, but rather, have the ethical responsibility to be unbiased backers of our product (e.g. price estimate). In the pursuit of additional business, some business appraisers depart from this ethical obligation.

Discount Factors

When determining which factors increase or reduce a closely-held company's marketability discount, several factors should be considered. Determining an appropriate marketability discount is an area of great debate, so I'll touch on some of the most popular topics. The IRS provides its valuation engineers a guide to follow in helping to determine the reasonableness of valuation discounts. While the service disclaims using the guide as a means to support a position, the publication provides insight into what they perceive as important and relevant.[30] You can view the full guide on the website **www.valuationforowners.com**.

In the tax court case "Bernard Mandelbaum et al. v. Commissioner – T.C. Memo 1995-255," the judge threw out both sides' positions (the IRS and the defendant). Lacking in substance, the judge (Judge David Laro – now famous in tax-related valuation circles) took it upon himself to right the ship. He came up with his DLOM factors that he believed to impact marketability, and hence, the DLOM.

---

[30] https://www.irs.gov/pub/irs-utl/dlom.pdf.

Known as the Mandelbaum Factors, they are:
1) Private versus public sales of the company's stock
2) Company financial statement analysis
3) Company divided history and policy
4) The nature of the company, its history, its position in the industry, and its economic outlook
5) The company's management
6) The amount of control in the shares transferred (shares being valued)
7) The restrictions on transferability (in the governing document of the closely-held company)
8) The holding period for the stock
9) The subject company's redemption policy
10) The costs associated with a public offering

Adjusting the DLOM according to each factor is intuitive. If, for example, the company's financial statement analysis demonstrates a poorly run company with grim prospects, the marketability adjustment (DLOM) would increase. On the other hand, if the company has a stable dividend-paying history, the marketability discount would be lowered (dividends are a form of liquidity).

Appraisers should use the best information available when supporting valuation discounts. I like what the IRS gives here because they spell out exactly what I've been saying throughout this book. The IRS isn't trying to wreak havoc and shut down the business valuation community. Quite the opposite is true. My experience in working with IRS engineers has been mostly positive. The service is understaffed and overworked. Provide them a supportable business appraisal and they'll move on to the next project.

A strength noted in the guide of the Mandelbaum Analysis is that it "raises the importance of the skilled application of differences/similarities of benchmark studies to the subject company."[31] Working through this type of analysis requires a competent appraiser's professional judgment to examine and adjust the important aspects impacting the closely-held interest's marketability.

In the same report, the service lists a weakness of the Mandelbaum Analysis in noting that to "attempt to cover all ten Mandelbaum factors might be difficult unless experienced." Even the IRS understands the

---

[31] Ibid.

difference between quality and cheap by recognizing appraiser experience as essential in applying a sound Mandelbaum Factor Analysis.

If you're so inclined to read further about other DLOM approaches, the IRS guide should quench your thirst. Because this book is intended to cover more than tax-related business valuation engagements, I will leave the option of further inquiry up to you. I use some of the methods noted in the IRS guide as sanity checks of my discount but rarely use them as a direct means to develop a valuation discount.

Total Discount Calculation

Discounts are multiplicative, not additive. When appraising a minority interest, the DLOC (lack of control discount) is applied first and the DLOM (lack of marketability discount) second. The difference between the end number and the pre-discounted number is the total discount, and it does not add up from a mathematical perspective. The formula that correctly calculates the total discount is as follows:

$$\text{Total Discount} = [1 - (1 - \text{DLOC}) \times (1 - \text{DLOM})]$$

According to this formula, a DLOC of 5% and DLOM of 30% would equal a total discount of 33.5%. Note how this differs from the sum of both discounts (5% + 30% = 35%). Adding the discounts together is incorrect, yet some appraisers are unaware of this vital concept (and mathematical principle). The following picture illustrates the difference between the correct and incorrect applications.

Correct Method - multiplicative		
Control Value		$20,000,000
DLOC	5.0%	($1,000,000)
Marketable Minority Value		$19,000,000
DLOM	30%	($5,700,000)
Nonmarketable Minority Value		$13,300,000
Total Discount	-33.5%	
Incorrect Method - sum of discounts		
Control Value		$20,000,000
DLOC	5.0%	($1,000,000)
DLOM	30.0%	($6,000,000)
Nonmarketable Minority Value		$13,000,000
Total Discount	-35.0%	

Other Discounts

Other discounts in addition to control and marketability discounts apply on a per-case basis. In general, they are less frequently encountered in closely-held business matters where the standard of value is fair market value. These other discounts typically pertain to a specific interest (blockage, size, quality, key person, composition of assets, etc.) and are beyond the scope of this book.

Discounts for Control Ownership Interests

Discounts for lack of control (DLOC) are inapplicable when valuing entities where the interest has control. However, discounts for lack of marketability (DLOM) deserve some attention. Two important points to hit on are the levels of control and the marketability of the subject appraisal interest.

Addressing the first, control (by definition) means ownership of greater than 50% voting control. Owning more than half of the voting shares allows, in most cases, the owner to materially influence corporate strategy. In other words, the controlling owner can "run the business" to his or her liking. On the other hand, many partnership and operating agreements –

if not most – require a "supermajority" vote to effect liquidation or other "major corporate action." A supermajority is usually two-thirds, or more than two-thirds of the voting shares (or all shares, including non-voting shares) outstanding. Major corporate action, by definition, ranges from liquidation to materially altering the capital structure. The list is endless and unique to each closely-held company. Regardless, an owner with 53% control has considerably less control than one with 95%. The former owner is absent the powers of liquidation, unlike the latter. Control has many shades of gray, and the company's governing document usually determines the tone.

Second, explicit costs are realized when a company creates or enhances the marketability of its equity, no matter the avenue chosen. Businesses that register for a public offering via an IPO pay fees to underwriters, accountants, brokers, and lawyers. Businesses that sell to other firms incur legal, accounting, brokerage and other costs. Liquidation, should a company liquidate, is also a cost-laden process.

I make these two points because no direct empirical evidence exists to support a DLOM for a controlling interest. Some business appraisers apply no discount for lack of marketability when valuing controlling interests. Others (I'm in this camp) believe an illiquidity discount should be considered and may be applied, depending on the facts and circumstances of the subject appraisal interest. Marketability refers to the ability to market the interest and receive funds promptly. Selling shares of stock trading on the NASDAQ will entitle you to low-transaction proceeds from your sale of marketable minority interest shares. A controlling shareholder of a closely-held private company, even with supermajority control, would have to incur liquidation costs in both time and money. Because the closely-held company is not marketable, the relative costs will be greater and the time will be longer to achieve liquidity.

Furthermore, liquidation is not the same as marketability. A controlling shareholder can "market" the company to other firms if he or she wishes to do so (governing documents and ownership will dictate the extent of marketability). Regardless of the intention – transaction or liquidation – an explicit cost will be realized to convert the interest from closely-held into cash. I call this discount an "Illiquidity Discount" in my valuation reports because it considers the explicit costs a company would sustain should it convert to cash. The size of the discount depends on the company's facts and circumstances. With that said, I am hesitant to apply an illiquidity discount of 15% unless the merits of the case strongly support it. Illiquidity discounts of less than 10% are more likely.

To reiterate, business appraisers butt heads on this matter and the logic on both sides is reasonable. Each has been upheld and refuted, making neither correct nor incorrect.

Control Premiums

If the subject appraisal is a controlling interest and the approach and method used provides a minority level of value, a control premium will be applied. We briefly touched upon control premiums earlier in this chapter. Control premiums are used to calculate implied lack of control discounts (DLOCs).

If the appraiser uses the guideline public company method, the resulting level of value is a marketable minority level. Because we need to climb the levels of value hierarchy ladder, a premium is applied, yielding a marketable control level of value. If the guideline company transaction method is used, no premium should be implemented. Transaction multiples include control and need no further control adjustments.

If using the income approach, a control premium may or may not be applied. Under the income approach, the numerator (free cash flow) dictates whether the level of value is control or minority. If the numerator is adjusted for control, no control premium should be applied. Some appraisers use cash flow projections provided by the company's management and make no changes to the management-provided cash flow projections. Making no adjustments assumes the interest has no say in operations and is, therefore, a minority level interest. In this case, a control premium may be warranted if the desired level of value is that of control.

The asset approach and excess earnings method provide control levels of value. Accordingly, no control premiums are applied to the value estimate using these methods.

Conclusion

Valuation discounts and control premiums are used to move a closely-held interest up or down the levels of value hierarchy. In Chapter 17 you will learn the importance of precisely specifying the level of value desired in your company's governing documents. Valuation discounts often pertain to tax-related valuations. Taxpayers (naturally) wish to pay as little tax as possible to the government. Estate planning strategies are available to administer efficient means of wealth transfer while minimizing taxes. Valuation discounts help facilitate tax minimization.

With that said, be cautious of business appraisers promising aggressive valuation discounts (this should sound familiar by now). Substantial discounts may be warranted if the case at hand justifies their use. Applying broad-based valuation discounts without consideration of the specific facts and circumstances of the subject interest can result in unwanted ramifications.

The business valuation industry has become more price-competitive, and to maintain revenue, some appraisers have positioned themselves as aggressive discount takers. Taking that position earns a reputation – a reputation that spreads locally, regionally, and eventually to the IRS. Don't fool yourself into believing the IRS doesn't monitor business appraisers. IRS engineers have a huge stack of business appraisals to sort through. Anything to help them segregate the "bad from the good" makes the screening process easier. Reputation matters in this line of work.

Finally, a business appraisal should read like a dissertation. Every adjustment should be supported and explained. Appraisers should also state all considerations given when appraising a company. If an approach or method was considered but refused, the appraiser should indicate that he considered the approach or method and explain why the approach/method was not implemented. Acknowledgment of said facts communicates to the reader that the appraiser gave considerate thought to all possible sources of information and used professional judgment in applying the selected adjustment, approach or method.

Chapter Fourteen

Navigating through a Business Valuation Report

Introduction

You learned in Chapter 3 about the four professional business valuation organizations. These groups confer valuation-related designations, prescribe rules for their members, and help promote the business valuation community. Because of the multiple (four) separate organizations, however, there are also four different bodies of rules governing valuation practitioners. Not only do the rules vary, but the methods by which each group allows its members to deliver an appraisal report differ. From oral reports to full, in-depth written valuation appraisals of 100+ pages, the delivery of valuation can take many forms.

A single chapter or sample appraisal report covering all available standards, levels, premises, reasons and delivery of valuation reports offered by the four organizations would be excessive. Fortunately, most appraisal organizations require their members to examine and discuss correlative criterion when providing a written appraisal report. This chapter will discuss the elements found in a full narrative appraisal report of a nonmarketable minority interest valuation. Nonmarketable minority interest appraisal reports require the practitioner to include additional substance to support valuation discounts.

As you read this chapter, keep in mind that the categories do not always have to be in a defined order, as long as the appraiser sufficiently communicates the information to the reader. Nonetheless, most reports I have read – and the valuations I perform – will follow a process similar to the one outlined in this chapter.

Navigating through a Business Valuation Report

Chapter 14 is the capstone of Sections One through Four, bringing everything together to ensure that you have the tools to navigate a valuation report. The foundation was poured in Section One. You then learned about the three primary approaches to valuation and their methods, along with a hybrid method (excess earnings method). Cost of capital, its components and importance were discussed. Finally, we examined valuation discounts and control premiums. From a high-level view, you've learned the pieces that together form closely-held business valuation. Now let's navigate through a hypothetical business valuation (appraisal) report.

I like to provide as much information as possible within the narrative section of the report to maintain a good flow for the reader. Many appraisals have "see Exhibit X" requiring the reader to finger back and forth through the report, searching for financial statements, graphs, and charts. Because most people don't enjoy this paper surfing task, I try to make the reader's life easy and include relevant exhibits within the report when discussed.

This chapter navigates through the critical sections you are likely to encounter in a business valuation report. Most reports do require a bit of paper surfing. As a result, this chapter has been outlined to accommodate what I believe you will encounter when reviewing a business valuation report.

Cover Page

The cover page will usually convey the name of the subject company being appraised, the interest being valued (e.g. 500 shares), the type of report, who the report is for and who performed the appraisal. Additional information is sometimes included, but the aforementioned elements are most common.

Transmittal Letter

This part usually resembles a memo-like format. If you are the individual being "engaged," the "memo" will be addressed to you. Its contents will state the standards used to appraise the interest, the interest being valued, the effective date, what the appraisal is for (its purpose) and the company's value conclusion. Most reports also disclaim that the report is subject to Assumptions and Limiting Conditions along with the Appraiser's Representations – which are usually inserted in the valuation's appendix at the end of the report. A signature bearing the appraiser's name, the appraiser's supervisor or that of the firm will be executed here. The valuation will only be signed when the appraiser issues the final appraisal report. Appraisers never signs draft copies (at least they shouldn't).

Executive Summary

This section is hit or miss – most often miss – in business valuation reports. If the IRS is going to read the appraisal, I highly recommend you push your business appraiser to include an executive summary. This suggestion is coming from the IRS's mouth, not mine. Here's where reputation can help a firm. Make the IRS engineer's life easier and you contribute to reducing the probability of a red flag. I'm not advocating aggressive, unjustifiable use of valuation discounts and then hedging the nefarious practice with an executive summary. An executive summary, when properly designed, will convey the salient parts of the appraisal without requiring excessive digging on the engineer's behalf. Including an executive summary is more of a suggestion to other appraisers, but as a business owner (or business owner's adviser) you want to see this included in your report. Points noted in an executive summary include:

- Company Description (brief)
- Interest being valued (4.5% limited partnership interest, for example)
- Standard, Premise, and Level of Value
- Effective date of the report
- Purpose and intent of the report (gift tax, estate planning, etc.)
- Valuation approaches used (with a brief statement why the other approaches were not used)
- Key inputs (discount rate, growth rate, valuation discounts and how they were determined)
- Major assumptions
- Conclusion of value
- Any subsequent event information or pertinent notes of disclosure

We're talking a page — two pages max. Summary letters provide intangible benefits to the reader (and client if the reader is the IRS) and to the firm itself.

Table of Contents

Depending on the appraisal and appraiser, this could be one to three pages.

Introduction

The introduction section is usually brief, covering:
- Description of the assignment (purpose of the appraisal, interest being appraised, effective date, standard of value, premise of value, disclosures required under the professional business valuation organization)
- Standard of value chosen and its definition (if fair value is used, the applicable definition of fair value is given)
- Premise and Level of value (under fair market value for tax purposes the level of value has already been defined in the standard of value so it may or may not be included here)
- Valuation date and reason for that date
- Type of report (full narrative report or a limited report)
- Scope of work performed
- Other required disclosures

Company Background

Here's where the reader will learn about the subject business. Background information, including a review of the firm's history, what it does, who runs it — everything a reader should know to gain an understanding of the subject company should be included in this section. Some reports follow Revenue Ruling 59-60 and define this part as "The Nature of the Business and the History of the Enterprise from its Inception." The ruling's headline explicitly tells the appraiser what to convey here. The corporate structure of the company (e.g. LLC, LP), business locations, customers (especially when concentrated customers exist) and ownership are laid out in this section.

Economic Outlook in General

Look for a third party or large economic data provider's language in this section. The outlook will be broad and will discuss the overall economy, and not that of the firm or industry. Don't get hung up here. Yes, the general economic outlook is essential, and the appraiser will consider it when valuing your company. However, the language used in this section is often purchased from a third party provider. An outlook of any type is inherently subjective, and viewpoints differ across the spectrum. Read the piece, but don't let it become a subject of argument between you and your appraiser. There's a good chance the appraiser also disagrees with parts of the outlook.

The Condition and Outlook of the Specific Industry in Particular

Now the information becomes more detailed. Industry analysis is an integral component of the valuation. If the appraiser doesn't understand your industry, how can he properly value your firm? This section should be thoroughly discussed and provide the reader insight into the industry's fundamental characteristics and features. Providing a brief history of the industry may be warranted. Discussion about key value drivers should be addressed. What makes the industry tick? Who are the major customers and suppliers? What causes the industry to grow and decline? Is the industry fragmented or concentrated? What direction is the industry heading? The industry section is significant, and the information included will depend on the company being appraised.

Business appraisers usually subscribe to industry research data providers. In my experience, the information from these providers is good but lacks in specificity. It's not granular enough to learn about what drives the subject company. Again, here's where quality and cheap separate. Cheap uses the high-level generic industry information. A copy/paste with a reference usually does the trick, and then the appraiser is on to the next job. Quality will ask the owner or senior management for technical journals that are most appropriate for the industry of the subject company. Trade and association journals provide the granular insight that appraisers need to understand a company's industry thoroughly. As an owner, you can help the appraiser by providing copies of trade journals or referring the appraiser to periodicals that will increase the appraiser's knowledge of your industry.

Financial Condition of the Business and Normalization Adjustments (If Made)

The appraiser will provide a study of your company's financial condition and operating performance. Most appraisals provide an analysis of the company's absolute financial standing and performance. In other words, the appraiser will provide a synopsis of the balance sheet position and usually include a trend analysis of how the balance sheet has evolved over the previous three to five years (or longer). The report will include a review of the income statement and the company's financial performance.

Normalization adjustments (if made) are typically next to follow in the appraisal. Normalization adjustments allow the appraiser to analyze the actual operating performance of the firm. Excess cash, for example, would be removed so as not to distort a financial ratio analysis. When normalization adjustments are required, I like to insert the adjustments made in this section of the narrative report instead of sticking them in the appendix. For companies with numerous adjustments, this saves the reader time from paper surfing and improves the flow of the report.

After making normalization adjustments, the appraiser will perform a relative financial analysis (relative to either peer group companies or industry data). Financial ratios will be calculated using the normalized financial statistics derived from the normalization process. Sometimes the appraiser will perform a brief comparative financial analysis before the normalization adjustment section. Comparing the company's financial variables to the industry or a peer group of publicly traded companies is how the appraiser determines what "normal" is. The relative financial analysis section and normalization section may also be combined. Regardless, the company's financial condition and performance will be compared to the industry or peer group companies to determine how well the company is performing compared to the other businesses in the same industry. If the appraiser uses the market approach and guideline public company method, financial data will come from the publicly traded companies selected. For other methods, third party industry data is frequently referenced.

Here's another area where problems can lurch. If the appraiser uses the guideline public company method, make sure the practitioner matches your financial performance and position to the period of the peer group companies. It's very easy to use different time spans instead of calculating a particular period that accurately reflects the performance and condition of your company compared to the peer group comparable companies. Timing becomes especially critical for businesses with high degrees of seasonality. Leaving out or including a quarter of performance can severely alter the relative ratios. Also, check to make sure the appraiser accounted for corporate tax, especially if your firm is a pass-through entity. Net income to a pass-through entity is pre-tax; whereas a publicly traded C-corporation's net income is after tax. Make sure everything is apples-to-apples.

Comparability problems can be especially exacerbated when using industry data. Many valuation practitioners obtain their industry data from third-party data vendors who acquire their information in various ways. Third party data providers collect company data from banks, tax returns, etc. Dates will not align, and survivorship bias can distort the data. Many providers use a calendar year-end date as the cut-off for industry financial information, so the appraisal date and industry information dates may conflict with each other. Information is also segregated by industry codes (SIC or NAICS). Industry codes are broad and can include businesses that have little economic correlation to your company.

A plethora of problems can arise when using general industry information. For many small and niche appraisals, however, the appraiser has little else to use. Valuing private closely-held companies using third party industry information can be particularly challenging because the industry information is private. It's tough to get. Sometimes appraisers have to use whatever they can obtain. In these circumstances, third party industry data is the appraiser's sole refuge.

Valuation Approaches (Approaches That Are Used and Those That Are Not)

The appraiser will list all three valuation approaches and then state which approaches and methods were chosen, followed by an explanation as to why he made the respective choice. For any approaches not selected, an explanation should be provided to clarify why the approaches were not appropriate.

Valuation Approaches – Implementation

The appraiser will walk through each of the valuation approaches used. This section is the meat of the appraisal report because the assumptions and forecasts are examined and discussed (including the cost of capital). Stepping aside from the masses for a second, I like to break this section into several parts. Valuation can be complex material, especially if performed well. Instead of confusing the reader, I prefer to make the information mentally digestible. Few appraisers spend much time talking about the cost of capital, which is one of the most important pieces in the report. Cost of capital, when appropriate, has its home in my reports. Some appraisers also walk this path, but most don't.

Valuation Discounts and Control Premiums

This section could make or break a tax-related appraisal. In Chapter 13 I told you to look out for this part, especially when there are ten-plus pages of boilerplate information referring to restricted stock and pre-IPO studies followed by a mere paragraph stating the valuation discounts selected. The discount for lack of control (DLOC), if applicable, should be discussed before the discount for lack of marketability (DLOM). Note, however, that if the appraiser lists each study and explains why the study is relevant (or not relevant) to the appraisal, this section becomes incredibly valuable. The discerning factor is not so much whether the studies are listed, but whether the appraiser considers each study with respect to the appraisal at hand and addresses its applicability, if any, throughout the appraisal. A Mandelbaum Factor Analysis can be very helpful when determining the discount for lack of marketability, and the appraiser would include it in this section.

Reconciliation of Values

If using more than one valuation approach, the appraiser will likely weight each approach by their respective merits. Professional judgment dictates the appropriate weights, but implementing arbitrary weights (e.g. 50/50 for no justifiable reason) is forbidden. The weighting must make sense. Valuation discounts established from the previous section are applied here, leading to the final value conclusion.

Test of Reasonableness

Few appraisals include this section and it's not always required. Just about all of my appraisals, however, include this section when feasible. Because an appraisal should read like a thesis, I try to make sure the reader is left believing that no other value conclusion could be possible. Here's where the unused approaches and methods can help out. If the market approach isn't reliable enough to be included as a means of determining the company's value, for example, it may have some value as a sanity check or a test of reasonableness. Guideline company transaction multiples, for instance, can be compared to the estimated value conclusion of the closely-held company to determine where the value lies in relation to the transactions (assuming the valuation is a control valuation). Alternative methods and approaches are available when appraising minority interests. Either way, a test of reasonableness enhances the quality of the valuation because it furnishes additional support that the appraiser's value estimate falls within an observable range of market values. It also shows the reader that consideration was given to all approaches and methods, even if the methods weren't reliable enough to directly value the company. Industry rules of thumb are often good candidates for this section.

Conclusion of Value
Usually just a paragraph or two, the appraiser restates the interest being appraised, effective date, standard, level and premise of value, and then provides the value conclusion reached. The appraiser, appraiser's supervisor or appraiser's firm will sign the final version of this page.

Appendices and Schedules
This section is where the paper surfing lives. Most appraisals contain few graphs, financial statements or charts within the narrative portion. Instead, the information is provided at the end of the report and referred to as "Exhibit X" within the narrative part of the appraisal. No narrative valuation report can avoid paper-surfing – minimizing it is the key and enhances the report's flow and readability. Customizing a report, however, takes time. Time is the enemy of the billable hour. As a result, most of the report's "meat" is likely to be buried here and referenced to within the report.

Common appendices and schedules include:
- Historical financial statements
- Adjusted (Normalized) financial statements
- Financial projections (for the income approach)
- Market approach comparable information
- Other (as needed) financial information
- Sources of information used
- Statement of Assumptions and Limiting Conditions
- The appraiser's representations
- The appraiser's qualifications (resume, papers published, other works, etc.)

Conclusion
A harmonious core of key topics are required by the professional business valuation organizations' standards. Topics covered depend on the purpose of the appraisal. Nonetheless, the items addressed in this chapter are core to most narrative closely-held business valuation reports.

Quality reports will include significant insight into each of the topics. No substantive matter will be ignored. Valuation approaches not considered will be discussed, along with the reasons for not using them. After reading a quality appraisal report, the reader should be left with no question that the value conclusion is reasonable.

Cheap reports will contain significant boilerplate language. The investigation of key topics will be absent or briefly touched on if not mandated by the appraiser's professional business valuation organization's standards. Little to no explanation will be given for selecting valuation discounts, costs of capital or why the appraiser chose certain approaches over others.

SECTION FIVE
THE LANDMINES YOU DON'T SEE

Demands for answers ignited this book's conception. Business owners frustratingly found themselves in a quagmire trying to understand the process of a business valuation engagement, let alone the valuation report when the engagement was over. A tool was needed to empower business owners and alleviate this seemingly endless perplexity. Few books have been published on the matter, and those books are even more restricted in scope. Nearly all are focused on educating valuation professionals and not business owners. The mission of this book is to provide you, the business owner, with the tools needed to not only understand a business valuation report and its components but also to know the difference between quality and nefarious business appraisals and gain additional insight into the industry from a practical point of view.

Section Five takes closely-held business valuation a step further. I know some readers of this book purchased it solely for Section Five. Unquestionably the most fulfilling part for me, I expose the landmines that almost every closely-held company has but either doesn't know exists or fails to remedy. In my experience working with business owners, most are altogether unaware of the problem. Owners who are aware typically convince themselves into thinking "it won't happen to me." Unfortunately, the data does not lie, and it does happen – even to the many owners who thought they had adequately planned for such an event.

First, a bit about my experience and what this section is going to cover. My clientele includes high net worth and ultra-high net worth individuals, families and business owners. In addition to business valuation engagements, I also advise ultra-high net worth individuals and families on private equity offerings. Furthermore, I'm frequently called on to review governing documents (e.g. LLC and Partnership Agreements), specifically the adequacy and thoroughness of transfer restrictions and price determination within these documents. My valuation practice is heavily focused on estate planning, gifting strategies and business succession planning. As a result, I've witnessed a healthy dose of valuation disputes between shareholders and beneficiaries. My goal is to prevent them. Moreover, I seek to "insure" a company and its shareholders against probable catastrophic events.

Accordingly, this section addresses the problems I see on a regular basis and the reasons why these problems exist in the first place. I'll discuss how you can "insure" your firm against these types of preventable disasters, and specifically how a buy-sell agreement, when correctly structured, is often the best insurance a closely-held company can have. Moreover, you will learn what to avoid and what to include in your buy-sell agreement.

In Chapter 18 you will learn why EBITDA is one of the most prevalent valuation multiples cited by business managers and appraisers. I will also tell you why it rarely belongs in valuation when used as an exit multiple in a discounted cash flow analysis. Despite its wide acceptance in business, when broken down and explained from a valuation perspective, EBITDA often serves as an anti-valuation multiple.

Finally, I'll give you the tools needed to select an appraiser that best matches your needs, including an insider's perspective of tips on how to secure the best bang for your valuation buck. You will no longer be left to believe what somebody else says is a "good price." Business appraisers have a relatively short amount of time to provide a fee quote to a potential client. In Chapter 19, you will learn strategies that most business owners (or any person seeking an appraisal) can use to influence high-quality business appraisers to lower their price. Chapter 19 alone – if you follow the instructions given – will save you money and speed up the valuation time frame.

Chapter Fifteen

Why Your Company Is in Danger

Introduction

Your company is in danger. Yes, yours. Most closely-held business owners believe they're immune to the danger. It's human nature to think that bad things only happen to others and that "it won't happen to us." The statistics, however, don't lie, and the odds of a grave scenario happening are very real. At this moment, right now, you and your company are in trouble. This isn't a scare tactic or sales pitch – it's the truth.

This chapter tells you what landmine, precisely, is lurking around the corner, just waiting to destroy everything you've worked to accomplish. Nearly all companies have landmines, and most are eventually triggered. Once triggered, the repercussions range from a slight financial setback to complete financial ruin. Families are torn apart. Businesses are dissolved or sold for a fraction of their values. Friendships are decimated.

Everything you're about to learn is real. Don't neglect the warning. Otherwise you, too, will face the horrific fate of becoming another statistic.

Most small to medium-sized private closely-held companies are structured as pass-through entities. Instead of being taxed at the entity level (like a C-corporation), these companies' earnings pass through the company level and taxes are borne by the shareholders of the pass-through entity. C-corporations, on the other hand, are taxed at two levels: first at the entity level and then at the shareholder level (on dividends received by shareholders). While this chapter applies to all closely-held enterprise structures, my aim is focused primarily on pass-through entities.

Operating and Partnership Agreements (*Governing Documents*)

The terms "Agreement" or "Agreements" are used interchangeably throughout this chapter. Attorneys practicing law draft Agreements. As a disclaimer: advice, suggestions or anything else in this chapter and book are not to be considered by the reader as legal advice. I do not practice law and am in no way intending to provide legal counsel. Lawyers do that – not me.

With that said, I regularly review Agreements drafted by attorneys. More specifically, I'm asked to review the valuation sections within Agreements. The area I focus on is the buy-sell clause, otherwise called a buy-sell agreement. Many companies have "Right of First Refusal" clauses in their Agreements. Do not fall into the trap in believing a right of first refusal and a buy-sell agreement are the same – they are not.

Look at your Agreement and search for the words "buy-sell agreement." You probably won't see them. A buy-sell agreement is typically a clause or collection of clauses within an Agreement, although it can be a standalone document as well. Most buy-sell agreements exist as clauses within governing document Agreements. Because the objective of a buy-sell clause(s) is to effect an agreement within the Agreement, despite usually being clauses and not a separate agreement, they're called buy-sell agreements. If you're confused, don't worry. A few years ago I gave a presentation on closely-held business succession planning to a group of attorneys. Most of the lawyers in the audience came from suburbs and rural communities. By nature of practicing in a small community, these lawyers tended to practice in a more general legal scope (as compared to a defined niche practice). The most asked question pertained to where the attorneys could find the buy-sell agreement within an Agreement. A few days after the presentation, one of the attorneys who was in the audience sent me a Partnership Agreement, swearing no buy-sell agreement existed within the Agreement. Why? The attorney couldn't find a clause titled "buy-sell agreement." Just as I recommend you find a quality business appraiser who focuses on your particular need, the same recommendation applies with legal counsel.

Side-note: As we begin this chapter, you will see "agreement" and "Agreement." These are not the same! When using the lower-case word "agreement," the reference is to the buy-sell agreement. I have done my best to incorporate "buy-sell" in front of "agreement" as much as possible, but there are times when it requires standalone usage. The upper-case "Agreement" refers to the Operating or Partnership Agreement (e.g. governing documents) that governs the company. So remember lower-case means buy-sell, whereas upper-case means governing document.

Buy-Sell Agreements

Buy-sell agreements dictate how the transfer of ownership proceeds when a triggering event occurs. A triggering event can encompass several things (e.g. divorce, bankruptcy, etc.), and we will cover triggering events later in this chapter. A buy-sell agreement should (but often fails to) provide four important features:

1) Establish a price for the shares in the event (a triggering event) shares are required, or need to be sold or otherwise transferred. The method determining the price should be understandable, current, and result in a price agreed in principle among the shareholders.

2) Provide marketability for the shares. The buy-sell agreement should create an orderly market for purchases and sales of shares of the closely-held company.

3) Be clear on the terms of the transaction.

4) Specify how financing will be established to create a market if a triggering event occurs. Companies without clear direction and protection can be wiped out if (and usually when) the perfect storm hits. The legal obligation to purchase shares with money a company doesn't have can lead to insolvency. A well drafted buy-sell agreement tackles this problem head-on.

Perhaps you're reading this thinking that your buy-sell agreement sufficiently covers all four of these features. A buy-sell agreement should include these, just like a new car should drive off a car dealer's lot. The problem is much deeper than "hitting all four" of the features. Remember that attorneys draft Agreements, and therefore they write the buy-sell clause (agreement) within the Agreement. From my experience, once a law firm – large or small – creates valuation language within a buy-sell agreement, the form remains static and becomes the company's go-to template used for all subsequent Agreements. Only the legal aspects that the attorney has been educated in and is familiar with are customized to fit the company's needs. Lawyers are great at what they do, and that is not valuation. Consequently, the buy-sell agreement wording is where I find serious flaws (landmines) in Agreements.

If business valuation were as simple as a paragraph or two, there would be no need for business appraisers. A buy-sell agreement is a function of valuation. Valuation is a prophecy of the future. Merely plugging a boilerplate number, multiple or formula into the Agreement ignores the complexity of business valuation. Moreover, it exploits the ignorance of authors who draft buy-sell agreements. I'm not allowed to practice law (a good thing). Why, then, are attorneys given a free pass to practice valuation? The problems discussed in this chapter predominantly arise from attorneys practicing as valuation experts.

And that is exactly why you must read this chapter and review the buy-sell clauses within your Agreement. If yours is a stand-alone buy-sell agreement outside of your Agreement, pull it out. Nearly all Agreements I've read contain at least one serious flaw. All have had at least one issue or ambiguous term that could lead to problems in the future. This chapter exposes the problems you need to look for.

Buy-Sell Agreement Price Mechanisms

To uncover the landmines, we must first identify what they look like. After defining each pricing method, you will learn the inherent flaws in each. The three major types of buy-sell pricing mechanisms ordinarily used in Agreements are:

1) Price is based on a formula
2) Price is fixed
3) Price is determined by a process (or processes)

• • •

THE BIG THREE

1. The Price Is Based on a Formula

Buy-sell agreements determining the price using a pre-defined formula are prevalent in many closely-held company Agreements. A multiple of a financial statistic is selected to establish the price when a triggering event occurs. For example, many companies use EBITDA as a valuation statistic. It's familiar, the calculation is straightforward, and rules of thumb are often based on EBITDA multiples. A typical example would read like "the price paid shall be six times the trailing twelve month EBITDA as of the most recent month end." In other words, the price is set at the previous twelve month EBITDA number multiplied by six. Book value (accounting book value) is also typical in pricing formulas.

Temporarily side-stepping the problems of using EBITDA as a multiple – which you will learn about in Chapter 18 – let's examine some of the critical landmines waiting to be triggered under the price based on a formula method. Note that this book covers landmines I have seen and reviewed, and does not exhaust additional landmines that have occurred outside of my view and could also arise.

The Flaws with Pricing Based on a Formula

1) Assuming your buy-sell agreement was drafted more than a year ago, the multiple is already stale. Multiples change over time as markets change. The more time that has passed since the buy-sell agreement was drafted, the more obsolete the price is. Price accuracy also fluctuates depending on which stage of the economic cycle your company is in. If last year was a record year, expect to pay a record amount to a seller if a triggering event occurs – even if last year's results are never projected to occur again. As a seller, if last year's results were unusually horrible, expect to receive a disproportionate price compared to what the company has historically been valued at and is likely to be priced in the future. Everything depends on the previous twelve months' results.

2) The conclusion of value using a price formula makes little economic sense. Price multiples are calculated from accounting information (as opposed to economic data). Take, for example, a price multiple of five times book value. According to the price formula, a triggering event would require the payment to the seller of five times the accounting book value.

Consider a hypothetical closely-held company whose line of business is providing professional services. When creating the buy-sell agreement, the closely-held company's owners agreed that five times book value made sense. At that one point in time, the company was reasonably valued at the agreed upon pricing multiple. Upon formation, the company decided to distribute excess cash proceeds to its owners on a quarterly basis into perpetuity. Also upon formation, the company purchased the land where its headquarters resides. Now assume that twenty years have passed, and an owner dies, triggering the company's buy-sell agreement.

In this scenario, two serious problems exist. Both are attributable to the disparity between economic and accounting value. First, the quarterly excess cash distributions reduce the book value (equity) of the company. Regardless of increasing and record-breaking cash flow, the price in the buy-sell agreement states that five times book value is to be paid to the seller (the decedent in this example). As a service company, the entity's balance sheet contains meager fixed asset balances. Excess cash is distributed quarterly to the owners. Yes, the real estate is there (we'll hit that next), but otherwise, the company has little substance in terms of accounting book value. Ignoring the cash flow generating history and future probabilities of the company is an economic aberration to the book value that the price is based upon (not to mention the company's value). One side (the buyer) is getting an incredible deal while the seller (the decedent's estate) will get shortchanged.

The second problem in this scenario emanates in the real estate used to calculate book value. Real estate is held at cost according to United States accounting rules (GAAP). The company owns the land where its headquarters resides, and the company paid $200,000 for that property twenty years ago. Many owners who have price formula methods in their buy-sell agreements assume they'll "get the value" when a triggering event occurs.

The buy-sell agreement said book value. Book value is an accounting term and represents the accounting equity – as opposed to economic equity – in the company. During the past twenty years, the metropolitan area where the company's main office is located grew exponentially. The $200,000 real estate parcel is now being assessed at $2 million (I'm not pulling the value from thin air – this happens). Yet, because book value – an accounting term – was used to determine the price, the real estate is valued at its accounting price of $200,000 and not its current economic value of $2 million. Real estate, held at cost, never changed values in the financial records.

For this second flaw, I provided one scenario using one hypothetical company and one multiple. To say I touched the tip of the iceberg is an understatement.

3) Formulas are predominately rules of thumb and rules of thumb change over time. Remember when inflation never happened for two decades? If not, perhaps you recall using a cell phone in 1970. No? Okay, those are silly statements. Economies change. Markets rise and fall. Automobiles destroyed the horse and buggy industry. Life happens! A price formula is a rule of thumb. Rules of thumb are almost always based on accounting figures. Accounting numbers do not equal economic reality. Valuation is a prophecy of the future and values change over time. A company valued at five times book value twenty years ago may be worth (economically) fifty times that amount today. When using a "multiple of…" the price ignores the underpinning of economics and finance. Its ease of understanding lacks teeth in economic reality.

4) A price based on a multiple doesn't account for changing capital structures within the business, and consequently, ignores the risk of the company. Increased relative financial leverage (debt) in a company's capital structure amplifies its risk, increases its cost of capital and lowers its current value, all else equal. No matter which multiple you choose, including EBITDA (especially EBITDA), the capital structure is completely ignored. Risk is ignored.

Imagine, for example, a company that had recently navigated through a rough period of performance due to an economic recession. To "hold its own" during this brief malaise, the company took on more debt than it preferred – but the debt was a necessity for working capital purposes. The recession is ending, and business is starting to pick up. Potential contract work is becoming more realistic, and the company's backlog is starting to build. At that moment an owner quits, triggering the buy-sell agreement. Business has yet to pick up enough to validate a five-times EBITDA multiple (hey, it made sense ten years ago) but things have changed. Paying five times EBITDA would violate the company's debt covenant that it entered into when working capital funds were needed. Also, the company can't afford to take on any more debt. Faced with a legal obligation to pay the owner according to the buy-sell agreement's price formula coupled with the legal requirement to pay the debt, you can only imagine what will happen (it's not pretty – it never is). Unfortunately, this scenario could have been entirely avoided with proper planning.

5) A price formula mechanism does not allow for gifting of the closely-held company's shares or equity interests. If the business owner desires to gift shares of the enterprise to facilitate generational transfers (the owner wants his son to run the business eventually), a pricing formula violates the requirements set in Revenue Ruling 59-60 and IRC Chapter 14 (as discussed in Chapter 10 of this book). Revenue Ruling 59-60 requires, among several other things, use of the fair market value standard of value. Try supporting a five-times-EBITDA value estimate in the tax filing. That's low hanging fruit for the IRS.

6) A culmination of the preceding problems is that the price is just inaccurate. Valuation cannot be correctly estimated using a formula inserted into a paragraph of an Agreement that's shelved for years without adjustment. I know the IRS and courts wish it could. Economics and reality, unfortunately, say otherwise. A winner and a loser will emerge when a buy-sell agreement contains a price formula mechanism. Which one will you be?

7) Nobody wants to revisit the buy-sell agreement. Thinking about divorce, illness, bankruptcy, strokes, death – it isn't a favorite topic at company meetings, family dinners, and social gatherings. Business owners are busy running their business. Who has time to revisit a buy-sell agreement that has (more or less) become an afterthought? After all, everybody is healthy, and you don't foresee anybody dying in the near future. You're fairly sure the other owners have great relationships with their spouses. It's just something you don't think about. Meeting this year's sales quota, making payroll – those are all more important. Your mind is on your business, not that other "stuff."

That is until you receive a call at 5 am from your brother telling you that your mom found your dad sitting unconscious in his favorite recliner. Ambulances raced to your parent's house. Your mom was worried that he was gone. Thank goodness the paramedics reached him in time and saved his life. While his life was saved, his brain was brutally damaged from a stroke. Your 60-year-old dad who owned a majority stake in the company he founded is legally declared "mentally incapacitated." Nearing the end of his career but in excellent health, a sudden stroke changed everything.

You've never seen your dad's Agreement but knew that a formula price mechanism was involved. Your mom told you about it a few years ago and that it was there "just in case" something happened to your dad. Mom said that dad reassured her that despite having little saved for retirement, the sales proceeds from the buy-sell agreement would guarantee their financial security should it ever be triggered – which he said would never happen.

The buy-sell agreement, however, had become more of an afterthought. Dad was planning to sell his shares in a negotiated offer in two years. Those two years never materialized. Now mom will have to take care of dad since he can't take care of himself. She's depending on the buy-sell agreement to provide the financial support that both her and your dad need – especially with the expensive (and ongoing) medical bills. Dad will never be the same and requires weekly physical and mental therapy to help regain some bodily and mental functions.

After much searching, the Agreement is located in a bank safety deposit box. Dad told you a few weeks ago he thought his share of the company was worth $7 million. Dad owned 70 percent of the company, and based on recent transactions in the industry; he calculated the company's total value to be about $10 million. His mental incapacity, however, is considered a triggering event in his business's Agreement. After reviewing the buy-sell agreement, your dad is entitled to receive five-times the previous calendar year's EBITDA. At that moment, you vividly remember dad saying how last year was the worst year in the company's history, but that business had turned around exponentially in the first quarter of this year. In fact, EBITDA for the first quarter exceeded all of last year's EBITDA.

Guess what – it doesn't matter. EBITDA this quarter was $1.5 million, a quarterly record for the company. Last year's total annual EBITDA, however, was $140,000. According to the buy-sell agreement, he – and now, more importantly, mom – will receive $700,000. Mom and dad, both 60 years old, are financially ruined. Dad based his retirement conservatively at $5 million. Knowing $7 million was likely two years away, mom and dad purchased a new home, a lake house, boats, jet skis – which in sum required them to take a $1.2 million loan.

It is with great sadness that I can personally attest that this story – and those similar to it – happens. The company that your dad founded and built over thirty years didn't fail him. Dad's uncomfortable attitude about mortality and unwillingness to acknowledge reality (the reality that "stuff" happens) has caused your parents financial ruin. All of this – the financial disaster – could have been avoided with a proper buy-sell agreement. All of it was avoidable.

2. The Price Is Fixed

Buy-sell agreements that contain a fixed price are completely illogical if not updated annually. Under this pricing mechanism, a fixed price of the company is written into the buy-sell agreement. Shareholders of the company agree on a price. The accepted price is then included in the Agreement as the applicable price if a triggering event occurs. As you might expect, the problems arising from this method are numerous.

The Flaws with a Fixed Price

1) The price may not be realistic. Lawyers practice law, doctors practice medicine, and business owners run their businesses – none specialize in the economic valuation of closely-held companies. In many circumstances, the owners agree on a price, and the price is memorialized in the buy-sell agreement. Is this price reasonable? Does it make sense? In my experience, the answer is overwhelmingly no. Politics often rears its ugly head into the mix when determining the price. Whether the price is too high or too low depends on the shareholder wielding the most power. Minority owners acquiesce to the value as long as it appears reasonable. The problem then becomes reasonableness. It's human nature to think our businesses are worth more than they are – unless a triggering event is likely to occur in the near future and you sit on the "buy" side of the equation. Undisclosed shareholder motives can dictate pricing for personal agendas.

2) The price may be set, but most buy-sell agreements with fixed price mechanisms lack the requirement of periodic updates (annually, for example). No matter the price set upon initiation, over time the economic value of the company will be different than the fixed price initially set – and the gap almost always widens as more time passes. For most businesses, the change in value is significant. Only when a triggering event occurs do the owners realize the mistake. One party will win (the buyer) at the expense of another (the seller). The consequences are dreadful, notably when family and close friends are shareholders.

3) The price has been agreed upon but the process requiring how the price is subsequently determined has not. Many buy-sell agreements using a fixed price mechanism call for the owners to agree upon a price when a triggering event occurs. The problem then becomes how this amount is decided.

Will it make sense? Can the parties agree on a fixed price? If not, how is the price determined? If no price is agreed upon, can the shareholder liquidate his interest because of the pricing dispute? If so, what is the applicable price of the shares? These are a few of many possible uncertainties that arise from fixed price mechanisms.

4) The price is not reflective of fair market value and will not allow for gifting. Many closely-held business owners gift shares to family members as part of their succession planning strategies. A buy-sell agreement fixed price mechanism violates the fair market value standard, among others.

The underlying problem of fixed price mechanisms is reasonableness. Owners sign an Agreement, agree to a price within the Agreement (the buy-sell agreement/clause) and lock it away. Only when a triggering event occurs, they realize the grave mistake made by using a fixed price mechanism. Furthermore, the price is not economically sound. A company's owners who specialize in their business (and not valuation) agree on a price they all like. That's it! No supportable evidence or reliance on a valuation expert to help provide practical price information. A fixed price, in my experience, proves disastrous for business owners. Unless an appraisal is performed by a valuation expert to establish the price and the valuation is periodically updated by a valuation expert, this mechanism provides the worst outcomes. The reality is that many companies having buy-sell agreements with fixed price mechanisms set a price upon the formation of an Agreement and fail to update the price.

3. The Price Is Determined by a Process (or Processes)

Buy-sell agreements that dictate price using a process are the most economically valid – yet costliest in fees – of the three pricing mechanisms. The buy-sell agreement will require that an appraiser values the company when a triggering event occurs. Many processes can be used in this type of pricing mechanism. Some buy-sell agreements, for example, provide that if a triggering event occurs and the buyer or seller rejects the value conclusion, either party may then select an appraiser of his choice. The second layer of appraisers then provides a value estimate. If the value estimates are within a defined threshold (say, five percent of each other) then the average of the two is used as the price. If the value estimates fall outside of the threshold, the appraisers are then required (per the buy-sell agreement) to agree on a mutual business appraiser. This third level appraiser (we're up to four valuations now) values the business. The value conclusion reached under the third business appraiser, or the fourth valuation, is binding on all parties.

This example illustrates one of several (emphasis on "several") processes used. Process agreements can be simple or complex. No matter the simplicity or complexity, process agreements share common faults.

The Flaws with a Price Determined by a Process

1) An unknown appraiser is selected to value your company. Buy-sell agreements with process mechanisms typically require an appraiser be hired, but fail to specify who the appraiser should be. Perhaps the local CPA who dabbles in valuation when tax season slows down could be the person selected to value your company. Maybe it's the majority shareholder's cousin who interned at an investment banking firm when he was in college ten years ago. No matter who is chosen, unless specified, the appraiser will be unfamiliar with your company. At some point in the process, you will be bound to a value estimate provided by an appraiser unfamiliar with your history, operations, key value drivers and intangible value.

2) The standard and level of value are absent in the buy-sell agreement. I have advocated strongly (and been published) on this topic, notably the level of value (we'll further examine the level of value problem in Chapter 17). Without a defined standard of value in the buy-sell agreement, the appraiser is left guessing and must make a subjective decision. Is fair market value used or fair value? If fair market value is the standard (which I recommend), should valuation discounts be used? If no valuation discounts are to be used, is it fair to compensate a minority level shareholder similarly to a control level shareholder? How about the level of value? If not defined, a control level of value determination can be used for a minority interest (and vice versa).

3) The price is a mystery to all parties until the appraisal is completed. Because the buy-sell agreement requires a valuation only when a triggering event occurs, the price is a mystical illusion until strife arises. Many companies have insurance policies to pay for stock repurchases in case an insurable triggering event occurs. How much insurance is needed to cover the stock repurchase? The liability cannot be adequately hedged with an unknown price.

4) The price eventually reached may be illogical. This is most prevalent when a single appraiser is used without the option of hiring additional appraisers to resolve the value quagmire. An appraiser unfamiliar with the nuances of closely-held business valuation – not to mention your company – is sure to make errors in the appraisal. Bound to a single value estimate, you lack the remedy of rebuttal. Will the erroneous value estimate favor you or the other party (or parties)? Nobody knows, and all you can hope for is the value to be in your favor (to the detriment of your fellow shareholders – something none of you ever intended to happen).

5) The shareholders not part of a triggering event may not be helpful in providing information to the appraiser. Even worse, the shareholder may provide information that benefits his side to your detriment. Assume, for example; you are a shareholder of a closely-held business along with other shareholders. Also assume that, for whatever reason, the other shareholders have a grudge against your wife. For several years, she has tried to gain their friendship to no avail. Now assume that you unexpectedly pass away. Under the buy-sell agreement, an appraiser is chosen to value the business. Your wife, the beneficiary, is relying on a reasonable value. The proceeds she will receive are needed to accommodate her well-being until her death. As the decedent triggering the buy-sell agreement, you (i.e. your estate) are the seller and the company is the buyer. You're gone, and the other shareholders don't care for your wife. As buyers, the shareholders are looking for the lowest valuation possible.

The less money they spend to buy your shares, the better. On the other hand, your wife needs the money to live – but you aren't there in her defense. The appraiser, not knowing a thing about your company before the engagement, has no choice but to believe management's forecasts. Because they (shareholders) want a low value, the estimates they give the appraiser will be biased downwards. Moreover, they will likely overstate the risk of your company. Collectively (smaller numerator and higher denominator), the value of the entity is negatively impacted. How fair are the estimates? Your wife has no idea. Only the remaining shareholders are in the know – and you're not around to debate their negatively biased forecasts. How many business owners do you know expect for this type of situation to happen? On the same token, how many times do you think this regrettable variety of scenario occurs?

6) No periodic or ongoing appraisal is performed. Accordingly, no gifting of company shares/equity interests is available unless you (personally) pay for the business appraisal. Moreover, the standard of value is not stated in the process of the buy-sell agreement. As you know by now, in nearly all cases, tax-related valuations require the fair market value standard.

7) The appraiser's qualifications and professional business valuation organization standards that must be followed are not defined. I've seen corporate finance professionals hired to provide business valuations (no joke). Is the appraiser qualified? Are professional business valuation standards being followed? If not explicitly defined, anybody can be chosen.

8) Of the three methods, this one tends to incur the greatest administrative and professional services costs. If only one process is used, then the cost is limited to only one business appraisal fee. But the detriment of using one appraiser can be paramount. Many buy-sell process mechanisms involve at least four appraisals – and accordingly, incur four appraisal fees. Exacerbating the problem is that as the processes move further along, time becomes a constraint. An appraiser will be required to "drop everything" and complete your appraisal. The first appraisal may have been reasonably priced, but each subsequent appraisal's cost will increase.

Triggering Events
Your buy-sell agreement remains dormant until a triggering event occurs. Business owners often carry the false perception of early death to be the primary culprit triggering a buy-sell agreement. Actuarial science tells us that the risk of disability is greater than the risk of premature death.[32] Then again, what defines disability? Every newly married couple evidently believes they will defy the odds of divorce, yet about 40 to 50 percent of married couples in the United States divorce.[33] Disability, death, and divorce are some of the most popular triggering events in buy-sell agreements. Notwithstanding the negligence in defining the appropriate price in a buy-sell agreement, the triggering events themselves are also neglected. Moreover, the statistical probabilities of a triggering event occurring are substantially greater than business owners perceive them to be.

---

[32] http://www.actuarialfoundation.org/consumer/disability_chartbook.pdf.
[33] http://www.apa.org/topics/divorce.

1) Closely-held companies often procure life insurance policies on shareholders' lives to hedge against premature death. Life insurance provides the funds needed to pay the decedent's estate when the triggering event (death) occurs. By now you understand that the three conventional buy-sell pricing mechanisms are flawed when determining the requisite amount of insurance. A lack of funds by inadequately insuring employee-owners can financially impair closely-held companies. Also, who owns the policies? Does the company own the policy or do shareholders take policies out on each other's lives? Does policy ownership impact the valuation? (Hint: it does.)

2) Disability occurs more often than premature death. Perhaps your buy-sell agreement is triggered when an employee-owner becomes disabled. Great, but what does that mean? Anxiety is considered a disability, yet millions of people with anxiety disorders can competently perform their jobs. If "disabled" is a triggering event in your buy-sell agreement, it must be specific. Personal injury attorneys thrive in the definition of "disabled" when ambiguously defined.

3) Turnover is a commonly neglected component in many buy-sell agreements. Then again, because employees never leave for other opportunities, and you (fortunately) have never had to fire an employee, this doesn't pertain to you. All joking aside, termination (voluntary or involuntary) is another event that triggers a buy-sell agreement. How likely is it that no employee-owners in your company will leave for greener pastures? Even worse, what do you do when an employee-owner is trying to sabotage your business and the rogue employee knows that you won't fire him because of the unfavorable (to you) buy-sell agreement? Triggering the agreement and forcing a payment to the employee-owner would compromise the company's financial picture. Knowing this, the employee-owner does nothing to improve the company's value but collects a steady paycheck every other week. Why not, what does he have to lose?

4) Perhaps your company has flourished throughout the years. You, along with five similar-aged owners grew the business beyond your wildest expectations. A second generation is lined up to run the ship, but all six of you are planning to retire in the next two years. How feasible is that? Where will the money come from? More important to you, what price will you receive? Take it a step further. In this day and age, how clearly defined is "retirement" after all? My father-in-law is an intelligent and successful engineer. He "retired" from his company years ago. As I'm writing this book, he's in another city consulting for that same company (and he continues to do so regularly).

Who's to say one of the founders of your firm won't "retire" before the rest of you. Perhaps the owner's motive is to receive both a fair sale price of his stock and future employment compensation. Knowing the company can't afford to pay all of you at once, he makes his "retirement" announcement official. The company, however, can't afford for him to leave right away. As a firm, you need his services for at least two more years or key clients will take their business elsewhere. The retired employee has the leverage because he's "cashed out" and knows you still need his services. If you're like most companies that have encountered this dilemma, you retain the "retired" employee on a contract basis.

(*Disclosure*: The example is intended to demonstrate how retirement today has changed from previous generations and the negative implications that can arise if not explicitly defined in your Agreement. This specific retirement plan is not what my father-in-law did. Nonetheless, my father-in-law has been retained on a consulting basis because of his in-depth knowledge and experience in a specialized area.)

5) Divorce is the biggest landmine in your buy-sell agreement. The statistics are not in your favor, especially when a group of several owners creates a company. Mathematically speaking, the probability of triggering your buy-sell agreement increases with the number of employee-owners. It only takes one divorce to trigger the buy-sell clause. If so, who gets the shares? Divorce courts seek equitable division among parties, and therefore, the spouse would be entitled to a portion of the employee-owner's interest in the company. What happens if the interest is a controlling interest? If the spouse receives the shares and gains control, what will happen to the firm? If your company is an S-corporation and you have 100 shareholders (the maximum number allowed to retain S-corporation status), what would happen if multiple divorces occurred and the courts split shareholder interests to additional parties, violating the S-corporation maximum shareholder threshold?

Of the triggering events discussed, death is the only event hedged by insurance. Most Agreements fail to define "disability," let alone have adequate insurance to protect against it. From a statistical viewpoint, premature death is the least likely event to happen, yet it's the only potential liability most closely-held companies hedge.

Other remedies used to hedge triggering events include sinking funds and notes. Sinking funds are like having a rainy day fund "just in case." Sinking funds are typically used to insure against uninsurable triggering events (non-life threatening events). Planning for the frequency and amount needed to fully subsidize a sinking fund can be problematic. Nonetheless, they are much better than a do-nothing approach. Companies also include notes, or the option to issue a note should a triggering event occur. Notes are debt, and debt has a tendency to accumulate at the worst possible time. Furthermore, many third party debt covenants restrict the issuance of notes and could potentially negate the issuance of a note when needed the most.

This section (and chapter) is meant to help you find the landmines in your buy-sell agreement. I hope your mind is now thinking about the havoc a triggering event would cause to your firm. Don't be like most business owners and put this aside. We've all heard the "it won't happen to me" response. That's always true – until it does. And according to statistical probabilities, the odds are not in your favor.

Conclusion

The purpose of this chapter is to show you the landmines that exist in your company's Agreement. The most valuable asset of nearly every business owner is the business itself. Why, then, is value (price) an afterthought – a neglected and overlooked piece to the very documents that govern the business? Using any of these three price mechanisms will guarantee problems. The extent of problems depends on the case at hand – but problems will arise. In any event, there will be a loser and a winner in the transaction, representing the very definition of a zero-sum game. Don't play it.

I have witnessed tragedy occur time and time again because of poorly written buy-sell agreements. Agreements, including buy-sell agreements within the governing documents, are drafted by attorneys. Valuation is not an attorney's forte. Seek guidance from a valuation professional when drafting your Agreement with a lawyer (or when drafting a stand-alone buy-sell agreement). The valuation professional should work with the attorney so that the buy-sell agreement makes economic sense. Every little facet should be specific, leaving no room for subjectivity. The next chapter gives you the resources to prevent these commonplace tragedies from dismantling you, your company, your fellow shareholders and, ultimately, your family.

Families are torn apart (many closely-held companies are family companies). Shareholders fight with each other. Businesses collapse because of financial and personal strife. The damage stretches beyond the owners and their families. Employees are also casualties of poorly written buy-sell agreements when economic implosion decimates the company (and they're left without a job). Their families, children, and spouses are all negatively impacted because of a poorly written buy-sell agreement.

Let me rephrase that point again: companies are forced to close their doors, families split apart, and people lose their jobs all because of a poorly written clause in an Agreement. Speaking from the depths of my soul, please do not let this happen to you.

All of It Is Preventable

Not only is it preventable, but the means to prevent it will increase your firm's value, provide all shareholders an awareness of company value, help benchmark performance, allow for tax-efficient succession planning, and provide economic equality to all parties when a triggering event occurs (to name a few of the benefits). The cost for this insurance pales in comparison to the value it creates. The Business Owner's Solution will give you a step by step plan to make all of this a reality.

It's time to find and dismantle the landmines in your buy-sell agreement. Let's do this.

Chapter Sixteen

The Business Owner's Solution

Introduction

You're probably a bit uneasy after reading that last chapter. You learned that your buy-sell agreement has some serious problems, or as I refer to them, landmines. As time marches on, somebody is bound to step on one, causing your buy-sell agreement to be triggered and everything to explode.

What if I told you that it is all preventable? Also, what if I said the method to prevent the landmines will also increase the value of your company?

There is a way to defuse the landmines in your buy-sell agreement, increase your firm's value and create a viable succession plan to the next generation, or maximize its value for sale. This chapter guides you, step by step, to help ensure that your company will be safe from unforeseen devastation.

What You Lack but Desperately Need

I tend to think of a buy-sell agreement as an insurance product. After finishing graduate school – and before entering the closely-held business valuation profession – I worked a two-year stint as an executive liability underwriter. Before accepting the job, I had little idea what the position specifically entailed. I was hired based on my financial analysis skills and told that I would "learn the rest later." Sure enough, I did – and if we're connecting the dots backward, the dots connect perfectly. The company I worked for was an insurance company, and the insurance that I underwrote was called directors and officers liability (D&O) insurance. As a business owner, you might be familiar with it, especially if your company has outside directors. D&O insurance indemnifies a company's officers and directors for losses stemming from the actions of its directors and officers. It gets a bit more complicated than a one sentence definition, but in general, that's the premise behind D&O insurance. My job was to underwrite (perform financial analysis on) publicly traded companies within the financial sector. I met with Fortune 500 CFOs and CEOs to obtain a better understanding of their business (sound familiar to what I do now?). Shareholder lawsuits were the primary "trigger" for a D&O policy to become active (much like a trigger event causes a buy-sell agreement to become active). The insurance we sold protected the company's officers and directors from other shareholders.

A well-written buy-sell agreement should function in a similar fashion. While no direct insurance product provides financial resources in the event a triggering event occurs (except for death and injury), a well-written buy-sell agreement is the business owner's tool to protect the company from financial ruin. It provides liquidity to those when needed in an orderly fashion. It protects the company's shares from falling into unwanted hands. A well-written buy-sell agreement is the core insurance required to retain an organization's constitution.

Note that I said a "well-written" buy-sell agreement and not just a buy-sell agreement. If not written correctly, the agreement is virtually worthless (and can be worse than having no agreement at all). A well-written buy-sell agreement protects your firm from both insiders and outsiders. In sum, a well-written buy-sell agreement is the most important insurance that your company must have but likely doesn't.

Because I cannot provide legal advice, you should seek counsel from an attorney for guidance. Also, consult with a tax accountant because the way you structure your buy-sell agreement (life insurance, for example) can have valuation impacts. If the subject were plain vanilla, I would write more about it. Due to the "no size fits all" attributes of buy-sell agreements, customized advice is required. No matter what you do, make sure the buy-sell agreement makes economic sense. To ensure this happens, consult with qualified business appraisers and have them review the buy-sell language. Buy-sell agreements are infrequently changed. Paying a highly skilled business appraiser (I recommend two) to assess the efficacy of the buy-sell language within your Agreement (governing document) – or stand-alone buy-sell agreement – is relatively inexpensive in price and carries a significant return on investment.

The Insurance You Must Have

You've learned about the three conventional buy-sell agreement pricing mechanisms and the flaws in each. Triggering events, and the potential disaster resulting from each were discussed in the previous chapter. Hopefully, you spent some time thinking about the consequences that could harm your company under the reign of your current buy-sell agreement. If it had been some time since you last reviewed your buy-sell agreement (which is common with most closely-held business owners), you probably uncovered some of the landmines that we examined in Chapter 15. If you haven't yet reviewed it, find it and look for the landmines. They're in there – I guarantee it.

To protect your company (shareholders, your employees, you, your family) from the existing landmines, you must take action. In this chapter, I will show you a way that not only protects your company and others from these landmines but eliminates the landmines and increases your firm's value.

Insurance isn't free – you pay a premium for the coverage. Under my recommended approach you will also pay an insurance premium. Unlike traditional insurance, however, the premium you pay using my approach increases your firm's value. When was the last time you bought insurance that increased your net worth?

The approach I recommend solves the problems found in the other price mechanisms. In summary, you, along with your co-owners, select a single appraiser to value your company. Appraisals will be performed annually by the chosen appraiser. Both the appraiser and your company will come to an agreement that this relationship is intended to be ongoing and long-term. This predetermined relationship must be communicated during the interview phase. As you will soon learn, stability and transparency are important in providing a solution that disarms the landmines in your company's buy-sell agreement.

The Business Owner's Solution

Summary

Adopting my approach, The Business Owner's Solution (herein also referred to as the "BOS"), you will meet with an attorney who will draft a buy-sell agreement using the steps that will soon be outlined in The Business Owner's Solution. Your attorney will customize the requisite language needed to fit your needs. Because I'm not an attorney and cannot provide legal counsel, I recommend enlisting an experienced attorney well versed in drafting buy-sell agreements. You may want the buy-sell agreement to be a stand-alone agreement (my recommendation), or you may include it in your Partnership or Operating Agreement (governing documents). The bottom line is to include the granular points noted in this chapter. Whichever method you and your attorney wish to accomplish that – either within your Agreement or as a stand-alone document – is up to you and your attorney. Ask your lawyer to read this chapter for greater clarity and to ensure that you're both on the same page. Having your buy-sell agreement correctly drafted is imperative. Don't pinch pennies for a lower quality attorney. Quality is non-negotiable.

The Business Owner's Solution prescribes using a single appraiser and having annual appraisals performed. Most of the work required by you will be done upfront to find the most qualified appraiser who meets your specific needs. As you're about to learn, the benefits increase over time. Your firm's value will become more accurately estimated. Performance benchmarks will be used to improve and increase your company's value. Observable management accountability standards will be implemented. Greater transparency will be provided to all stakeholders. Succession planning will be facilitated (if desired). Your company will always be operating at its optimal value.

And in many cases, the cost of this annual "premium" will decrease over time.

You might be thinking that this sounds too good to be true. Keep reading and you will learn how this annual insurance premium – by proxy of a business valuation – may be the greatest return on investment you will ever experience.

The Screening Phase

Step 1:
Conduct a thorough screening process of qualified business appraisers. The end goal is to select a single appraiser, but for now, you need to find four or five qualified business appraisers. Using this book as a tool, you will know the particular type of appraiser to choose. Have each of your co-owners read this book (or at minimum this section). Once finished, determine the qualifications required to perform an appraisal of your business. Don't settle – keep the standards high. Your personal wealth (via the company) is at stake here.

To find a Qualified Business Appraiser that meets the requirements needed to implement The Business Owner's Solution, adhere to the following guidelines:

1) **Minimum education requirements**
   a. Sound knowledge of economic and finance theory is a must. Depending on your location, you might have problems finding a local business appraiser holding the requisite credentials to fulfill this need. Don't limit yourself to a local area if you can find a higher quality appraiser elsewhere. Remember, this is your firm's value. Getting this right the first time is paramount. Accordingly, here are the minimum qualifications I recommend.
      i. Business valuation credential from one of the four credentialing organizations. My personal recommendation would be to screen for ASA or ABV credential holders. The organizations that confer these designations are globally known and respected.
      ii. An individual holding the CFA® charter or a Ph.D. graduate with an emphasis in finance or economics. You are seeking somebody who has demonstrated an advanced knowledge of finance and economics through rigorous testing. Appraisers who have passed all three levels of the CFA® Program and earned the charter, or appraisers who have successfully defended a doctoral thesis in a relevant field helps ensure your appraiser understands the fundamentals of valuation.

1. Unfortunately, finding individuals holding the CFA® charter or a relevant Ph.D. combined with a business valuation credential (the first criterion) is often challenging. If you find yourself in this position, the secondary filter would be to search for a CPA who specializes in business valuation, or a graduate of a respected graduate school (MBA or Masters in Finance from a prestigious school). Regardless of whether a CPA or a graduate school candidate is chosen, the candidate must have a credential from one of the four business valuation organizations. If a CPA is selected, make sure the CPA's role is devoted solely to valuation work and that the CPA doesn't get pulled away every spring to "help out the tax department." A word of caution when selecting a CPA – be sure the individual has the requisite finance knowledge to perform your appraisal at a high level, otherwise the benefits that The Business Owner's Solution delivers will not be realized in full (if at all). I've completed both the CFA® and CPA programs. The difficulty and body of knowledge between the two are immensely disparate. Nonetheless, there are CPAs who, through decades of experience and relentless self-education, have obtained sufficient finance knowledge to perform your business valuation adequately. I also have an MBA and know the general nature of the degree, grade inflation and pressure on administrators to rank high with publications such as U.S. News and World Report. In summary, if you need to filter beyond an individual holding the CFA® charter or a Ph.D., tread lightly and be diligent.

2) **Minimum relevant work experience**
   a. This one is trickier than it appears. CPAs who dabble in valuation work on the side can claim to have decades of experience, yet the CPA who has devoted his entire career (even if it's five years) is likely to be infinitely more qualified. Measuring expertise by quantity of years is not always the best indicator of quality experience. Relevant work experience should take precedence. Make sure the appraiser has sufficient experience performing appraisals and that the appraiser does nothing but valuation work. You will get a feel for the appraiser's experience level when you interview him.

3) **Field of expertise – no generalists!**
   a. If your company sells shoes, don't hire a business appraiser who values auto manufacturers. The valuation industry is transcending into a field of specialists. You may have to broaden your search (geographically) to find somebody specializing in your industry. Don't limit yourself because of convenience. Set that bar high!

4) **Consider the appraiser's age**
   a. The solution I'm providing requires a long-term commitment from the appraiser. Many closely-held business owners expect their companies to exist for a long time – and many transfer the business to their children. The appraiser you choose needs to be alive for an extended period. An appraiser in his late 50s or 60s has fewer service years remaining than one in his 30s or 40s. Age shouldn't be the defining factor, but it is something you should consider given your long-term objectives. You're doing the hard work now to reap rewards over the next couple of decades (or longer). Hiring an appraiser who is five or ten years from retirement will require you to revisit this entire process again and will cost you more in time and money down the road. I'm hesitant to recommend filtering an appraiser on age, but my recommended approach requires a long-term relationship. Not mentioning the consideration would be an injustice to you.

Step 1.9:
Interview the appraisers that meet the minimum qualifications. Don't spend an elaborate amount of time and resources here. Focus on getting to know the appraiser's personality, experience, etc. The other owners should do the same with their candidates. Phone interviews or Skype/Webcam will work if needed. This step is Step 1.9 and not Step 2 because I don't want you to invest a significant sum of time here. 90 percent of your time should be spent on research and 10 percent on interviews. Finding candidates who meet the minimum requirements in Step 1 will probably eliminate nearly everybody because of scarcity, so spend time ensuring all the requirements in Step 1 are met. Once your group has been filtered, you will then need to interview each of them. What I'm about to recommend requires a life-long commitment. Invest the time now and reap the benefits for decades. Any business appraiser refusing an interview should be immediately crossed off the list for consideration. You demand the best. At this stage give the appraiser an overview of your intentions and communicate that this will be a long-term relationship. Be forthright with what you are looking for so the appraiser can also decide if the relationship would be agreeable from his perspective.

Step 2:
At this point, you and your fellow business owners have interviewed several appraisers using the minimum qualifications outlined in Step 1. After conducting the interviews from Step 1.9, you will each have four or five appraisers that meet your requirements. In Step 2, each owner narrows the number of qualified appraisers down to three. If your business consists of yourself and two other owners, for example, the total number of appraisers selected would be nine. At this point, the owners meet and compare the appraisers selected. Discuss the advantages and disadvantages of each candidate. Spend an ample amount of time discussing, critiquing and analyzing all of the candidates selected.

During this meeting, you will discover that a natural consensus builds around two or three appraisers. If it happens to be more, that's okay. The point here is to vet the merits of each appraiser and receive feedback from the other owners.

Once the field is narrowed (assume you have narrowed the pool to three candidates), arrange for another interview with each of the remaining candidates. This time, all of the owners should be involved in the meetings. Let the appraiser know that the other owners will be in the meeting and that they will have questions. If possible, prepare and deliver some questions to the appraiser in advance so that he can provide you an informed answer. Do not submit all of the questions, however, because you need to observe how the appraiser responds to unfamiliar questions. If the appraiser claims to specialize in your industry, ask him on-the-spot questions that test his knowledge of your industry. This exercise isn't meant to be rude (and don't be). You are choosing a long-term business partner that you can rely on during good times and bad. If the appraiser lacks character, integrity, honesty and other important traits – you will find out pretty quickly when the appraiser is under duress.

Step 3:
Come to an agreement with your fellow owners on a single appraiser. When selecting the appraiser, rank them numerically from the consensus favorite to least favorite. If you and your co-owners have done a sound job vetting appraisers, this will be a difficult process. Ranking the finalists gives you piece of mind for a "just in case" event. Think about the time and effort you've invested up to this point in finding the perfect appraiser. Now imagine if that person dies prematurely. Don't let the time and effort go to waste. Keep the number two (and possibly third) appraiser's contact information handy "just in case."

Implementation

During the interview phase, you will have informed the appraiser of the intended relationship. Your buy-sell agreement should reflect the desire that your company's value will be determined by the value estimate provided by this appraiser. Since the relationship will be long-term, your company's pricing will become transparent, and planning (estate, retirement, etc.) will be simplified. I recommend having the attorney who is drafting your buy-sell agreement include a clause that provides a backup appraiser "just in case." Yes, this is where the number two person comes into play. In the unlikely event your appraiser is no longer available, or a supermajority number of shareholders deem the appraiser to be unqualified, you will want the second-ranked appraiser to be the de-facto person deciding your company's value. This clause is intended solely to provide insurance should your chosen appraiser pass away (or retire, if you've chosen a "senior" appraiser). It's also meant to give the majority of shareholders the option to say "we hired a bad apple" and to remedy the problem in a cost-effective manner. Since you've already invested the time screening and ranking appraisers, you won't have to spend additional time in selecting another appraiser.

If you use The Business Owner's Solution screening process, the probability of hiring a poor appraiser is highly unlikely. Nonetheless, it provides an "out" should it be needed. I also recommend that a supermajority vote be required to remove the appraiser, although the percentage of voting shares required will depend on each firm's ownership structure. The company-appraiser relationship should be broken only by reasonable means and not over petty arguments. Requiring a supermajority vote protects this relationship and allows for the company's owners "as a whole" to change direction – and only for good reasons.

Drawbacks to This Approach

A typical response I hear from business owners is "this is going to be expensive." Business valuations aren't cheap (unless you hire a cheap appraiser – which becomes expensive later). The annual business valuation is another expense that must be added to an already razor-thin budget. At first glance, this does appear cost prohibitive. I empathize with that concern. The fallacy with the cost-focused approach (focusing on explicit costs and ignoring opportunity costs) lies in the misunderstanding of the implicit costs that are significantly greater than the price of a business appraisal.

In Chapter 15, you learned about the landmines that exist in your buy-sell agreement. You also read some examples illustrating what happens when buy-sell agreements contain the traditional pricing mechanisms. Aside from curing the problems in Chapter 15, the annual business appraisal cost factor can be mitigated in many ways.

- Create a payment plan. If your company's business is seasonal, ask the appraiser to consider receiving fee payments (or the bulk of the fee) when your business is cash-rich. Monthly or quarterly payment plans may also be arranged with the appraiser.
- The cost will decline over time. As the appraiser becomes more accustomed and knowledgeable with your company, less time is required to perform the appraisal. I expect to charge less over time as the years go on, and I become better acquainted with the company. From a business appraiser's view (mine, in this case), having a good relationship – a good client – has an implied premium. The first few years are priced at standard rates, but after a few years of becoming acquainted with the firm and how it operates, I typically reduce the annual price without being asked to do so. If it's a client I enjoy working with, after gaining a full understanding of the company, I

want to make sure we maintain the relationship. Having a customer call me and say that I mistyped the price when sending over an engagement letter — and then saying that I didn't (it's lower than the previous year) — is a great feeling. Yes, I'm receiving less money for the project, but I'm rewarding the company for choosing me to be its trusted valuation expert. The relationship goes both ways.

- Envision the business valuation for what it is: insurance. Not only is it a form of insurance (theoretically), but it improves the value of your company and helps eliminate the potential landmines from your buy-sell agreement that will eventually trigger and explode. Not having it is costlier than having it. From a value perspective, you may never receive a better return on investment than your annual business appraisal (especially when a triggering event occurs).

If cost remains a concern despite learning about the catastrophic repercussions of using the price mechanisms in Chapter 15 (what is likely in your current buy-sell agreement), let's examine the benefits that you, your company, fellow shareholders, employees, your family, and employees' families will receive by implementing The Business Owner's Solution.

Thrive with The Business Owner's Solution

The advantages of implementing the BOS are almost limitless. You are about to read the typical benefits of this approach. Because I'm bound to confidentiality of specific details, I can assure you that in almost every buy-sell triggering event where one of the three approaches in Chapter 15 was used, my answer is "it could have been avoided using my approach," which is The Business Owner's Solution. Buy-sell agreement triggering event disagreements or problems typically gravitate towards the value derivation outlined in the buy-sell agreement. When the price is the variable of contention, I cannot think of one instance throughout my career where the BOS approach would not have solved (or at a minimum, significantly reduced) the problem.

- The appraiser gains a comprehensive understanding of your company. As an appraiser, perhaps the most challenging and time-consuming issues are obtaining a fundamental understanding of the enterprise and the company's key value drivers. Gaining an understanding applies primarily to new engagements of closely-held companies (as opposed to investment partnership valuations). The valuation cost for "one-off" appraisals will include the additional time required by the appraiser to gain an understanding of your firm. Remember, you know your company better than anybody. Your business appraiser, even as a specialist in your industry, doesn't know that "Roger is a key-man" to your firm's success and without him you would be in trouble. Despite interviews with management and an on-site interview of your company's premises, the appraiser can't see what kind of office politics exist or know what the intangible value drivers are. This is one of the primary drawbacks of choosing an appraiser when only a triggering event occurs. Using the BOS, the appraiser will become accustomed to how your firm operates. Over time, the appraiser will learn the nuances that make your company unique – the parts that you and your firm know but can't describe or quantitatively display. The intangible pieces that should be incorporated into your discount rate, but aren't because they can't be supported without a clear understanding. By learning how your company operates and what the key value drivers are, the appraiser's value estimate will improve as critical variables (tangible and intangible) are accounted for in your company's valuation. More than half of the business owners I meet with say their business is "different" and therefore will be "hard to value" because there are either few other companies like them or none at all. The BOS solves this dilemma.

- You will learn how the appraiser values your company. Business valuation, as you've read throughout this book, is a niche field. Perhaps the company you own operates in a niche market. Each year the appraiser will provide you a business valuation of your company. You get a third party's perspective on what impacts your firm's value. Not just a third party, but because you followed my steps in selecting an appraiser, you're getting an incredibly knowledgeable and experienced valuation professional's perspective. Early in the relationship, you might think the appraiser missed something when valuing your company. Perhaps you believe an element of value exists that can't be quantified. Knowing how the appraiser values your business, you will be better suited to provide the appraiser feedback about the value drivers you believe to be important. Remember, you know your business better than anybody. Using the BOS, the knowledge gap between owner and appraiser narrows, resulting in greater consistency, a more rigorous appraisal report, and a more accurate value estimate.

- Company pricing becomes transparent to all parties. Because an annual appraisal is performed, all shareholders know what the price of the company is on a yearly basis. The benefits to price transparency are both profound and numerous. Accordingly, we'll cover them later in this chapter. Price transparency is the critical flaw of the process method discussed in Chapter 15 (in addition to multiple appraiser fees, with appraisers all under time constraints to value a company they're unfamiliar with).

- I recommend using fair market value as the standard of value for your buy-sell agreement. Using the fair market value standard clarifies any confusion as to how the business should be valued. Fair market value is also the standard of value prescribed by the IRS when making gifts. Because succession planning is an important piece to most closely-held business owners, you will be allowed to use the valuation for gifting purposes. However – and this is important – the valuation used for your firm (for the buy-sell agreement) should not be the valuation sent to the IRS when supporting a gift. A separate valuation that applies specifically to the interest being gifted must be used. Fortunately for you (if using the BOS), the appraiser is already familiar with your firm from performing the company's annual valuation. The additional time required to appraise a minority interest in your company will be minimal. As a result, the cost will also be small – and much lower than using an outside appraiser unfamiliar with your entity performing a "one-off" appraisal. If succession planning is essential to carry on your firm's legacy, no better method exists than the one I'm recommending. I have yet to see a more accurate and cost-effective way when performed collectively.

- The appraiser is not influenced by individual shareholders or other parties. If your buy-sell agreement requires an appraisal upon the occurrence of a triggering event (and only then), how do you know the appraiser selected will be qualified to perform a competent appraisal? Not only is the appraiser unfamiliar with your company (which will increase the cost of the valuation and decrease the value estimate's reliability), but the method for selecting an appraiser is often absent in the buy-sell agreement. When a buy-sell agreement is triggered, the reason causing a triggering event is typically not pleasant. Death, divorce, disability – all are tragic in some fashion or another. A triggering event requires the price to be calculated. If the price is fixed or based on a formula, the problems will be paramount but fall outside of an appraiser's judgment (because an appraiser will not be used). If a process mechanism is the defined method in the buy-sell agreement, an appraiser will be employed to perform the appraisal. Assume, for example, one of the company's shareholders passes away, triggering the buy-sell agreement. The shareholders required to purchase shares from the decedent will want to pay the least amount possible for the decedent's interest to the detriment of the decedent's beneficiaries (estate). Because no method other than "select an appraiser" is outlined in the buy-sell agreement, odds are the purchasing shareholders will search for an appraiser who can be influenced to provide them a favorable value estimate. The methods used to influence (or control) the appraiser take many forms, but include providing biased information that favors a value estimate, not providing the "whole picture" to the appraiser, selecting a close friend of one of the shareholders to perform the valuation, etc. Influence is used in many ways to benefit the remaining shareholders and is specific to the situation. The BOS eliminates this problem because the appraiser already knows your company, the politics within your firm, shareholder dynamics, value drivers and other company-specific factors. Time won't be an issue because the appraiser already knows what to expect and isn't required to gain an understanding of the company (he already has it). Shareholders can review the appraiser's previous appraisals of the firm to ensure consistency with how the valuation is performed. The BOS helps eliminate influence and shareholder conflict while the other methods promote or exacerbate these problems.

- The cost is minimal - and in many cases decreases over time. We've touched this already, but it deserves additional attention. The price of a valuation is minuscule compared to the opportunity costs (landmines) of not having one. As the appraiser becomes more familiar with your company, the appraisal price will likely come down. I mentioned earlier that I usually lower my price after a few years once I'm familiar with the company and my time requirement decreases. The time required decreases because the appraiser isn't required to gain an understanding of your business, a process that consumes a considerable amount of time. Instead, the appraiser will check to see what changes have been made that would impact his current understanding of your firm (much less time consuming). If your appraiser doesn't lower the price after three or four years, you should ask for a price decrease. You are likely to receive one, too. Note, however; the price probably won't be lowered much (if at all) after that. To produce a quality appraisal, the appraiser will still need to invest a considerable amount of time on your engagement. Haggling the price each year is not recommended and could spur a toxic environment that benefits nobody. I suggest asking for a price decrease after three or four years and then leaving the pricing alone. Also, if you leverage the appraiser for ancillary services, and the appraiser doesn't charge extra for them, heed caution at asking for a price reduction. The appraiser is likely building in these services into the annual appraisal fee. Use your best judgment.

- The accuracy and efficiency of life insurance planning are increased as your company's value is known. Many companies have life insurance policies to insure against an insurable triggering event (death in this case). Unless a current price is known, the amount of insurance required to cover the repurchase obligation in the event of death is unknown. No other pricing mechanism provides the assurance of matching liability coverage with the economic responsibility that would be due. The BOS helps ensure that the right amount of life insurance coverage is secured. A lack of life insurance funding to pay for the buy-sell liability can and does negatively impact closely-held companies. Many companies lack the funds to cover the liability and are required to borrow funds to satisfy the amount due. This additional leverage increases the financial risk of the firm, which in turn increases its cost of capital and lowers its value. Ramifications that nobody saw before usually trickle beyond the already tragic event (death of a shareholder). Using the BOS, the company will continue to operate without issue and will adequately fund the decedent's estate without negatively impacting the business and its value. Instead of focusing on "how are we going to pay for this," the attention is focused where it should be – grieving the loss of a friend or family member.

- Hedging for non-insurable triggering events is improved. Many trigger events are non-insurable. Knowing the value of the company beforehand allows for proper planning. Such knowledge prevents the company from being held hostage by rogue employee-owners who have leverage because of a poorly worded buy-sell agreement that places the company in a situation where it can't "buy-out" the rogue employee without facing financial malaise. Whether it is a note, sinking fund or other means of financing, management can adequately plan for unforeseen events that would otherwise paralyze a company's financial position and destroy employee morale. Having an accurate price helps reduce rogue employee lawsuits and facilitates management's ability to let go of poor employee-owners without harming the company's financial stability. The company will be ready to handle and prosper through the unexpected and unwanted.

- The standard of value is known. Many buy-sell agreement price mechanisms ignore the standard of value, leaving it up to the appraiser's judgment. As you know from reading this book, the differences between investment value and fair market value are significant. If left blank, however, the appraiser is free to use whichever standard of value he believes to be applicable. Additionally, this is where the politics and leverage of the remaining shareholders can rear its ugly head. To obtain the most economically sound value or price, owners on the buy-side of the transaction can wield their influence to help lower the value estimate. I recommend using fair market value for reasons already stated. Either way, the standard of value – key to any valuation – is known to all parties and eliminates confusion and the opportunity for others to alter the value. The BOS solves these potential problems from the start.

- The valuation process is known to all parties. In Sections Two through Four of this book you learned about how the business valuation process works. You know that information transparency is critical to the appraiser when calculating an accurate value estimate. If you didn't read this book, however, you may have had a much different reaction when the appraiser asked for sensitive financial information. Business owners, having their business appraised for the first time almost always question why I need a particular document or documents. Some are appalled that I would request such information, but later understand why the request was made. Closely-held private businesses are just that – private. I have yet to meet a business owner who liberally gives out copies of annual financial performance to strangers. Privacy is an appealing feature that owners of closely-held private companies cherish and protect. Yet, the business valuation process requires owners to let go of that very information. Using the BOS, you will learn why the appraiser needs certain documents and will minimize the number of people who see it. After a few appraisals, you will be able to put together a packet of information, knowing what specifically the appraiser is going to want. In return, the appraiser saves time trying to obtain important documents. Requiring less time from the appraiser gives you another reason to request a fee decrease after four or so appraisals have been performed. Also, you will have asked for a Non-Disclosure Agreement (NDA) to be executed by the appraiser, legally binding the appraiser not to release any information (remember Chapter 4?). I recommend you contact an attorney to draft a custom NDA. A sample NDA is available on the website **www.valuationforowners.com**.

- The valuation time frame is reduced because the appraiser knows your company. We've touched on many of the benefits of using a single appraiser to perform annual appraisals of your company. Of these benefits, several involve knowing your business. The familiar phrase "time is money" rings entirely true in business valuation. If your buy-sell agreement has a process method, an appraiser is selected following a triggering event. The effort needed to gain an understanding of your firm requires considerable time, and increases the cost of your appraisal. Most buy-sell agreements with process mechanisms allow for an additional process to proceed if the shareholders dispute on the value estimate from the first appraiser.

These buy-sell agreements often stipulate a maximum amount of time that the second round of appraisers have to complete their respective valuations. Because of the time constraint imposed, a premium will be charged to you by the business appraisers. Using the BOS, if a triggering event occurs and your buy-sell agreement requires a valuation as of the triggering date, the appraiser already has an understanding of your firm. Also, the appraiser also has nearly everything needed to perform the appraisal. In these circumstances where the effective date (triggering event date) differs from the annual appraisal date, and the buy-sell agreement requires (or provides the option) to have an appraisal performed as of the triggering event date, the time needed to carry out the valuation is minimal. Think about it like this: the appraiser performed a valuation for your company with an effective date of December 31st. Three months have passed, and a triggering event occurs. Your buy-sell agreement allows the shareholder to request an appraisal as of the effective date (say April 3rd). The appraiser has your previous financial data already in his models. Forecasts likely haven't changed much since the last appraisal, and the cost of capital adjustments (if any) will probably be minimal. The point is that the appraisal won't be time-consuming, and the price will be considerably lower.

Business owners sometimes ask if having an appraisal performed as of the triggering event should be included as an option. The answer, if you haven't guessed already is, "it depends." How comfortable are you and your fellow shareholders using an annual appraisal as the buy-sell price when a triggering event occurs in-between appraisals? My suggestion is to come to a consensus one way or another and agree on it. Leaving an Agreement open-ended is an invitation for litigators. You don't want that (trust me on this!). For most closely-held companies, the change in value between years will be minimal, or smoothed. Even if the company had a gangbuster year in sales, all facts would be considered when valuing the company. If sales are expected to continue to skyrocket infinitely, the appraisal will naturally reflect that change in direction. In this case, you would probably want to provide, or give shareholders the option of having an appraisal performed as of a triggering event. If a shareholder dies and has a taxable estate, an appraisal will be needed as of the effective date or an alternative date (which is six months after the date of death). Collectively as owners, and with your attorney, come to a consensus with how you desire to move forward. Remember that by implementing the BOS, the additional comfort of including such an option is the lowest cost (appraisal cost, opportunity cost or both) compared to the other buy-sell price mechanisms.

- The closely-held company is always prepared for the unexpected. Triggering events are inherently unpredictable, and they often occur when least expected. Sometimes they happen at the worst time possible. Perhaps your company is seasonal, and a triggering event occurs during the busy season. Or maybe one of your key employee-owners unexpectedly announces he's leaving the company. Any number of reasons could cause your buy-sell agreement to be triggered. When triggered, time will be spent determining the price of your company. Because many business owners lock their Agreement away after it's drafted (and with it the buy-sell agreement), finding where the Agreement is physically located may take a considerable amount of time. Scenarios like these are fairly common, especially with companies that hire attorneys on a "one-off" basis instead of maintaining a relationship. After the lowest-priced attorney uses his boilerplate language to create the company's Agreement, one of the owners files it away. It becomes an afterthought because running the business becomes a priority. Years later when the triggering event occurs, the owners have to find where the Agreement is located. Finding the Agreement pulls the owners away from running the business and enhancing its value. Once found, the buy-sell pricing mechanism is reviewed, and mayhem ensues. Here's where disputes over pricing arise because the owners know that the price agreed upon twenty years ago is nowhere close to that in the buy-sell agreement. Bound to a legal contract, there is little room for remorse. If the BOS is implemented, company owners would not only know where their Agreement is, but they wouldn't have to worry about preparing information for an appraiser and other time-consuming tasks (let alone the shock of having a value that makes no economic sense). The BOS minimizes time spent away from value-enhancing activities and significantly reduces the opportunity costs to the firm and its owners.

- Managers gain insight into factors that increase valuation, and as a result, the company's value will increase. Earlier in this chapter, I told you that the "premium," or annual appraisal's cost, is dissimilar to traditional insurance in a meaningful way. Unlike other insurance products, the valuation fee not only protects (insures) your firm from significant opportunity costs, but it also gives you tools to increase your company's value. Protecting your firm and increasing its value are additional reasons as to why you must find a business appraiser who is exceptionally well versed in finance and economics. To maximize the economic utility of your appraisal dollar, make sure the appraiser you select has a proven education in finance and economics.

The Business Owner's Solution recommends using the CFA® charter or Ph.D. with a related emphasis as a "must-have" qualifier when selecting your appraiser. These individuals are trained through their respective programs and curriculums to thoroughly understand the fundamental sciences that valuation is built upon. Moreover, these people have been trained to understand the key components that increase a firm's value. When reading your first appraisal report, have the appraiser walk through areas within the report that impacted value. If not obvious, ask the appraiser how the value determination was decided. Ask how the firm's value could be increased. A quality appraiser will be more than happy to explain these to you. On the other hand, an appraiser lacking such knowledge will try to avoid these questions or give you wrong answers. Nobody likes to be asked questions they can't answer, especially when the questions pertain to the field they are supposed to be "experts" in. Assuming you have implemented the BOS and chosen a quality appraiser, over time, you will likely uncover gems in your own backyard. In other words, you will learn about value drivers within your company that you otherwise were unaware of. Or perhaps you were aware of them but didn't understand the magnitude the value drivers had in determining your business's value. Using the BOS, you have an outside party, well educated in valuation, finance, and economics, providing not just a more accurate value estimate – but also providing insight into your company that you didn't know existed. The appraiser will also be able to keep you up to speed with changes in value drivers and offer suggestions on how to increase your company's value.

- Firms can benchmark performance based on valuation metrics that drive economic value. Once the key drivers are known and better understood, the company can begin benchmarking performance. Say, for example, that your firm's value is dinged because of the negative impact poor working capital management had on your company's performance relative to industry peers. By increasing your company's working capital management, more favorable contract agreements with suppliers can be procured. Doing so gets you better terms and improves your bottom line (this is one of many examples). Qualitative features may also negatively impact your firm's cost of capital. A lack of succession planning or management depth is standard with closely-held companies that fail to plan. Consequently, the company's cost of capital is increased as unsystematic risk, or firm-specific risk, is greater. Increasing the discount rate (cost of capital) decreases the company's value. Using the BOS, you will know both the quantitative and qualitative factors that impact value. With that knowledge, your company can implement measures to improve the key value drivers and reduce the negative factors that are depressing your company's value potential. As a result, your business's value will increase. Additionally, by having benchmarks you can measure the rate of change and hold managers accountable for executing change. Owners gain a clear understanding of value factors. Benchmarking these factors transparently demonstrates the tangible progress that has been made to enhance the firm's value. Accountability for business development is no longer a question – it's on paper and can be measured.

- The firm's value is always maximized. Using the BOS, key value drivers are known. Benchmark values are created, along with plans to improve upon baseline values. Managers are given measurable goals and are held accountable for reaching those goals. The objective is to create efficiency within your firm akin to that of a publicly traded company. Publicly traded company financial information is disclosed to analysts and investors to read, model and make buy-sell decisions. Each firm has a cost of capital, determined by markets and the company's specific, or unsystematic risk. Companies that execute on the primary value drivers realize greater share prices. Businesses that don't are punished with lower stock prices and higher costs of capital.

Closely-held companies not listed on an exchange aren't given the luxury of price measurement afforded to publicly traded companies. By deciphering, benchmarking and improving key value drivers, your firm will be rewarded with an increased share value. Having an appraiser well educated in valuation – which requires a deep understanding of securities markets – is the best way to help guarantee your firm clearly and correctly identifies observable key value drivers (as observed in publicly traded companies). As those value drivers change, you will be kept abreast of the significance each has on value through your annual business valuation. Annual planning and benchmarking are improved. Instead of falling behind (like most closely-held companies), you will stay ahead of your competition. Instead of guessing which actions you "think" will be best for your business, you will know what value decisions investors have rewarded and those that investors have punished.

- The Business Owner's Solution results in increased sales proceeds upon the sale of a company. I've performed consulting and valuation work for companies in search of a buyer. When I'm approached by company shareholders looking to sell their business, the conversation usually begins with the owners stating their desire to sell their firm in a few years (although the sooner, the better). Shortly after stating their intent to sell, the conversation's direction usually turns to short-term or intermediate actions that the owners believe they can implement to increase their firm's value (and sell for a high price). I call this window dressing, and most buyers will see right through it and move on to the next purchase opportunity (or pay a much lower price than the owners expected to receive). Even if you aren't looking to sell your company now, chances are someday you will. Perhaps you want to keep the business within the family. If that's the case, what happens when your child doesn't want to run the company (a very common situation)? Another scenario is when a company is approached to sell their firm at a time they don't want to, but for some reason (divorce, financial struggles, etc.) they have no other option and receive a lower than market rate price. Whatever the situation is, as a business owner you should always be operating "as if" you are planning to sell today. If you want top dollar, the buyer must be convinced your company is worth it. Two distinct benefits are worth examining here.

First, by operating as if your firm is selling today you're always working to increase its value. Operating "as if" has an exponential impact over time and is similar to the snowball effect. Owners seeking to sell their company work exceptionally hard to maximize their firm's value drivers. However, many decide to implement the measures recommended under the BOS (identification of value drivers, benchmarking, adjusting measures when needed to increase firm value) just before selling the company. Imagine if the company wishing to sell would have implemented these measures twenty years earlier. Each year the company would have grown incrementally larger. The rate of growth would increase exponentially as the growth rate compounds over time (2% of $1 million is better than 2% of $100,000). Adopting the BOS creates a pro-growth company culture. Value drivers are identified, benchmarked, measured and improved. Opportunities that would otherwise not have been available become attainable. Brand awareness grows, and the firm's reputation improves – both lowering the company's cost of capital and increasing the company's value. When the time comes to sell, you're ready – because that's how your company operates. Always at its peak, always capitalizing on improving key value drivers, your company is always ready to sell and will command top dollar in the marketplace.

The second benefit considers the due diligence that will be conducted by the buyer. A company that runs "business as usual" for decades and then wishes to increase its value over the course of two to three years to receive top dollar is in for some sad news. Depending on the company (industry, age, the reason for purchase, etc.) the potential buyer will be reviewing a history of financial performance. A company in business for twenty years will need to provide a minimum of ten years' financial statements. Imagine reviewing a company's financial statements and noticing a relatively constant (low) growth rate for almost a decade and then seeing significant improvements in the most recent two to three years. This practice is called seller's window dressing, and astute buyers will look right through it. Companies can improve cash flow multiples for short periods of time to improve value. Over time, however, these adjustments cannot persist, and the multiples will decline. Delaying capital expenditures to improve free cash flow is one example. For capital intensive firms this can improve short-term free cash flow and enterprise value. Eventually, however, money will be required to fix and replace the fixed assets. Free cash flow will be reduced. A company operating "as if" it's selling today doesn't have this problem. Buyers will see a history of progress supporting the firm's value. Moreover, because the company has always operated "as if," the compounded growth rate will be higher. Remember, over time, the value will have snowballed into a much larger amount. The firm is not only more valuable but has a history supporting the persistence of value. A buyer won't be dismayed by short-term performance window dressing because there isn't any to see. Firm value is always maximized under the BOS. When the time comes to sell, convincing buyers that your company is "worth it" will be comparatively easy. You have the history to prove it.

- Shareholders and their families have a clear understanding of their economic worth, assisting them in estate and retirement planning. Instead of a triggering event preceding planning (and possible catastrophe), shareholders can implement estate planning strategies and plan for retirement. Retirement is a common triggering event in buy-sell agreements. You learned about the tragic flaws implicit in the modern buy-sell price mechanisms. The BOS, on the other hand, provides a recurring (annual) transparent price to all shareholders. When a shareholder retires, there's no questioning how much the retiree will receive. The company will also be able to plan for such liquidity events and know how much capital will be needed. If a shareholder dies and the buy-sell agreement is triggered, the living spouse won't have to worry about not receiving the $5 million her and her husband planned for because the buy-sell agreement had a nefarious pricing mechanism producing an economically unjust price. Personal insurance planning is simplified and more accurately hedged as the shareholder's real economic wealth in the company is known. Using the BOS allows the company to plan and insure against insurable liquidity events with accuracy.

Non-insurable liabilities can also be hedged with precision because the company's value is known. Greater planning is involved, and the extent of hedging will depend on the complexities of the closely-held company. The hedge (sinking fund, for example) should be adjusted each year to compensate for the change in the enterprise's value, along with any shareholder departures or internal liabilities that would require an adjustment. The BOS protects both the company and the employee-owners, provides more efficient and effective planning and reduces the total risk for all.

- Finally, the BOS makes the most economic sense – both in value and in cost. The economic value estimate's accuracy using the BOS far exceeds the other methods. Valuing a firm based on a multiple (five times EBITDA, for example) ignores the risk elements and economic growth potential of a firm (along with many other problems). Multiples also change over time and become inapplicable and economically unsound. A fixed price mechanism quickly becomes stale and incorrect. Unless the company, its components, industry, the general economy, etc., never change, the value will be wrong using a fixed price mechanism. Furthermore, the fixed price customarily varies substantially from the actual economic value when a triggering event occurs. Pricing determined by a process (or processes) is the most precise method of the three. Nonetheless, the process method can invite non-qualified appraisers to determine the company's value. Even if a qualified appraiser is selected, the appraiser will need to gain an understanding of your firm and its key value drivers. Gaining an understanding takes considerable time, and time is something typically not afforded to the appraiser when a triggering event appraisal is needed. In essence, the value estimate – even when using a qualified appraiser – will be less precise than one familiar with your company. Moreover, if subsequent processes are exercised, additional costs will be incurred as more appraisals will be performed. The BOS requires a single annual appraisal fee that decreases over time. Price accuracy of the company improves as the appraiser becomes more familiar with your firm and its key value drivers. You benefit from the appraisal by recognizing the key value drivers, implementing benchmarks, measuring progress and growing your company's value.

Conclusion

The opportunity costs of not implementing The Business Owner's Solution are significant. Not only is your buy-sell agreement's value component economically sound and transparent, but your firm will increase in value. Follow my recommendations and watch your company's value increase exponentially as you focus on the key value drivers that grow economic value. Eradicate the fear of "how are we ever going to sell the company for $XXX?!" and the ill-fated strategy of window dressing by instead operating "as if" your company is always for sale, maximizing its value at all times.

The Business Owner's Solution delivers a win-win method that generates the most value from a business appraisal by performing thorough due diligence upfront, selecting an expert in valuation (i.e. finance and economics) and using that appraiser as a de-facto consultant. Many owners view the business appraisal as a byproduct of the relationship and instead consider the appraiser's expertise on value-adding solutions that increases the firm's value as the primary benefit of the BOS. The opportunity costs of not implementing The Business Owner's Solution as laid out in this chapter are significant. You can't afford not to.

Chapter Seventeen

Eliminating the Level of Value Quandary in Your Buy-Sell Agreement

Introduction

This chapter addresses the level of value in your buy-sell agreement. If you implement The Business Owner's Solution, this information will be helpful in determining and specifically detailing what level of value you desire when triggering events occur. Minority interest levels of value are less marketable and void of power compared to controlling interests. As such, you may wish to allow for valuation discounts to be used for minority interest transactions. On the flipside, you will also need to address control interests and the respective control premiums that should (or shouldn't) be used. Both valuation discounts and control premiums are purely up to you and your fellow owners. This chapter, however, addresses a crucial point that the most astute buy-sell clauses frequently lack. Even if you decide to continue with your current buy-sell agreement, this chapter merits your attention.

Parts of this chapter may seem redundant, but that's for good reason. Much of this chapter was published in a highly circulated publication in March 2016. For readers who decide to forgo implementing The Business

Owner's Solution and forge ahead with their current buy-sell agreement, I decided to keep much of this article's constitution intact. Modifications include additional insight and pointers, along with reduced technical jargon so that you (the business owner) can easily understand and communicate to your attorney what needs to be done when modifying your current buy-sell agreement. Even if you decide to keep your current buy-sell agreement, you will need to add or change some parts of it to avoid some very dangerous pitfalls. This chapter provides that guidance.

Eliminate the Level of Value Quandary in Your Buy-Sell Agreement

Whether you have an Operating Agreement (LLC) or Partnership Agreement, you likely have a buy-sell agreement (think of it as a clause or group of clauses) within your "Agreement." Many business owners fail to recognize the existence of a buy-sell agreement within their governing documents because of the separate term "Agreement." Most business owners aren't attorneys, and those who are often fail to catch the crucial details that could lead to a ticking time-bomb if not adequately addressed. As you read this chapter, understand that buy-sell agreements are almost always within your Operating or Partnership Agreement (depending on your legal structure). Buy-sell agreements are not always a separate document – despite the term "agreement" which throws off many business owners (and attorneys, accountants, etc. – you aren't alone!).

Note: *Unless capitalized, the term "agreement" and "buy-sell agreement" are used interchangeably.*

Defining value in buy-sell agreements of closely-held businesses is frequently a dubious practice for attorneys and business appraisers alike. Articulating the standard of value (e.g., fair market value, fair value) receives disproportionate attention to the peril of somewhat obscure valuation concerns, notably the level of value. Despite the attention the standard of value receives, the concluded value definition is frequently illogical. Whether erroneously defined, ambiguous or absent altogether, correctly defining the client's intent of value remains unnecessarily problematic.

The cardinal objective of this chapter is to examine the levels of value in buy-sell agreements and the importance of accurately defining the level of value intended by the company's owners. The following paragraph is relatively standard language taken from an actual buy-sell agreement:

> "'Fair Market Value' means the amount agreed to in writing between the Company and the selling Shareholder within thirty (30) days after the date of the Triggering Event. In the event no agreement is reached within such period, "Fair Market Value" means the amount a willing buyer would pay a willing seller for the Shares being purchased under all the circumstances, using commercially reasonable valuation standards, without taking into account premiums for control or change of control (what a strategic buyer would pay) and without applying discounts for minority interests and lack of marketability. The determination of Fair Market Value shall be determined by an appraiser selected by the Company."

Now let's take a closer look. The clause tells us that no adjustment for the price should be applied, whether the adjustment is a premium or discount (of any kind). Here's where the fault lies: an implied discount or premium is embedded in the value by default, depending on the valuation approach and method used. Therefore, the buy-sell agreement's desired level of value must be precise for the appraiser to select the proper approaches and methods when performing the business valuation.

Take an example where the interest at hand is a 10 percent (minority) interest in a going concern, closely-held operating company. Typical normalization adjustments have been made. Abiding by the agreement, no cash flow or multiple adjustments have been made to elevate the level of value from minority to control. Considering three conventional approaches to business valuation (Market, Income, and Asset Approaches)—and some of their respective methods (noted in Exhibit I) — provides the following levels of value conclusions. In adhering to the language of the buy-sell agreement, these value conclusions are reached without applying discounts or premiums.

Exhibit I		
Approach	**Method**	**Level**
1. Market Approach	Guideline public company method (MAGPC)	minority
	Guideline company transaction method (MAGCT)	control
2. Income Approach	Discounted cash flow method (IADCF)	minority
3. Asset Approach	Adjusted net asset method (AAM)	control

Exhibit II is a graphical rendition of the levels of value hierarchy. The left side delineates the levels of value (range) whereas the right side represents the level of value conclusions under the approaches and methods from Exhibit I.

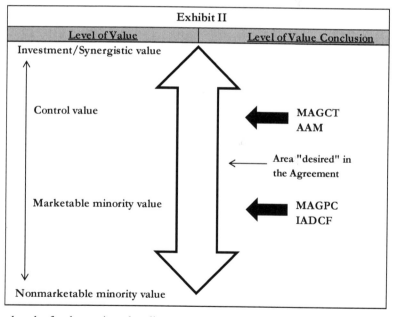

The level of value using the discounted cash flow or guideline public company methods is that of a minority shareholder. No controlling adjustments are permitted per the buy-sell agreement. The cost of capital used to discount the cash flow streams under the discounted cash flow method is based upon publicly traded, minority interest shares, as are the multiples used for the guideline public company method. This level of value is lower than the level of value desired in this example.

In contrast, the level of value using the guideline company transaction or adjusted net asset methods is that of a controlling shareholder. The guideline company transaction method uses multiples from observed control transactions, providing a control level of value. The adjusted net asset method substitutes the company's assets' book values to current prices and nets out the present value of existing debt. The residual—or adjusted net asset value—is a control level of value. Only a controlling interest level would have the ability to liquidate and realize the residual. This level of value is higher than the level of value desired in this example. Other methods could also be justified and still provide divergent levels of value.

The fair market value standard defined in Revenue Ruling 59-60 states that "A sound valuation will be based upon all the relevant facts, but the elements of common sense, informed judgment and reasonableness must enter into the process of weighing those facts and weighing their significance."[34] This sentence encapsulates the heart of business valuation. It is both an art and a science, with subjectivity and latitude expected to be used by the business appraiser in harmony with the ruling's guidelines. The following situation exemplifies the subjectivity appraisers will use without specific guidance.

Continuing with the previous example of a 10 percent interest and the buy-sell agreement language, assume that two appraisers are hired to value the company. The standard of value is fair market value, as defined in the buy-sell agreement, and no valuation discounts or control premiums are to be applied. Appraiser A uses the income approach and the discounted cash flow method. Appraiser B uses the market approach and the guideline company transaction method. The former method uses discount rates obtained from minority interest publicly traded equities (resulting in a minority level of value conclusion), whereas the latter method uses acquisition multiples from transactions that have occurred in the company's industry (yielding a control level of value conclusion). An implied discount is included in the former compared to an implied premium in the latter. Exhibit III illustrates the alarming valuation differential that can occur because the level of value was not explicitly specified in the buy-sell agreement.

---

[34] Internal Revenue Bulletin 1959-1 CB 237, IRC Sec. 2031.

	Exhibit III	
	Appraiser A	**Appraiser B**
Approach:	Income Approach	Market Approach
Method:	Discounted cash flow method	Guideline company transaction method
Estimated Value:	$5,000,000	$5,750,000

In accordance with the buy-sell agreement, the appraisers were instructed to abide by the following:

"Fair Market Value' means the amount a willing buyer would pay a willing seller for the Shares being purchased under all the circumstances…"

Ambiguous wording begets subjective interpretation to what "all the circumstances" truly means. The 10 percent interest would usually be considered a minority interest. However, assume one of the shareholders owned 41 percent of the company. Purchasing the 10 percent interest would convert the purchasing shareholder from a minority shareholder to a controlling shareholder. If the appraiser believes the 41 percent shareholder may buy the 10 percent interest, how does she determine the level of value for the 10 percent interest? As indicated in Exhibit III, control value is a bona fide premium shareholders pay for.

"…without taking into account premiums for control or change of control (what a strategic buyer would pay) and without applying discounts for minority interests and lack of marketability."

No control premiums or valuation discounts should be applied. Not applying premiums or discounts is perfectly acceptable if the level of value is specified. Because different approaches and methods implicitly result in diverging levels of value without applying premiums or discounts, this guidance is flawed. The appraisers were left to choose the level of value.

Consequently, an implied 15 percent premium is embedded in the value conclusion of Appraiser B relative to Appraiser A's value conclusion. The company's industry ascribes a 15 percent premium for a controlling level of value compared to a minority level. The document's language failed the client by not directing the appraisers to a specified level of value, and thus, the appropriate method to use. Appraiser A believed the income stream projections were sufficient to perform a discounted cash flow value method. Appraiser B preferred quantifiable observable transactions and opted to use the guideline company transaction method. After reviewing the financial information and the buy-sell agreement, and discussing why each appraiser selected her respective approach, the conclusion was: they were both correct.

The next step was to review control premiums and transaction premiums for the industry to determine which method was more reasonable in this case. Accepting the median control premium transaction multiple as reasonable, the premium (17 percent) could then be converted into a discount for lack of control (DLOC). This process is shown in Exhibit IV.

Exhibit IV	
DLOC = 1 - 1 / (1 + Premium)	
Median premium	17%
Implied DLOC *(rounded)*	15%
Actual Implied DLOC = 14.53%	

The observable median industry premium of 17 percent implies a 15 percent discount for lack of control (rounded). Remember, the discounted cash flow method used by Appraiser A produced a minority interest level of value. To check the reasonableness of Appraiser B's value estimate (a control value), a discount for lack of control must be applied to determine the minority level of value.

Exhibit V		
	Appraiser A	**Appraiser B**
Approach:	Income Approach	Market Approach
Method:	Discounted cash flow method	Guideline company transaction method
Estimated Value:	$5,000,000	$5,750,000
Implied DLOC of ~15% to control value:		($835,470)
Minority level of value:	$5,000,000	$4,914,530

A mere 2 percent variance exists between the value conclusions when calculated on the same level of value. The document's ambiguity in determining what fair market value meant left a sinister amount of subjectivity, and neither of the appraiser's methods—nor the reasons they selected them—were unreasonable.

Moving Forward

Including language in the buy-sell agreement that prescribes the specific approaches and methods to be used is one way of alleviating the level of value quandary. However, this can be highly problematic. For example, the income approach relies on a firm's ability to project cash flow streams into the future with a high degree of certainty. If income is erratic or a company is unable to project cash flows with an underlying degree of certainty, the income approach may not be deemed appropriate by the appraiser. Likewise, the market approach relies on finding either comparable publicly traded guideline companies (the guideline public company method) or transactions that "make sense" within the company's industry (the guideline company transaction method). Not every approach is appropriate, given the nature and circumstances of the business being appraised. For these reasons, the approaches and methods used should be left to the appraiser's professional judgment.

The best way to solve the level of value problem may be to define it, then let the appraiser do her job in deciding which approaches and methods are most suitable. Use a graph to define the levels of value (as shown in Exhibit II) and include that in your agreement for further clarity. Defining the level of value in text and visually depicting your intent leaves no room for interpretation.

Final Takeaways

I would be amiss without deliberating a brief appraisal of two notable flaws in the aforementioned buy-sell agreement. My expertise is that of a business appraiser specializing in business valuation and business consulting. I am not an attorney and do not render legal advice. With that said, my recommendations should improve specificity when drafting the text governing a business owner's (your) most prized possession – and remove potential headaches when a triggering event occurs.

1) "Fair Market Value" is too vague as presented and should be defined by reference. IRS Revenue Ruling 59-60 defines Fair Market Value as:

> "...the price at which a property would change hands between a willing buyer and a willing seller when the former is not under any compulsion to buy and the latter is not under any compulsion to sell, both parties having reasonable knowledge of relevant facts. Court decisions frequently state in addition that the hypothetical buyer and seller are assumed to be able, as well as

willing, to trade and to be well-informed about the property and concerning the market for such property."[35]

The ruling provides eight specific factors the appraiser must consider when valuing an interest under the fair market value standard. By referencing the ruling (and fair market value definition) in your buy-sell agreement, subjective interpretation by the appraiser (or other parties) is mitigated. I advise fair market value as the standard of value for most buy-sell agreements. The devil is in the details, not the intent.

2) The phrase "using commercially reasonable valuation standards" is too broad and open to conflicting interpretation. Using this undefined phrase, the controlling shareholder of the company could apply any standards (or none), adversely impacting you – or other shareholders – who are bound to the agreement. I've reviewed business valuations completed by un-credentialed business appraisers stating their business valuations were performed "in accordance with professional business valuation standards" – an ambiguous phrase lacking credibility that adheres to no professional appraisal organization's standards. To eliminate the possibility of differing standards (or none at all), specify the appraisal standards that must be used in the business valuation.

Credible professional appraisal organizations were discussed earlier in this book (e.g. standards include the AICPA's SSVS No. 1 or the ASA's USPAP). Defining credible appraisal standards protocol in your buy-sell agreement increases the quality of work and minimizes the odds of a botched business valuation.

Conclusion

Make sure to have your buy-sell agreement reviewed by a professional, and if possible, multiple professionals who are well versed in drafting or reviewing buy-sell agreements. Attorneys are exceptionally gifted at their craft – and that craft is not valuation. Your company's value is one of the most important factors in your Agreement. Remain steadfast and do not blindly accept what has merely been provided.

---

[35] Internal Revenue Bulletin 1959-1 CB 237, IRC Sec. 2031.

If you haven't noticed by now, this is important and complicated stuff. Seek the right professionals for guidance and avoid the preventable headaches and financial bleeding that most owners discover all too late.

One thing I didn't mention in the article, but that you should know as a reader of this book, pertains to the author of the buy-sell agreement referenced earlier. The attorney is a senior partner in the trust and estate planning division at a very large and prestigious law firm. The individual is well respected nationwide – and I have great admiration for this person as an estate planning attorney. This buy-sell agreement came from one of the best law firms in the United States, authored by a highly-educated, elite attorney who is excellent at providing legal guidance on estate and business succession planning purposes. Yet, the Agreement's valuation component was riddled with flaws.

Do I blame the attorney? Absolutely not. All of the firm's Agreements contained similar buy-sell agreement language. As I said earlier in this book, law firms typically retain what they believe is the best buy-sell agreement language and use it interchangeably. Attorneys are not valuation experts. The language becomes boilerplate with small adjustments made when needed.

The buy-sell agreement language in this chapter originated from one of the best law firms in the United States, and it contained fundamental errors filled with landmines. How many landmines do you think exist in your buy-sell agreement? Don't leave disaster to chance when it is entirely preventable. If you choose not to implement The Business Owner's Solution, at least have a valuation professional (or two) experienced at reviewing Operating and Partnership Agreements review your buy-sell agreement. The cost will be minimal compared to the potential landmines that are waiting to be triggered. Nonetheless, The Business Owner's Solution remains the most effective and least costly alternative to eliminating the level of value quandary in your buy-sell agreement.

Chapter Eighteen

EBITDA: The Anti-Valuation Multiple

Introduction

EBITDA. Whether you pronounce it "E-bitda," "E bit Daa," or some other variation, it all means the same. Add back interest, tax, depreciation and amortization expense to net income and you have EBITDA. EBITDA is one of the most spoken multiples when discussing value. No matter what industry your company is in, you have heard the term used at least on occasion. Investment bankers and business brokers are quick to use EBITDA when discussing sales prices (e.g., "5 times EBITDA is what companies like yours sell for"). While EBITDA has its uses, chiefly when comparing companies in similar industries requiring similar working capital and having similar capital structures (did you get all that?) – I'm taking action against its use in business valuation.

Perils of EBITDA in Valuation

Perhaps you've seen it yourself, either as an owner looking to sell (target) or seeking to buy (acquirer). A business broker sits you down and turns on a large projector screen filled with lavish excel spreadsheet models with circular references galore that astonishingly sync together. You review the cash flow projection model and agree with its presentation (perhaps not so much the estimates, but that's another story). After a few scrolls, you seemingly notice something at the end. It irks you. You aren't quite sure what to make of it, but it doesn't feel right. Yep – it's a multiple of EBITDA at the end of the projection period as the exit multiple. So much for that free cash flow model...

Let's walk through an example. Assume the analyst projected seven years of free cash flow to equity (FCFE), with the seventh year being the terminal year (last year projected). Valuation theory instructs us to maintain an apples-to-apples comparison so as not to bastardize or otherwise misconstrue the product. Seems logical, right? If so (and let's be simple here); you're looking for the terminal value to be the model's final period of cash flow increased by the long-term sustainable growth rate, divided by the cap rate (discount rate minus the long-term sustainable growth rate, the denominator), discounted back to the present value at the appropriate cost of capital.

Note: *If you were confused by that last paragraph, go back and re-read Chapter 8 (The Income Approach). Pay specific attention to the two-stage model example provided in the chapter. Everything from the previous paragraph was deconstructed and explained, piece by piece, in the Chapter 8 example.*

So when you see a multiple of EBITDA as the terminal value (an exit multiple) instead of the terminal value methodology discussed in Chapter 8, your intuition ably served you.

Perhaps you're saying, "Great, so what does that mean?" Happy you asked.

Since this isn't a treatise on explaining formulas, let's hit the differences between the two and how they impact you as a business owner.

Before examining the differences, remember what EBITDA is: earnings before a bunch of expenses. Depreciation and amortization are non-cash expenses. You can't see them, but they are real costs. Assume you purchase an asset (say a car) and drive it 50,000 miles a year. That assemblage of metal will eventually need to be replaced. In the business world – assuming the car is a business asset – you can depreciate, or expense an amount each year to account for erosion of the car's economic utility. While the depreciation expense isn't a cash outlay each year, time will come when the piston blows through the roof and money will be needed for a new car. Never push aside depreciation or amortization as afterthoughts or imaginary expenses.

Now let's discuss the touchy-feely expenses. The expenses you can smell as cash leaves your hand – and this time, your cash is going to the bank in the form of interest expense on debt. An example will demonstrate the axiom of why EBITDA can be perilous when comparing two companies. Assume both companies A and B as shown (Exhibit I) have the same EBITDA. If that's the case, what's different?

Exhibit I

	Company A	**Company B**
Total Assets	$10,000,000	$10,000,000
Liabilities (L)	$1,000,000	$5,000,000
Equity (E)	$9,000,000	$5,000,000
Total L + E	$10,000,000	$10,000,000
Interest Rate on Debt = 7%		
Interest Expense	$70,000	$350,000

One of EBITDA's fundamental shortcomings is that it fails to compare capital structures between companies. As noted in Exhibit I, Company A's debt ($1 million) is a fraction of Company B's ($5 million). Company A is subject to less financial risk than Company B, yet per our assumption, both have the same EBITDA. An apples-to-potatoes comparison, if you will. From a valuation perspective – all else equal – each company's individual cost of capital will be different, resulting in different values. Company B is more susceptible to financial risk by having greater financial leverage. If both companies suffered critical but equal revenue impairments, Company B is at a higher risk of insolvency. Accordingly, Company B's cost of capital is higher than Company A, all else equal. A higher cost of capital (denominator) equates to a lower present value.

If the appraiser uses a multiple of EBITDA in the terminal value of a discounted cash flow model, the rules of finance have likely been broken. As discussed throughout this book, the numerator and denominator must match. EBITDA is a product of accounting and is not representative of actual economic cash flow. Using free cash flow as the numerator throughout the projection period up until the terminal value mismatches economic cash flow with accounting income and discredits the model. A multiple of EBITDA as a terminal value is a rule of thumb. You know that rules of thumb change over time and should not be used to value a company directly. Finally, the numerator and denominator do not match.

If EBITDA is used as the terminal value, the cost of capital must be an accounting equivalent denominator that matches the EBITDA numerator. Now the appraiser has introduced two costs of capital and two sets of numerators – free cash flow and accounting income (EBITDA). Moreover, the exit multiple is a speculative rule of thumb that ignores fundamental components of a company's cash flow. Considerable adjustments must be made to the cash flow model to make this theoretically and practically sound – and even then the appraiser is relying on a rule of thumb to estimate a significant component of the company's overall value. In practice, I have seen EBITDA used as an exit multiple and have never seen the discount rate adjusted to account for both accounting income (EBITDA) and the discrete cash free flow streams leading up to the terminal value. Investment banks are privy to using EBITDA as exit multiples. EBITDA is easy to calculate, understand and communicate to business owners. Unless you're a large company undergoing an initial public offering using a bulge bracket investment bank, chances are the EBITDA exit multiple will be erroneously applied if a multi-stage discounted cash flow model is used to value your firm.

Let's move on to another touchy-feely expense. Instead of the bank, this time it's the government and those taxes you eagerly pay each quarter. Without diving into the differences between actual cash tax expense and accounting tax expense, EBITDA assumes you don't pay tax. The EBITDA multiple (by adding back tax expense) implicates that the government gives you a free pass and extrapolates a value based on an unrealistic number (because taxes are real). As a business owner, you will have to pay taxes at some level no matter how you're structured (C-corporation, S-corporation, LLC, LP, etc.) – and those are real expenses. The premise to adding back taxes is to compare companies with different capital structures, and consequently, different effective tax rates. Unfortunately, that negates the cost of capital rule when using a discounted cash flow model. It also distorts the comparability between closely-held companies, especially when comparing C-corporations to pass-through entities. The former are taxed on corporate earnings at the entity level whereas the latter organizational structures are taxed at the shareholder level. Tax credits, carryovers and deferral rules are different between the corporate structures. How can comparability occur amongst the entities when different tax rules apply? Without enormous time spent making subjective adjustments, they can't.

Okay, so we've touched on the "add-backs" or the ITDA of EBITDA. High-level stuff so far, nothing granular…yet.

For the majority of discounted cash flow (DCF) models, the largest component of value is the terminal value. Using EBITDA as the terminal value – a non-cash flow item – materially distorts the value of a company.

When you abandon free cash flow for EBITDA (here comes the granular stuff) you:
- Completely dismiss the deduction of income taxes (a cash item).
- Omit the deduction of interest expense when discounting back cash flows (compute the present value), ignoring a real cash item.
- Ignore capital expenditures. Remember the last time you didn't need to buy or replace assets? Neither does any other business owner.
- Forget working capital – the money you need to run the ship. Companies are increasingly seeking to improve working capital management efficiency to increase net margins.

By using EBITDA instead of cash flow, you're left with a company that:
1) Has no debt (adding back interest expense),
2) Doesn't pay taxes (adding that back, too),
3) Has no capital expenditures, and
4) Has no change in net working capital.

When the terminal value in a discounted cash flow model is a multiple of EBITDA, the cost of capital is either ignored or (likely) incorrectly applied. However, the cost of capital is one of the most important elements (if not the most important) to consider when valuing an enterprise.

EBITDA is useful for rule of thumb comparisons and ratio analysis. It is also helpful in the market approach because the comparable companies or transactions should be similar (if your appraiser does a good job they will be). Furthermore, the comparable companies in the market approach have a growth element built into the EBITDA ratio. Using the market approach, EBITDA isn't a rule of thumb because the multiples are obtained from the market as of a specific date (i.e. the "effective date"), in contrast to a subjectively chosen exit multiple.

Conclusion

In closely-held business valuation, EBITDA is an easy, crude way to measure value when used as an exit multiple. It's a rule of thumb approach that fails to withstand the rigor of a thorough free cash flow exercise. EBITDA is the overweight couch potato that longs to be the free cash flow fitness model but doesn't want to put in the hard work to get there. Use it as you wish, but its place in valuing companies as an exit multiple in discounted cash flow models is flawed if not accounted for properly.

Chapter Nineteen

Choosing an Appraiser (and Getting the Most Bang for Your Buck)

Introduction

In Chapter 16, you learned what to look for when selecting an appraiser to implement The Business Owner's Solution that diffuses the landmines in your company's buy-sell agreement. The selection criteria provided in that chapter, however, applies to any appraisal. If you want a quality appraiser to perform your business valuation, use the suggested minimum qualifications to ensure you select an experienced appraiser well versed in finance and economics.

This chapter expands on the selection process. At this point, you have learned the minimum guidelines when choosing a quality appraiser. Now it's time to find out how to locate a quality appraiser and keep the cost as low as possible. I'll give you tips on how to reduce your cost and how to help assure that your valuation is performed without encountering problems that commonly arise.

Choosing an Appraiser

Deciding who to appraise your business can be intimidating and overwhelming. You have many constraints, yet want the best person possible. Once a business owner decides a business appraisal is needed, the owner typically has the following needs and wants:

- An appraiser who can perform the valuation for gifting purposes (or some other purpose – the particular reason will vary)
- The best appraiser in the area
- The appraisal to be completed in one month
- At a cost of no more than $X

The last bullet point (cost) is typically the central point of the conversation. The budget, for example, is almost always too small to get the first three wants fulfilled. Why?

Quality appraisers earn a reputation of exclusiveness through decades of education and experience. Like any other professional service (doctor, lawyer, etc.), you get what you pay for. Second, the time frame requested by the business owner to have the appraisal completed is frequently too short. Valuing an operating entity can take months. On your end, finding and selecting an appraiser that best matches your specific needs will take at least a few weeks (if you want it done right, or if this is your first time searching for an appraiser). The appraiser will need to review your company's financial information, gain an understanding of your business, and read through and analyze governing documents and tax information before providing fee a quote. For a quality business appraisal to be completed, one month is too little time (for most engagements).

Once an appraiser is selected and all information has been provided (which alone can take a week or more), expect six to eight weeks for the appraisal to be completed. Many valuations require the appraiser to perform a site visit. On the site visit, the appraiser will view the premises and talk to management. As discussed in Chapter 4, plan on the site visit to take at least a half day. A single day is typical for most companies, but if your company or the project is complex and extensive, appraisers may need to spend several days.

Perhaps the most important tip for selecting an appraiser – and one that is often ignored because of advertisement or sticker shock – is to find a specialist in your field. You do not want to be somebody's mistake or learning experience. Many appraisers are jacks of all trades, masters of none. If you own a veterinary practice, find an appraiser who specializes in valuing veterinary practices. You will pay more to a specialist versus the CPA down the street who performs a few valuations when tax season is over, but you want quality. For most business owners, their closely-held company constitutes the largest asset of their net worth. Moreover, the business is also a "personal" asset. It's more than just a business. If you weren't the founder, your family (likely) risked their livelihoods to build the business. It's personal. To get the value right, you should demand the best.

Imagine if the following scenario played out.

Chest pains have been ailing you for the past few days – and they're getting worse. You decide to visit your local urgent care to see if they can figure out what's causing the problem. After some examinations, they discover that a valve in your heart is partially blocked. You need heart surgery to remove the blockage. Unless you have the surgery and clear out the blockage, the doctor assures that you will die prematurely.

Fortunately, you have options. The general surgeon at your nearby hospital (only 5 minutes away!) dabbles a bit in heart valve clearings. Technology has improved, and he's taken a few classes on how to get the stint into the valve and relieve the blockage. Last month you saw on his website that he started advertising this service. Because you've seen him before for some minor issues – one-off type of procedures – you know he's relatively inexpensive.

The urgent care doctor tells you about a surgeon in the city, which is an hour away. According to the urgent care doctor, this surgeon does nothing but heart surgeries. Moreover, he specializes in valve clearings – the exact procedure you need. He performs thirty of them a week. The surgeon isn't cheap, but you know you're in the best hands by driving into the city and visiting the specialist.

Assuming you value your life (hopefully, that's the case) the answer is a no-brainer. You have a problem. The consequences of not fixing your problem are significant. Sure, the general surgeon might do an okay job. He might even fix it. But if he doesn't get it right, either (1) you're going to die or (2) you will have to pay the specialist a visit later to have the procedure performed correctly to fix the general surgeon's failed attempt. If you don't die and have to visit the specialist after the procedure is done incorrectly by the general surgeon, you will pay the specialist in addition to the general surgeon. If you visited the specialist first, the problem would have been remedied sooner, and you would only incur a one-time payment. Both your health and wallet would have been better off.

Maybe you're thinking "comparing life and death to an appraisal is nonsense." You're right; this isn't life and death. But the analogy is one I frequently encounter when I'm forced to fix something because a generalist botched the job.

Examples tend to resonate with people more than analogies, so let's walk through an example.

A CPA who specializes in income tax returns called me one evening. His client had an appraisal performed by a local firm that generalizes in all valuation areas. The appraisal was a nonmarketable minority interest of a family limited partnership for estate tax purposes, and the client insisted they use a local company. Not knowing any better, the CPA agreed, and the appraisal was completed by the client's chosen appraiser.

Months later, the IRS sent the client's CPA a deficiency notice for tax due. What was originally a non-taxable estate (the valuation fell below the taxable estate threshold) had become a taxable estate. Instead of zero tax due, the client now owed nearly $200,000. The CPA had 90 days to respond to the deficiency (but sat on the letter for over a month before taking action).

What happened? The IRS has a team of engineers, or valuation specialists, who review appraisals submitted for tax-related purposes. The appraiser who performed the appraisal did not follow the guidelines outlined in Revenue Ruling 59-60. In fact, the appraiser – when later asked – didn't even know what Revenue Ruling 59-60 was. Large valuation discounts were applied, reducing the value of the interest far below a supportable fair market value estimate. The IRS rejected the valuation, eliminated all discounts, and wrote the assets up to their market values. Consequently, the total value of all assets was increased above the taxable estate threshold. The amount above the limit was taxed (at ~40%), and interest was also added to the tax deficiency.

The Consequences. I feel horrible for people who find themselves in this situation. The CPA's client was sold on the appraiser. We later found out the appraiser promised a substantial valuation discount. Not only is this unethical, but it fundamentally conflicts with the appraisal community's ethos. As appraisers, we are advocates of our work, unbiased by clients or sales. Our mission is to provide an empirically supported value estimate, tested with rigor and challenged by precedent, justifiably convincing the reader that no other conclusion could be reasonable. The appraiser, in this case, sold an unrealistic (and unethical) dream. Sometimes these appraisals get through the cracks. I've seen appraisers sell clients on past work, knowing they're selling a game of Russian roulette. In other words, these appraisers are showing potential customers significant valuation discounts that have successfully made it through the IRS. Sometimes these are the result of the IRS being overwhelmed while other times the valuation discounts are appropriate to the subject interest.

With $200,000 in taxes and interest suddenly due, but without the means to pay it, the client was distressed and vexed. After speaking to the CPA, the client contacted the appraisal firm to get answers. Oddly enough (not really) the appraiser's voicemail answered the call. After several attempts – and messages left – the appraiser returned the client's call, blaming others and giving excuses as to why the IRS had challenged the appraisal. Ultimately, the appraiser agreed to redo the valuation, but the fee would be double because of the time constraints imposed by the IRS.

Now what? Fortunately, the client stopped the bleeding. Instead of making a bad situation worse, he declined the generalist's offer and contacted the CPA for guidance. I was fortunate enough to have presented at a conference the CPA had attended on a similar subject matter. The CPA remembered my presentation and contacted me. I agreed to review the original appraisal and either write a rebuttal letter in support of the original appraisal or perform another appraisal altogether. I also suggested the client contact an attorney to work with the CPA and myself to extend the time period and make sure the customer squared away the tax delinquency for good. Because of the now significant tax delinquency, hiring an attorney was a comparably small expense and the client agreed. The attorney ultimately retained specialized in estate planning, knew the local IRS personnel, and was able to extend the period without any penalties.

Some things cannot be saved, and the original appraisal was non-salvageable. I agreed to perform a new appraisal, which was then submitted to the IRS as the CPA's rebuttal position. The IRS accepted the new appraisal estimate. My estimate was higher than the original valuation because the valuation discounts initially applied were unsupportable. Under my estimate the estate was taxable, but the valuation discounts applied were supported and accepted by the IRS, whereas the original appraiser's valuation discounts were altogether thrown out. The result was a $40,000 tax instead of $200,000. While the accepted valuation estimate saved the client $160,000 in taxes, it cost the client $30,000 in additional expenses (not including taxes) and other headaches that persisted for almost a year. What the customer originally thought was a "done deal" became an emotional and financial disaster that lingered on much longer than necessary.

Instead of paying a specialist to perform the business appraisal, the client chose a generalist. Rather than paying the specialist's price of $10,000, the client wanted the generalist who charged $5,000. After the IRS had rejected it, the client had to pay the CPA additional money for his time. The attorney sought after to ensure closure was an added expense. My fee increased because of the time constraint.

The original appraisal fee was a sunk cost. For an additional $5,000 (hiring a specialist), the client could have saved a princely sum that could have been allocated towards paying the tax due on the estate (when including the added expenses incurred by using the generalist). Instead, the total amount due (taxes and fees – knowing the estate was taxable to begin with) increased markedly because of the additional expenses and sunk costs. Rather than paying a total of $50,000 in taxes and valuation fees (specialist), the client spent $75,000 in taxes and total fees by using the generalist. The cost of using cheap is demonstrated below. (The first column indicates the total costs that would have been realized if a specialist was initially hired. The second column shows the actual total fees incurred by using the generalist and then having to get the deficiency "cleaned up." Using the "cheap" appraiser increased the total cost by $25,000, or 50 percent.)

	Specialist	**Generalist**
Valuation fee	$10,000	$5,000
Tax	$40,000	$40,000
Additional fees		$30,000
Total Paid	$50,000	$75,000
Difference in cost	50%	

This example is not intended to toot my own horn. I'm regularly asked to perform appraisals out of my niche – and I decline every single one of them. I'm well connected to specialists who I know do an excellent job in their respective niches, and I'm happy to refer clients to specialists who can accurately complete the assignment. I provided this example so that you fully understand what happens when you choose price over substance and fail to perform diligence on the appraiser. You have every right to interview the appraiser – and should do so. If more than one appraiser fits your criteria, interview all of them. The appraisal process requires communication and trust. Do the work upfront and the appraisal process and the result will pay off exponentially.

While this book covers several valuation topics, I want to stress to the reader that the IRS is not the "bad guy." A considerable amount of my valuation practice focuses on gift and estate tax valuation work. Most of my interactions with the IRS have been positive. From a business appraiser's perspective, the key to establishing a good working relationship with the IRS is to: (1) give them what they need in a supportable valuation that makes sense, (2) make it easy for them to find the information they require, which can be accomplished with a well written executive summary, and (3) be polite and responsive. In other words: do a good job, help make the engineer's over-worked and understaffed job easier by spending a few extra minutes writing an executive summary letter, and be respectful.

• • •

How Much Will It Cost?
Here's the part you want to know. If it's not the first question I get, it's schematically embedded in the question list – and always the one that receives the greatest attention.

The answer (of course) is: "It depends." Stick with me and I'll show how you can get the price down without sacrificing quality.

Your appraisal's cost will depend on:
- Complexity
- Type
- Purpose
- Quality
- Timing
- You

Complexity. This one is relatively easy to understand. A company with several subsidiaries, ownership in other operating entities, foreign corporations, irregular transfers between entities and specialized fields requiring a high degree of specialist knowledge will be more expensive to appraise. Recapitalizations, changes in legal structure (C-corporation to S-corporation/LLC/LP), the recent loss of key personnel, partial sales, infighting amongst owners, high executive turnover – these, too, increase the complexity of valuing your company. Expect to pay more.

Type. A full narrative appraisal will cost more than a "light" valuation engagement. I'm using the word light because each credentialing body assigns its term to the lighter version(s) that each allows its members to produce. A full narrative valuation almost always requires more time and resources than a light valuation. All else equal, the full narrative appraisal will cost more.

Purpose. Purpose goes hand in hand with type. The purpose of your appraisal will dictate the type required. Expect to pay more if litigation is (or will be) part of the engagement. Marital dissolution valuations often become expensive quickly because of the start/stop/wait process dictated by the judge presiding over the case. Also, controlling interest appraisals will usually cost more than minority interest appraisals. A controlling interest has greater autonomy to change the operations of the company. Consequently, the appraiser must gain an understanding of a controlling owner. A minority interest, conversely, has little or no control over business operations and is forced to accept the controlling owner's operational decisions. Accordingly, there is greater subjectivity in a controlling interest compared to a minority interest, resulting in more time and resources needed to complete the control interest appraisal.

Quality. Like any professional service, exceptional quality commands a higher price. A specialist will command a higher price than a generalist, and vice versa. Focus on the quality of the appraiser's experience, credentials and practice niche. Interview appraisers to get a better feel for their charisma and how they operate. An appraiser refusing an interview is not worth your time no matter the specialty (or lack thereof). Business valuations are not inexpensive. Any appraiser not willing to give you their time for questions isn't worth a cent of your money.

Timing. Quality appraisals require a considerable amount of time to complete. There are, however, instances when a business appraisal is promptly needed. If you find yourself in the position of needing an appraisal with a short deadline, expect to pay more.

You. Yes, you dictate the price – or even whether or not the appraiser will accept your engagement. If you choose a specialist, the aforementioned price determinants are quickly understood by the expert when determining the fee element associated with each factor. Akin to the heart surgeon who specializes in valves, the valuation specialist has enough experience to know what's coming (for the most part). Unlike the heart surgeon (where you're asleep during the procedure), the appraiser will need your cooperation throughout the process.

With quality appraisers, the interview process is a two-way street. As you interview them, quality appraisers will also be interviewing you to get a feel for how you work. Quality appraisers are in demand and consequently, are forced to adhere to stringent timelines. Despite the strict deadlines, however, quality appraisers will always make sure they deliver a quality product no matter the time required. They do it because it's the right thing to do. Many quality appraisers price appraisals based on the value provided to you instead of time spent completing the project. Again, do you care how much time is spent assembling your car (e.g. billable hour) or are you concerned with its quality?

Because I want you to get the best bang for your buck, follow these tips to help make the process go as smooth as possible and reduce your cost.

Be clear about what you expect. Appraisers are not mind readers. Many clients just nod their head in agreement without fully understanding what they're getting – only to review the draft report and say "this isn't what I wanted." Be crystal clear in defining what it is you need. Often, having an attorney present is desirable to help explicitly determine what's needed, but this depends on the type of engagement.

Provide information as soon as possible. Before providing a price quote, the appraiser will need to review your company's financial statements, governing documents, etc. Send the information as soon as practicable. Doing so tells the appraiser you're responsive and easy to work with as a business partner.

Cooperate. During the appraisal process, the appraiser will probably need additional information that wasn't requested upfront. He doesn't know your company as well as you – so be prepared to answer questions that help the appraiser better understand your business, industry or other entity-specific dynamics. Some questions may put his work to a halt until answered, costing him time and delaying your report. The appraiser wants to get the job completed as soon as possible to please you. Failing to cooperate hurts both you and the appraiser.

Be Respectful. Respect is a two-way street. You wouldn't hire an appraiser that treated you like dirt. Don't do the same to the appraiser. If you and the appraiser have agreed to an eight-week completion date, don't call three weeks in asking when the appraisal will be finished.

In my experience, failing to provide requested information on a timely basis and being overbearing are the easiest ways to get overages (additional billable hours or fees) when the final bill is due. As a business owner, you understand the importance of having a solid professional reputation. Like you, the appraiser also wants to maintain a stellar reputation. People like working with individuals who are good to work with. A damaged reputation increases your intangible cost of capital.

How well you and the appraiser connect will generally affect the price between 20%-50%. Many appraisers decline to provide quotes to individuals who have reputations of being difficult to work with. The hassle of pulling teeth isn't worth the headaches, especially when good clients are asking for the same thing. Some appraisers intentionally price themselves out of engagements (or hope to do so) by doubling or tripling their standard rate (or more) compared to what they'd charge a favored client.

In summary, be clear about what you expect from the start, provide information when requested (otherwise the appraiser can't do the job), be responsive to questions, don't be overbearing, abide by the contract between you and the appraiser, and be respectful. You may think this list sounds like common sense – but in reality, it isn't commonly practiced. The chief complaints I hear from appraisers are poor communication (slow to provide information) and lack of respect (demanding and overbearing). Assuming you approach a quality appraiser, these tips will help get you the appraiser's best price, giving you the best bang for your buck.

Conclusion

If you were looking for a dollar amount for "how much will this cost" – the answer really is, "it depends."

"Light" valuation reports are less expensive than full narrative appraisal reports. Pricing will depend on the appraiser performing the work. A nefarious appraiser who fills the report with boilerplate language will cost much less than a rigorously conducted, customized narrative appraisal completed by a competent specialist. The difference in price can range from a few thousand dollars to tens of thousands of dollars.

Full narrative valuation reports of Family Limited Partnerships (e.g. Investment Partnerships) consisting solely of liquid assets (or non-liquid assets with current appraisal reports – for example, real estate) usually cost less than full narrative valuation reports of operating companies.

Full narrative valuation reports of business operations vary considerably. Control valuations will be costlier than minority valuation reports, all else equal. The difference in price between minority and control valuations is usually significant because of the additional time and resources required to perform a control valuation. Nonetheless, minority interest valuations also require considerable time and resources to be valued correctly.

Do your research when seeking business appraisers. Don't give a free pass to referrals from trusted advisers. While your trusted advisers are likely to guide you in the right direction, you simply don't know the relationship between the two. Moreover, the adviser may not know the ability and skill set of the appraiser, but has used them because "that's who we've always used." Aim for quality and conduct thorough due diligence before hiring the appraiser who will work best for you. Use the tips in this chapter to secure a quality appraiser for the least amount of money.

ABOUT THE AUTHOR

Zach is living proof of the saying that in life "the dots always connect backward." Shortly after graduate school, a stroke of luck landed Zach in his dream job – an equity research analyst for a large international fund company. Fate, however, had different plans.

After years of living with his wife in a large city far from home, a "surprise" pregnancy urged Zach to find work closer to family. This new career in a newfound industry provided an unforeseen life change that led him to discover his ultimate calling, and what initially appeared to be an unsatisfying role turned out to be what he never knew he wanted. Instead of analyzing publicly traded stocks, Zach now consults with business owners of closely-held private companies on numerous facets of valuation. Zach's never-ending pursuit and passion are helping business owners reach their goals by helping them protect and grow their company's value.

Zach played football at Lake Forest College in upstate Illinois where he majored in business. Working as a graduate assistant, he received his MBA from Southeast Missouri State University, graduating with academic distinction. Zach is a CFA® charterholder, a licensed CPA and is Accredited in Business Valuation (ABV) by the AICPA. He is an international speaker and published author on matters of valuation and valuation-related topics.

Zach performs business valuation engagements, assists high net worth individuals with buy-sell agreements, consults on private equity investments, and helps individuals on other matters related to company value. He has also presided as interim president and served as a director for several closely-held company boards. You can find more about Zach and his work at **www.thevaluationexpert.com**.

Made in the USA
Middletown, DE
30 May 2018